Advance Praise

The book *The Leadership Odyssey: From Darkness to Light* has shed new light on management style and leadership. Case studies, coupled with interviews with senior business leaders from both private and public sectors and people from various sections of society, provide invaluable insights on the human experience and will greatly help understand what leadership is and how it is practised.

I find the book very interesting, well written and contains practical and sound advice with emphasis on self-reflection and holistic understanding of the leader at the physical, intellectual and spiritual levels. I have no doubt this book will not only inspire the readers but will also serve as an important reference book for all aspiring to be virtuous leaders.

—*Harsh Pati Singhania*, **Managing Director, JK Paper Ltd**

The Leadership Odyssey: From Darkness to Light is a great book to be read by all those desirous of becoming virtuous leaders. It is a unique work in that it deals with the contours of both toxic and virtuous leaders. It powerfully highlights the road map which can enable toxic leaders to move towards virtuous leadership. Most importantly this book emphasizes the role of holistic leadership to become a virtuous leader and this can only be achieved by encompassing all the core elements—physical, emotional, intellectual and spiritual—of leadership.

—*I.S. Jha*, **Chairman, Power Grid Corporation of India Limited**

The master thought leader Dr Pritam Singh and his co-authors Dr Asha Bhandarker and Dr Snigdha Rai have brought out a unique work that provides a beacon to leaders in all walks of life, on how to move from unconscious conspiracy and lead consciously, governing with conscience and deep empathy for humanity. In my opinion, the book rightly emphasizes the key role of spirituality to become a virtuous leader. The book has been written in a captivating style and brings out various nuances of toxic and virtuous leadership. A must-read for leaders and leaders to be, today and tomorrow.

—*S.K. Acharya*, **Director (HR),**
Neyveli Lignite Corporation Ltd, Chennai

This is a perfectly timed book to help the world community to address the existing global leadership crisis. The authors have beautifully blended their intellectual depth and rich experience in this work and have provided a simple 'tool kit' for us to identify and develop virtuous leaders.

—*Atul Sobti*, **Director (Power),**
Bharat Heavy Electricals Limited (BHEL)

This book synthesizes research with narrative about real leaders. The authors have, for the first time in published literature, boldly profiled the dark characteristics of leaders. The toxic characteristics of leaders are vividly narrated for all of us to take serious note of. They have co-held this very well with the virtuous characteristics of leaders. They have chosen to distil both the dark and illuminating characteristics distinctively, as the dominant characteristics in their many protagonists. I am sure, they, while doing this, are also drawing our attention to the presence of both the illuminating and the dark characteristics of leadership, in all of us. All of us, including those the authors have profiled, have both the set of characteristics; while one of these two sets may be dominant. They have left it our choice on which ones, we would want to be dominant and deploy more often, given the consequences, we seek. They make it amply clear that to expect creating illuminating consequences with dominant dark characteristics is delusory. Overall a serious yet enjoyable read, with deep insights, if we choose to reflect about ourselves.

—*K. Ramkumar*, **Executive Director, ICICI Bank Limited**

In the contemporary world, all institutions—whether political, social or economic—are plagued by the severe crisis of leadership. There is a preponderance of toxic leaders over virtuous leaders. In this perspective, the book, *The Leadership Odyssey: From Darkness to Light,* is a landmark contribution. It deals with both the toxic and virtuous leadership phenomena which reside within us all, albeit in varying degrees. The challenge according to the authors lies in conquering the toxicity in us by increasing the power of virtuousness that lies within. The uniqueness of this book is the clear road map which leaders can follow, to move from toxicity to virtuousness. The book strongly brings out that it is possible to become a virtuous leader, only by integrating the physical, emotional, intellectual and spiritual aspects, which constitute the core elements of leadership. This work is a great contribution in the domain of leadership. In my view, this book must be read by all who aspire to play virtuous leadership roles in their lives.

—*S.Y. Siddiqui*, **Chief Mentor, Maruti Suzuki India Ltd**

This book is a significant contribution to understanding the crisis of leadership in the contemporary world and the need for spiritual and ethical values; it then highlights what needs to be done to restore the confidence in our leaders in the corporate world.

The authors draw from the ancient Indian wisdom, from empirical research and case studies to illustrate the two extreme styles of leadership: that of toxic leaders and that of virtuous leaders. A model-based comparison of their attributes enables readers to understand the differences between the two and how to make a successful transformation from toxic leader to virtuous leader. The empirical research is very convincing. I think this book is a must for all aspiring managers who intend to transform their companies in the modern competitive world. What I like about the book is its positive approach to leadership; it explains in very clear terms how one can make a successful journey from a toxic leader to a virtuous leader.

It was a great pleasure for me to read the book and I would recommend that not only all aspiring managers should read it, but it should also be a guide for the senior management.

—*Jyoti Gupta*, **Professor, ESCP Europe**

In the 'New Normal' characterized by a perennial VUCA gale and countervailing pushback by stakeholders, organizations need to show sustained outperformance while simultaneously showing extreme care for all stakeholders. This is not possible unless leaders combine competence with values and purpose, and the real source of such leadership is the deep inner space, the mother font from which everything else emanates.

Those who are not connected with their true inner self are unlikely to be successful transformational leaders in the Brave New World.

This well-researched book explores these issues, is a powerful exposition of the journey from unconscious to conscious living, and explores how we can train our energy to consciously move from the toxic to the virtuous state by getting clarity about the meaning and purpose of existence through continued self-reflection and mindfulness. I am sure that the combination of insightful analysis and powerful stories in this outstanding book will inspire and guide those leaders who are committed to making a positive difference by unleashing the potential of the people and the organizations they are associated with.

—*Rajeev Dubey*, **Group President (HR & Corporate Services)and CEO (After-Market Sector), Member of the Group Executive Board, Mahindra & Mahindra Ltd**

Pritam Singh and Asha Bhandarker have done it again. This time, with the contribution of Snigdha Rai, they have written an excellent management book on a very important and highly sensitive subject: toxic versus virtuous leadership. On one hand, toxic leadership is a major source for the dismal picture in many businesses, as well as of the corruption and inequity in the world today. On the other hand, virtuous leadership, coming under the forms of transformational, inspirational or charismatic leadership has long been recognized as a major source for bringing the best out of people, and therefore a major source for prosperity at both the corporate and national level. How do we eliminate toxic behaviour, and how do we transform toxic leadership to a virtuous one? This is the question that the authors address, and they do so very successfully.

Through rigorous and objective analysis, and by combining existing knowledge on leadership, of which they are masters, the authors come up with new knowledge about the characteristics of toxic and of virtuous leaders, analyze the impact of these behaviours at the individual and organizational level, present thorough case studies of toxic and of virtuous leaders that could serve as role models to avoid (in the case of toxic leaders) or to follow (in the case of virtuous leaders), and outline a detailed roadmap for the 'odyssey to leadership' i.e. for moving from toxic to virtuous.

A very enjoyable and useful book, that should be in the library of every academic or leader, whether in business or in politics.

—*Gregory Prastacos*, **Dean, School of Business,**
Stevens Institute of Technology, USA

The potential of an organization is often limited by its leaders; which is why we need great leaders but the unfortunate reality is that they are in short supply. This book is a very timely and important piece of work because it identifies profiles of toxic and virtuous leaders and provides a roadmap for becoming a virtuous leader. The author team of Dr Pritam Singh, Dr Asha Bhandarker and Dr Snigdha Rai draws on its rich real-world experience in leading and transforming organizations coupled with systematic research to provide insights that should help all managers and students of leadership to move towards a better version of themselves. The book's insights apply universally and it should be a must-read for everyone who wants to understand and nurture virtuous leadership skills.

—*Sunil Mithas*, **Professor, Robert H. Smith School of Business,**
University of Maryland and author of *Making the Elephant Dance:*
The Tata Way to Innovate, Transform and Globalize

It is not only the rich quantitative and qualitative empirical work that makes this book valuable but also the message—it brings the often unconscious toxic side of leadership to the awareness of managers, and it encourages and inspires them to discover the strengths of virtuous leadership. Great leaders in business are important for the organizations they serve as well as for society at large. Therefore, the authors are to be applauded for a very humanistic, enlightening approach to leadership that contributes to a better world.I strongly recommend the book to managers as the leaders of today and to students, aspiring to become the leaders of tomorrow.

—*Professor Stefan Schmid*, **Chair of International Management and**
Strategic Management, Academic Dean Executive Education,
ESCP Europe

In the plethora of leadership literature, the book *The Leadership Odyssey: From Darkness to Light* 'stands out' in the real sense of the term. This work brings out some of the undesirable realities of contemporary organizations. Dr Singh and his co-authors have been able to conclusively establish that when 'Aham' (self-centricity) becomes larger than 'Om' (entirety), the consequences can be disastrous for individuals and organizations. The uniqueness of this book lies in laying down a clear trajectory to move from arrogant, egocentric and toxic to virtuous leadership by practising holistic leadership, that is, integrating all the components of leadership—physical, emotional, intellectual and spiritual. This book is a must-read for both current and aspiring leaders.

—*Pushp Joshi*, **Director-HR, HPCL**

This work goes to the soul of what it means to lead. The authors explore the landscape and mindscape of leadership with sharp empirical lenses. The research architecture used to write this book is transparently shared. This book is genuinely evidence based. The research sample includes a constellation of international executives, Indian public sector executives and Indian private sector executives. One of the key elements of this book is the identification of toxic leadership that results in demise and disintegration of institutions. This work is not eulogistic. It does not celebrate arrogance and narcissism that wears the mask of leadership. The most significant contribution of the authors to leadership literature is perhaps this: laying down a clear pathway for emergent leaders from philosophy and purpose to behaviour and style. This is a path-making and a path-breaking book. This is an illuminating read that is reminiscent of our perennial wisdom: *tamaso maa jyotirgamaya*.

—*Debashis Chatterjee*, **Author of** *Timeless Leadership*

A wonderfully crafted book which takes us through the journey of true leadership, from darkness to light, from toxicity to virtuousness—in public service as well as in business. Theory and empirical research are here woven into an extraordinarily persuasive argument which should help academics to teach, students to learn, as well as inspire practitioners worldwide to lead collaborators at all levels.

—*Alfredo Behrens*, **Professor, Intercultural Leadership, FIA, Sao Paulo**

This is a unique and distinctive book on leadership; in its self-actualization and transformation approach, use of nuggets from Indian and Western philosophical thoughts (purpose of life, values, beliefs and attitudes), and in its detailed research of measurable behaviour of successful as well as not so successful contemporary business leaders. The detailed case studies and analysis of positive and negative experiences are fascinating and absorbing. The overall objective and theme is to discover oneself and then move from toxicity to virtuousness in leadership.

I consider *The Leadership Odyssey*, based on holistic understanding of leadership at the physical, intellectual, emotive and spiritual levels, to be a gem among the plethora of books available on this subject.

—*General V.P. Malik*, **Former Chief of Army Staff, India**

Leaders, in any walk of life, need a visionary purpose, personal optimism, boundless energy, innate ability and the courage to execute dreams. *The Leadership Odyssey*, the book authored by Drs Singh, Bhandarker and Rai, aptly captures the need to move leadership from a toxic to a virtuous trajectory, providing examples rooted in Indian mythology relevant even today. Dr Singh, in his inimitable style, effectively highlights how times may change but what is right does not change. An insightful read that tells us that doing the right thing, even if none demand, is what differentiates us from the rest. It is a great book to be read by all aspiring to be virtuous leaders.

—*N.S. Rajan*, **Member, Group Executive Council and Group CHRO, Tata Sons**

In the current landscape, the leadership encapsulates an enigmatic mind-set that includes passion, charisma, moral authority, courage, vision, elocution, ability to motivate, and drive for results. On the flip side, it is also more associated with ruthlessness, egoism, blind ambition, impatience with differing views and an absence of compassion. It is in this context that the current research and findings are very timely. The trend now is towards developing a 'philosophy of leadership' with more emphasis on emotional intelligence than just hard number-crunching. This makes for conscious leadership.

The Leadership Odyssey: From Darkness to Light, written by seasoned thought leaders on management, does a commendable job in urging leadership to move away from this narrow self-centred toxic view to a wider, more virtuous perspective of greater good. In my view, this book is a must-read for all those who believe in leadership and management.

—*P. Dwarkanath,* **Independent Director, GlaxoSmithKline Consumer Healthcare**

The Leadership Odyssey: From Darkness to Light is a book with a difference. You will be able to relate to the practical experiences shared by the authors regarding both toxic leadership and virtuous leadership. The research is grounded in Indian realities and it will change your awareness about holistic leadership and its various dimensions. A must-read for leaders and to be leaders.

—*Kamal Singh,* **Director General, National HRD Network**

The Leadership Odyssey

The Leadership Odyssey

From Darkness to Light

Pritam Singh
Asha Bhandarker
Snigdha Rai

SAGE

Response
Business Books

www.sagepublications.com

Los Angeles • London • New Delhi • Singapore • Washington DC

First published in 2016 by

SAGE Response
B1/I-1 Mohan Cooperative Industrial Area
Mathura Road, New Delhi 110 044, India

SAGE Publications Inc
2455 Teller Road
Thousand Oaks, California 91320, USA

SAGE Publications Ltd
1 Oliver's Yard, 55 City Road
London EC1Y 1SP, United Kingdom

SAGE Publications Asia-Pacific Pte Ltd
3 Church Street
#10-04 Samsung Hub
Singapore 049483

Published by Vivek Mehra for SAGE Publications India Pvt Ltd, typeset in 11/13 pt Baskerville by RECTO Graphics, Delhi, and printed at Chaman Enterprises, New Delhi.

Library of Congress Cataloging-in-Publication Data Available

ISBN: 978-93-515-0736-9 (HB)

The SAGE Team: Sachin Sharma, Alekha Chandra Jena, Rajib Chatterjee and Ritu Chopra

To the most special people in my life—my dear grandchildren—Anvit, Virat, Viraj, Varun, Vihan, Nishank and Krish. Above all to Akansha—my most loving and caring granddaughter.

~Pritam Singh

To three great, unusual and very special people in my life—my late grandmother Lakshmi Devi, my mother Vilasini and my father Venkatesh—who have continuously inspired me to follow my dreams.

~Asha Bhandarker

To my mother Madhuri Sharma, my father Sadanand Sharma and my husband Nitin whose precious love, steadfast support and consistent encouragement helped bring out the best of me.

~Snigdha Rai

Contents

List of Tables		ix
Foreword by Jagdish N. Sheth		xv
Acknowledgements		xix
Prologue		xxiii
1.	Peaks and Valleys of Leadership	1
2.	Toxic Leader Profile	47
3.	Virtuous Leadership	126
4.	Leading Consciously: A Road Map for Moving from Toxic to Virtuous Leadership	279
Epilogue		317
About the Authors		321

List of Tables

1.1	Sample Details of Questionnaire-based Research	28
A1.1	Leadership Inventory	29
A1.2	Emotional Distress Inventory	30
A1.3	Coping Inventory	32
A1.4	Resilience Scale	34
A1.5	Work Locus of Control Scale	36
A1.6	Personal Values Scale	38
2.1	Toxic Leadership Attributes: Overall Frequency, Percentage and Rank	51
2.2	Toxic Behaviours from Interview Data	82
2.3	Psycho-social Response to Toxic Leaders	83
A2.1	Toxic Leadership Attributes by Age Categories: Frequency, Percentage and Ranks	87
A2.2	Toxic Leadership Attributes by Work Experience: Frequency, Percentage and Ranks	89
A2.3	Toxic Leadership Attributes by Educational Qualification: Frequency, Percentage and Ranks	91
A2.4	Toxic Leadership Attributes by Gender: Frequency, Percentage and Ranks	93
A2.5	Toxic Leadership Attributes by Family Type: Frequency, Percentage and Ranks	95
A2.6	Toxic Leadership Attributes by Resilience: Frequency, Percentage and Ranks	97
A2.7	Toxic Leadership Attributes by Work Locus of Control (LOC): Frequency, Percentage and Ranks	99
A2.8(a)	Toxic Leadership Attributes by Values (Egalitarian and Humanistic): Frequency, Percentage and Ranks	101

A2.8(b)   Toxic Leadership Attributes by Values
          (Hedonistic and Personal Development):
          Frequency, Percentage and Ranks   103
A2.8(c)   Toxic Leadership Attributes by Values (Pride and
          Materialistic): Frequency, Percentage and Ranks   105
A2.9   Toxic Leadership Attributes by Organizational
          Sector: Frequency, Percentage and Ranks   107
A2.10   Toxic Leadership Attributes by Industry Type:
          Frequency, Percentage and Ranks   109
A2.11   Toxic Leadership Attributes by Nationality:
          Frequency, Percentage and Ranks   111
A2.12   Descriptive Statistics   113
A2.13 F-Test (Age as Independent Variable and
          Emotional Distress as Dependent Variable)   113
A2.14 F-Test (Work Experience as Independent Variable
          and Emotional Distress as Dependent Variable)   114
A2.15   Independent Sample t-Test (Educational
          Qualification as Independent Variable and
          Emotional Distress as Dependent Variable)   114
A2.16   Independent Sample t-Test (Gender as
          Independent Variable and Emotional Distress
          as Dependent Variable)   114
A2.17   Independent Sample t-Test (Family Type as
          Independent Variable and Emotional Distress
          as Dependent Variable)   114
A2.18   Independent Sample t-Test (Resilience as
          Independent Variable and Emotional Distress
          as Dependent Variable)   115
A2.19   Independent Sample t-Test (Work Locus of Control
          as Independent Variable and Emotional Distress as
          Dependent Variable)   115
A2.20   Independent Sample t-Test (Values as
          Independent Variable and Emotional Distress
          as Dependent Variable)   115
A2.21   Independent Sample t-Test (Organizational
          Sector as Independent Variable and Emotional
          Distress as Dependent Variable)   116

A2.22   Independent Sample *t*-Test (Industry Type as
         Independent Variable and Emotional Distress
         as Dependent Variable)   116
A2.23   Independent Sample *t*-Test (Nationality Type
         as Independent Variable and Emotional Distress
         as Dependent Variable)   116
A2.24   *F*-Test (Age as Independent Variable and
         Coping Strategy as Dependent Variable)   117
A2.25   *F*-Test (Work Experience as Independent Variable
         and Coping Strategy as Dependent Variable)   117
A2.26   Independent Sample *t*-Test (Educational
         Qualification as Independent Variable and Coping
         Strategy as Dependent Variable)   118
A2.27   Independent Sample *t*-Test (Gender as
         Independent Variable and Coping Strategy
         as Dependent Variable)   118
A2.28   Independent Sample *t*-Test (Family Type
         as Independent Variable and Coping Strategy
         as Dependent Variable)   119
A2.29   Independent Sample *t*-Test (Resilience
         as Independent Variable and Coping Strategy
         as Dependent Variable)   119
A2.30   Independent Sample *t*-Test (Work Locus
         of Control as Independent Variable and Coping
         Strategy as Dependent Variable)   120
A2.31   Independent Sample *t*-Test (Egalitarian as
         Independent Variable and Coping Strategy
         as Dependent Variable)   120
A2.32   Independent Sample *t*-Test (Humanistic
         as Independent Variable and Coping Strategy
         as Dependent Variable)   121
A2.33   Independent Sample *t*-Test (Hedonistic
         as Independent Variable and Coping Strategy
         as Dependent Variable)   121
A2.34   Independent Sample *t*-Test (Personal Development
         as Independent Variable and Coping Strategy
         as Dependent Variable)   122

A2.35   Independent Sample *t*-Test (Pride as
        Independent Variable and Coping Strategy
        as Dependent Variable)   122
A2.36   Independent Sample *t*-Test (Materialistic
        as Independent Variable and Coping Strategy
        as Dependent Variable)   123
A2.37   Independent Sample *t*-Test (Organizational
        Sector as Independent Variable and Coping
        Strategy as Dependent Variable)   123
A2.38   Independent Sample *t*-Test (Industry Type as
        Independent Variable and Coping Strategy
        as Dependent Variable)   124
A2.39   Independent Sample *t*-Test (Nationality
        as Independent Variable and Coping Strategy
        as Dependent Variable)   124

3.1   Virtuous Leadership Attributes: Overall Frequency,
        Percentage and Ranks   129
A3.1   Virtuous Leadership Attributes by Age: Frequency,
        Percentage and Ranks   252
A3.2   Virtuous Leadership Attributes by Work Experience:
        Frequency, Percentage and Ranks   254
A3.3   Virtuous Leadership Attributes by Educational
        Qualification: Frequency, Percentage and Ranks   256
A3.4   Virtuous Leadership Attributes by Gender:
        Frequency, Percentage and Ranks   258
A3.5   Virtuous Leadership Attributes by Family Type:
        Frequency, Percentage and Ranks   260
A3.6   Virtuous Leadership Attributes by Resilience:
        Frequency, Percentage and Ranks   262
A3.7   Virtuous Leadership Attributes by Work Locus
        of Control: Frequency, Percentage and Ranks   264
A3.8(a) Virtuous Leadership Attributes by Values
        (Egalitarian and Humanistic): Frequency,
        Percentage and Ranks   266
A3.8(b) Virtuous Leadership Attributes by Values
        (Hedonistic and Personal Development):
        Frequency, Percentage and Ranks   268

A3.8(c)   Virtuous Leadership Attributes by Values (Pride and
          Materialistic): Frequency, Percentage and Ranks   270
A3.9   Virtuous Leadership Attributes by Organizational
          Sector: Frequency, Percentage and Ranks   272
A3.10   Virtuous Leadership Attributes by Industry Type:
          Frequency, Percentage and Ranks   274
A3.11   Virtuous Leadership Attributes by Nationality:
          Frequency, Percentage and Ranks   276

Foreword

I am very pleased to write this foreword for *The Leadership Odyssey: From Darkness to Light* for three reasons. First and foremost, the book is authored by world-class thinkers and educators who have not only conceptualized but clinically observed and impacted hundreds of business leaders, and especially the public sector leaders and executives.

In my view, public sector leaders are the unsung heroes of India but often they are in the shadows of the private sector promoters, entrepreneurs and CEOs since the economic reforms of 1991, which unleashed the power of capitalism and entrepreneurship.

Second, *The Leadership Odyssey* is a unique blend of qualitative and quantitative research. The quantitative survey of more than 700 respondents is supplemented by an in-depth analysis of several world-class leaders from public sector enterprises as well as NGOs. The book documents that the single most differentiator for the success or the failure of an organization is its leadership. Either the toxic leaders tend to destroy the value of the enterprise or they are unable to unlock its potential. At the other end, an inspiring leader transforms the organization that has become complacent or is trapped into an ecosystem which is unfriendly or at best, constraining.

The book clearly demonstrates that leadership is all about motivating people in the organization; that what matters most is neither the financial capital nor the technology but organization's culture as reflected by its human capital. Igniting the human talent is the real competency of all successful leaders.

Most successful enterprises acquire seven bad habits on their way to success. They are: (1) Denial of new realities such as competition from the private sector or from non-traditional competitors; (2) Arrogance especially among the founders and pioneers; (3) Competency dependency which means that what was a core

competence at one time has become a core liability. This is happening to all companies that are anchored to analogue, mechanical or chemical technologies as the markets are shifting to digital
technologies, such as digital cameras; (4) Competitive myopia which
makes the organization focus too much on the obvious competitors
and ignore the non-obvious or disruptive competitors. The recent
examples of the growth of e-commerce retailers as opposed to brick
and mortar retailers are obvious; (5) Complacency: Does success
breed failure? The evidence is overwhelming that it does. This is
particularly appropriate for state-owned enterprises and public
sector monopolies. The book has several good case studies about
complacency; (6) Volume obsession which believes in the myth of
economies of scale and encourages cross subsidies and marginal
pricing tactics; and finally (7) Internal turf wars. Managers waste a
lot of energy and time in internal conflicts and politics instead of
using them to battle external challenges.

Great leaders are like great doctors. They have great diagnostic
skills and a keen sense of observation. They are hands on and they
love to wander around the organization and listen to their employees, customers, suppliers, community and other stakeholders.

The third and final reason for me to accept the invitation to
write this foreword is that search for leadership excellence is a journey and not a destination. It is similar to search for the meaning of
life. The journey is as important, if not more so, as the destination.
And even if you don't reach the destination, you feel a sense of fulfil-
ment and satisfaction that comes from learning.

The Leadership Odyssey provides enlightenment to our understanding of leadership especially for public sector leaders. It is full
of insights and 'a-ha's'. It is also a great checklist of self-diagnostics
to assess whether you are a toxic or enlightened leader.

In my own research and writings, over many decades, I have
concluded the following about leadership:

- You can neither manufacture nor buy leadership. You must
  earn it.
- Great leaders are great doers. They have a knack of organizing
  and inspiring followers. Often they generate cult-like loyalty.
- When followers are ready, the leader will show up. Therefore,
  in times of crisis, uncertainty and chronic dissatisfaction,

unexpected people become leaders, especially in politics and social movements. This was the case with Nelson Mandela, Martin Luther King and Mahatma Gandhi, as was also the case with Winston Churchill, Franklin Roosevelt and Abraham Lincoln. In short, ordinary people become extraordinary leaders.

- Great leaders are driven by purpose and passion. They derive boundless energy from their passion and purpose. For them, leadership is all about people. Management is all about stuff.
- Great leaders not only promise the future but deliver it.
- Great leaders are great architects. Like good architects, they imagine something unique, enduring and inspiring. Examples of such enduring architecture are: the pyramids and the ancient temples, mosques and churches. More recent examples are the Opera House in Sydney, the Bird's Nest Olympic Stadium in Beijing, the Putrajaya, the new capital of Malaysia and the new Botanical Gardens at the Bay in Singapore.

There are three universal qualities of all great leaders: passion, care and capability. Interestingly, this is also true of great educators. Dr Pritam Singh and his colleagues (Bhandarker and Rai) clearly embody these three traits in their thought leadership. I want to congratulate them for their extraordinary contribution through this research-based book.

Jagdish N. Sheth
Charles H. Kellstadt Professor of Business
Goizueta Business School
Emory University

Acknowledgements

Every work of research comes to fruition because of myriad enablers, supporters and advisors, each having contributed at different stages of the work. First, we thank many toxic leaders who have provided us with deep insights into toxic leadership and its impact on ruining individuals and destroying organizations.

We now make an attempt to acknowledge some of the people in our lives who have provided us with meaningful understanding of virtuous leadership. We acknowledge with profound humility the following individuals: B.M.L. Munjal (Chairman Emeritus, Hero Group), Adi Godrej (Chairman, Godrej Industries), Nripendra Misra (Principal Secretary, Prime Minister of India), Atul Chaturvedi (Chairman, PESB), M. Damodaran (Ex CMD, UTI and IDBI), K.M. Birla (Chairman, Aditya Birla Group), S.K. Rungta (Ex CMD, SAIL and Vedanta), R.K. Tyagi (Ex CMD, HAL), Susheel Tripathi (Ex Secretary, Ministry of Petroleum and Natural Gas), M.V. Nair (Ex CMD, Union Bank of India), M. Narendra (Ex CMD, Indian Overseas Bank), Arup Rai (CMD, SAIL), B.P. Rao (CMD, BHEL), Baba Kalyani (Chairman, Kalyani Group), A.M. Naik (Chairman, L&T), Anil Khandelwal (Ex CMD, BoB), Late Shri Hari Shankar Singhania (former President, JK Group), Late Shri Aditya Birla (former Chairman, Aditya Birla Group) and Shubhalaxmi Panse (Ex CMD, Allahabad Bank).

Others who have inspired us and played a significant role in sustaining our motivation are: R.P. Singh (Ex CMD, Power Grid), S.K. Chaturvedi (Ex CMD, Power Grid), R.N. Nayak (CMD, Power Grid), Dr M. Ayyapan (CMD, HLL Life Care), Rajiv Sharma (CMD, REC), Rajiv Dubey (Director, HR M&M), Ram Kumar (Director, ICICI Bank), P. Dwarakanath (Advisor, Max Group), S.Y. Siddiqui (Chief Mentor, Maruti Suzuki), Rajneesh Bawa (Director, HR CNH), Santrupt Misra (CEO, Carbon Black and Group Director HR),

N.S. Rajan (Group President, Tata Sons), Ram Narayan (DIG UP), S.K. Acharya (CMD, NLC), Pushp Joshi (Director HR, HPCL), Cherian Verghese (Director HR, Indian Oil Corp.), Biswajit Roy (Director HR, Oil India), Dr A.K. Dubey (Additional Secretary, Ministry of Coal), Ajay Shankar (Ex Secretary, Industries), Dr K.M. Abraham (Principal Secretary Finance, Kerala), Girish Chaturvedi (Ex Secretary, Banking), Anil Sardana (CEO, TATA Power), Veena Swarup (Director HR, EIL), Pankaj Bansal (Founder CEO, People Strong), G.P. Rao (Ex HR Head, Reliance Overseas), Kamal Singh (DG, NHRDN) and Dhananjay Singh (Ex Director, NHRDN).

Special thanks are also due to Anurag Batra (Chairman, *Business World*), Shamni Pande (Senior Editor, *Business Today*), Prem Palety (CEO, C *fore*) and Ester Martinez (CEO and Editor-in-Chief, *People Matters*).

We would also like to acknowledge some of our colleagues for their kindness and help in many ways: Professors A.K. Rath, B.A. Metri, Subir Verma, J. Das (Director, FORE), G.K. Agrawal, R.R. Sharma, Devashish Chatterjee (Ex Director, IIMK), Harivans Chaturvedi (Director, BIMTECH), Arun Jain (IIML), Roshan Raina (IIML), Ravi Kumar (IIMB), Laxman Prasad (IIMB) and C.N. Narayana (Director, Kirloskar Institute of Management).

Dr Bhandarker and Dr Rai would like to profusely thank Dr B.H. Dholakia (DG, IMI) for extending wholehearted support in completing this work. They also extend special thanks to their colleagues at IMI, Professors Bhupen Srivastava, Kshitija Wason, Afsha Dokadia, V. Chandra, Shailendra Nigam, Mamta Mohapatra, Richa Awasthy and Sriparna Basu.

The senior author, Pritam Singh, would like to acknowledge with deep gratitude the lifelong contribution and guidance that he received from Professor A.K. Shah—his mentor, philosopher and guide. It was he who inculcated in Pritam the quest for knowledge. The second author, Asha Bhandarkar, owes a debt of gratitude to T.L. Sankar who encouraged the cultivation of independence of thought and an academic temperament.

Some people in our lives have sacrificed, ungrudgingly and silently, and have supported us throughout the journey of this work. The senior author would like to begin by mentioning his wife Saroj Singh; his daughters-in-law Mamta, Indu, Priti and Radhika; and his daughters Savita and Alka. Regular inquiry from his sons—Vikas,

Vidhan, Vivek and Vipul—kept the work on track and put moral pressure to complete it as soon as possible.

The second author would like to express her deep gratitude to her loving sisters Sudha and Vidya and to their spouses Venkataramana and Sarwat Hussain. Her brother Vivek and his wife Sharmila supported and helped with their gentle inquiry and encouragement. The next-generation Bhandarkers—Ashish and Advik—gave plenty of joy and pleasant diversion to sustain this work. Heart-felt thanks from the second author to her life-long friends, the 'Ya-Ya' sisters, Anita Ratkalkar, Linda Cordeiro, Shakila Dausi, Malavika Melkote, Arundati Sarvottam and Archana Paranji, who have been a strong anchor of support over the years. Special thanks are due to Aruna Bahuguna (DG, National Police Academy) for her consistent concern and friendship. The third author, Snigdha Rai, would like to express her deep gratitude to her grandmother for her eternal love and inspiration to do the best in life. Also, special regards are extended to her father-in-law, Mr Ramji Rai, for his unconditional support and encouragement. Last but not least, she would like to thank her brothers, Abhishek and Ashish, and sister Neha for their precious love and support.

Above all, we would like to express our deep appreciation to Mr Vinod Rai, Mr R.V. Shahi, Major General D.N. Khurana, Mr M.D. Mallya and Mr R.K. Dubey for having spared endless number of hours for this work. They have handled our many enquiries and questions very patiently, sometimes even at odd hours.

Thanks also to Professor Reeta Raina of FORE School for editing this work despite her hectic schedule. Mrs Bhanumathy, IMI, deserves kudos for having patiently and unhesitatingly done the word processing of this book multiple times.

Mr Anup Sharma, librarian IMI-Delhi, was most supportive and helpful in procuring all relevant materials and to him go our warm thanks.

Last but not least, the authors would like to profusely thank the National HRD Network for all their support and encouragement during the execution of this work.

Pritam Singh
Asha Bhandarker
Snigdha Rai

Prologue

Aao Phir Se Deep Jalaayein
(Let's light the lamp again)
—Bharat Ratna Shri Atal Bihari Vajpayee,
former Prime Minister of India

The above line from a poem by the former Prime Minister of India significantly highlights the perennial human quest for enlightenment that moves from darkness to light. Such a quest leads to the creation of an enlightened society which promotes happiness, peaceful coexistence and progress, which are the basic goals of humanity. In pursuit of these goals, through centuries, people have been struggling to find leaders and rulers in various walks of life. There is an anecdote in the Mahabharata which powerfully amplifies this human quest. While replying to a riddle posed by Yaksha, 'Which path should be followed?' Dharmaraja stated, '*Mahajanohjenoh Gatah Sa Pantah*'—that is, when one is confronted with the dilemma of what to do and what not to, one should unhesitatingly follow the path shown by great people. The immortal lines '*Lives of great men all remind us, we can make our lives sublime and departing, leave behind us, footprints on the sands of time*' by Henry Longfellow[1] powerfully echo the same wisdom. In other words, through centuries, virtuous rulers and kings have contributed significantly to building and leading societies. While in present-day democracies, people link their aspirations with leaders' capabilities and elect them accordingly; in history many good kings and rulers were also selected by a group of wise elders for their virtuous qualities and conduct. Governance and leadership capabilities, such as valour, courage, compassion, honesty, evolved aesthetic sense, ethical and philosophical orientation, were assigned priority in the selection process.

Many centuries ago, King Janak—one of the most revered of Indian Kings—known as Raj Rishi; Bhishma—the most respected patriarch of the Mahabharata; and Plato—the philosopher icon—highlighted that kings and rulers must combine governance capability with philosophical orientation. Plato, in his *Republic*,[2] said,

> *Until philosophers are kings or the kings and princes of this world have the spirit and power of philosophy, political greatness, and wisdom meet in one; and those commoner natures who pursue either to the exclusion of the other, are compelled to stand aside; cities will never have rest from their evils no, nor the human race as, I believe ... and then only will this our state have a possibility of life and behold the light of day.*

A similar paradigm—Tian or Mandate of Heaven—heavenly support for virtuous leadership qualities, was in vogue in Ancient China, while selecting kings and emperors. In fact, the kings who were evil or toxic were overthrown regardless of their royal lineage. Similar measures were also adopted by the Greeks, Romans, Egyptians, Babylonions, and others. A fine Indian example is that of King Bharat who chose Bhumanyu, son of Rishi Bharadwaj, to succeed him (despite having nine sons) because of the latter's virtuous qualities to lead and govern.[3]

In the contemporary world, leaders such as George Washington, Thomas Jefferson, Eisenhower, Gandhi, Nehru, Sardar Patel, Charles de Gaulle, Lenin, Roosevelt, Winston Churchill, Nelson Mandela, Martin Luther King, Lee Kuan Yew, Gorbachev, Vajpayee and A.P.J. Abdul Kalam were the front runners of renaissance and transformation, characterized by both philosophical orientation and deep concern for the well-being of the people. Similarly, there is a galaxy of leadership icons in the corporate world—Lee Iacocca, Ford, Andrew Carnegie, Fulbright, Akio Morita, Jamsetji Tata, J.R.D. Tata, Toyoda, G.D. Birla, H.P. Nanda, Soichiro Honda, B.M.L. Munjal, SriRam, Jack Welch, Jeff Immelt, Steve Jobs, Bill Gates, Andy Grove, Percy Barnevik, Baba Kalyani, Kiran Mazumdar, K.V. Kamath, Sunil Mittal, Satya Nadella and others—who have made significant contributions to the nation and the society.

Viewing the contemporary business world using the lens of the qualities of the virtuous leader described above, however, unfortunately, shows a dismal picture. A large number of leaders across all walks of life are today characterized by arrogance, hunger for power, hedonistic excesses, blatant display of selfishness and primitive drives for domination and subjugation.

On the political plane, there are many examples of destructive and toxic leaders. The exploits and acts of leaders such as Saddam Hussain, Richard Nixon, Berlusconi, Sarkozy, Idi Amin, Hitler, Osama Bin Laden, Pol Pot, Ayatollah Khomeini, Mussolini, Stalin, Kim Jong Un, to name a few, reveal the dark and negative side of leadership. The silence displayed by the erstwhile Prime Minister of India, Manmohan Singh, in the face of many misdeeds of the government emboldened Indian politicians to become brazenly corrupt. These were people in powerful positions who through their acts of commission and omission failed to live up to the expectations of the people, and did enormous disservice to the masses. In fact, today, politics is just another profession driven not only by ideology but also by opportunity for amassing power and wealth. There are many political leaders, such as Mayawati, Laloo Prasad Yadav, Mulayam Singh Yadav, Karunanidhi, Sharad Pawar, Jayalalita, Om Prakash Chautala, Yeddyurappa and many more, whose styles and behaviour have proven the above point. Extreme hypocrisy is obvious in the ongoing infighting in the Aam Aadmi Party (AAP), which came to power on the plank of the ideology of serving society through honest governance. Similar hypocrisy is clearly evident across all political parties, as indicated by the yawning gap between what they profess vis-à-vis what they practise. Alas! What a letdown!

Instances of corruption in India—the CWG scam, the Coalgate, the 2G scam, parking of slush money in Swiss bank accounts, the Vadra scam, LaMo gate and Vyapam, to name a few—all reflect the excess of lust and greed to hoard wealth by a nexus of corrupt politicians, bureaucrats and corporate executives in leadership positions. The existence of a thriving parallel economy in India also reveals the greed to make money by any means, among members of the business community. They do not hesitate to make money by hook or by crook, with scant concern for stakeholders. The disproportionate rise in salaries of top-level executives vis-à-vis other levels in the organization, the golden parachutes which top-level executives get regardless of their poor contribution to the companies they head, excessive incentivization of performance of the CEO, reflecting poor corporate governance, all yet again indicate avariciousness and hunger for power as well as the pursuit of selfish interests, which seem to have possessed the minds of many of those occupying high positions.

It is no wonder that India ranks 94 out of 148 nations on the effectiveness and competitiveness of corporate governance.[4] It is ironical that while, on the one hand, India's competitiveness has slipped down from 65 to 94, on the other hand, the number of multimillionaires has grown remarkably. Today, India boasts of having the fifth largest number of multimillionaires globally, ranking after the top four countries—USA, China, Germany and UK.[5] It has been globally accepted that gender diversity at the board level leads to better corporate governance and effectiveness. It is with this perspective that SEBI has mandated Indian companies to hire independent woman directors on corporate boards. According to Prime database,[6] even in this area, companies are managing to retain dominant control of the boards and are at the same time complying with SEBI rules to hire women, by nominating family members and relatives as directors. According to this report, only 305 women out of 567 women board members are truly 'independent' directors, indicating a systematic subversion of the SEBI intent. As regards the Indian judiciary, the less said the better. Although their judgements may be sound, the manner in which most cases linger on for decades is shocking. The timelines in reaching a verdict are interminable as observed in the cases of Mayawati, Mulayam Singh Yadav, Laloo Prasad Yadav, Jayalalitha and others. Things have come to such a pass that even lawyers have themselves become critical of the glacial timelines in giving judgements.

The American Federation of Labour and Congress of Industrial Organizations[7] has shown that the salary of a CEO in America was $11.7 million in 2013, whereas the annual salary of an American worker was a paltry $35,293. The gap between the two salaries is a mind-boggling 331 times. The situation in large Indian corporations, especially family-owned organizations, is much worse, with the prevalent salary of CEOs ranging from ₹15 crores to ₹50 crores per annum (an average of 20 crores), as against ₹1.20 lakhs to ₹5.00 lakhs for workmen (an average of 3 lakhs per annum).

The difference between the two average salaries is a whopping 1300 times, which means the salaries of CEOs in India is approximately 700 times more than that of workmen. The situation becomes even more grim when the salary of CEOs is compared with that of workmen in the unorganized sector in which workmen are paid a pittance for their hard labour.

Christine Lagarde, the Chief of IMF, in her speech in London, has recently said that the richest 85 persons in the world own the same amount of wealth as the bottom half (50%) of the world's entire population, which is again another indicator of the shocking levels of inequity flourishing in the contemporary business world.[8] The above data bring out the alarmingly extreme inequality in the world and this can certainly pose the biggest threat to peace on the planet. Through their excessive and lavish lifestyles, their scant concerns for the plight of the masses, today's super rich are behaving in ways which may well incite another social breakdown, upsetting the very foundations of their power. This may take the form of agitations, attacks on and kidnapping of the rich, and other forms of criminal activity. The Anna Hazare movement has been an example of how collective public force (among other things) became the backbone of the downfall of the mighty Congress party toppling many heavy-weight politicians.

It may be worthwhile noting that the fall of great empires, and likewise great business organizations, has occurred in different parts of the world because of the closed and despotic mindset and behaviour of the people in power. Such factors might have contributed to the fall of the mighty Chou dynasty, the Roman, British and Moghul empires, which fell especially because of the overwhelmingly short-sighted, self-oriented, arrogant, whimsical and sometimes downright cruel behaviours of kings and emperors who took their subjects for granted. In fact, the famous anecdote attributed to Marie Antoinette, the French queen, who remarked 'Let them eat cake' when told that the people did not have bread to eat, reflects how out of touch can rulers be from ground reality. Many corporate houses such as the Modis, Escorts, DCM, Kanorias, Bangurs, some of the Birlas, Bank of America, HP, Merck, Motorola, Rubbermaid, JPM, which featured in the top bracket at one time, simply slid into decline over the years. Jim Collins[9] who analysed the downfall of many of these erstwhile mighty corporations concluded that factors such as hubris borne out of success, arrogance, close-mindedness and poor learning orientation led to their decline and downfall. Toxic leaders, greedy corporations and growth models focused primarily on wealth creation and economic development have resulted in people experiencing normlessness, powerlessness and consequently meaninglessness and dehumanization. In fact, economic development and wealth creation without adequate focus on equitable distribution is not sustainable in the long run, since inequity triggers forces of revolt, rebellion and revolution.

The above treatise powerfully brings out that existing leaders in all walks of life have, in many cases, failed miserably. There is therefore a dire need for a new form of leadership, moving from the toxic trajectory to the virtuous trajectory.

The authors have started asking questions about the raison d'être for the enormous crises of leadership in the contemporary world. Is it lack of skills and competencies? Is it lack of information and knowledge? Is it lack of appropriate value systems or attitudes? Is it lack of philosophy and purpose in life?

It may be worthwhile mentioning that a leader's philosophy and purpose of life, values, beliefs and attitudes have a far-reaching role in making a person a leader. This has been clearly demonstrated in writings on great leaders such as Lincoln, Roosevelt, Martin Luther King, Mandela, Gandhi, Jamsetji Tata, J.R.D. Tata, G.D. Birla and Jack Welch.

The technological innovations and knowledge explosion in the last 50 years is unparalleled when compared to any other period in human history. At the same time, however, one wonders whether there has been a significant evolution in value systems, attitudes and philosophy of life of the people in keeping with the technological and knowledge advancements. Although physical strength and capability as well as mental abilities have seen tremendous growth as compared to earlier generations, the same is, however, not true with regard to the enhancement of emotional and spiritual power. A growing awareness of this gap has appeared, as indicated by the greater emphasis on enhancing spirituality and positive emotions to develop virtuous leaders. Good business schools at the global level have launched compulsory courses in business ethics and corporate social responsibility in the last decade. Clearly, there is a growing awareness about the need to inculcate ethical–spiritual–value systems while grooming leaders.

Virtuous leaders nurture and help institutions grow through their overarching vision and dream, entrepreneurial zest, integrating horizon with ground realities, connecting the dots, empowering approach, demonstrating high degree of humility, sensitivity to people, ethical and moral values, etc.

Our counselling and mentoring sessions with hundreds of leaders over the years have revealed that many of the CEOs are well aware of the importance of spiritual and emotional growth to become better leaders. They are, however, grappling with the challenges of moving from toxic to virtuous leader behaviour, and they do not know how to achieve this growth. In fact, our own experience shows that many of the leaders are either unaware of their toxic impact or are in denial about their toxic behaviour. The plausible explanation for this phenomenon lies in there being unaware of the dark side of one's nature. The greater the lack of self-awareness, the greater the grip of the 'dark' side on the leader, that is, the 'unconscious' aspect of their 'self' drives their behaviour.

The purpose of writing this book has been to enable leaders and various role holders to embark on their journey of moving from darkness to light, in order to live and lead consciously. The primary thrust and accent of this work is self-level transformation. The following quotes poetically capture this process of self-transformation:

> *Let a man raise himself by hisself,*
> *Let him not debase hisself,*
> *He alone indeed is his own friend,*
> *He alone is his own enemy.*
> > —Bhagavad Gita[10]

Similarly Buddha[11] articulated,

> *Be ye lamps unto yourselves, Be your own reliance,*
> *Hold to the truth within yourselves as to the only lamp.*

Both these quotes categorically bring out the role of 'self' in creating one's own leadership destiny and in scripting one's own future as a leader. The famous lines from the poem Invictus by Henley[12] made immortal by Mandela—*I am the master of my fate and the captain of my soul*—yet again bring out the pre-eminent role of the self for transformation.

In other words, to lead consciously and become a fully functional and productive leader, the journey of self-transformation is a necessary prerequisite. This is, however, possible only by becoming fully aware of one's self and understanding the purpose of one's existence. This has been powerfully articulated by Nathaniel Branden[13]—*Know Thyself, Own Thyself and Change Thyself.*

After much deliberation among ourselves and also after discussing with some thinkers and scholars on leadership, we decided to title this book *Odyssey to Leadership: From Darkness to Light.* The term 'odyssey' has been used because it symbolizes a long journey, characterized by overcoming difficulties and obstacles, and by vanquishing enemies before reaching one's destination. Viewing the journey as an odyssey becomes relevant when we view the dilemma of being a human and at the same time of being continually jostled by the dualities of one's own nature—good and evil, angels and demons, *tamoguna* and *satoguna* as well as ignorance and enlightenment. *The Leadership Odyssey*, therefore, represents the inner quest and journey to move from darkness to light and from toxicity to virtuousness. Thus, it is a process of moving from the grip of unconscious conspiracies to living and leading consciously.

Therefore, the key focus of this work is to delve deeper and throwing some light on the leader's odyssey from unconscious to conscious living and leading as well as on tapping the positive potential which lies within the unconscious self. We hope that this book will inspire those who hold leadership positions, as well as those who aspire to become leaders.

The book has been organized in four chapters:

- Chapter 1, Peaks and Valleys of Leadership, which deals with a panoramic view of leadership across the range from toxic leadership to virtuous leadership. It also presents the methodology used to conduct this research.
- Chapter 2, Toxic Leader Profile, which reports empirical findings regarding toxic leader behaviour and its impact on followers.

- Chapter 3, Virtuous Leadership, which describes the virtuous Leader profile.
- Chapter 4, Leading Consciously: A Road Map for Moving from Toxic to Virtuous Leadership, which deals with a road map for moving from toxic to virtuous leadership.

REFERENCES

1. Brainyquote.com (2015). Henry Wadsworth Longfellow Quotes. Retrieved from http://www.brainyquote.com/quotes/quotes/h/henrywadsw124600.html (accessed on 30 June 2015).
2. Wolfe, R.P. (1969). *Ten great works of philosophy*. New York, NY: Penguin Books.
3. Vasudev, J (2015). *Bharata: Rhythm of a Nation*. Available at http://www.ishafoundation.org/blog/lifestyle/bharat-the-power-of-a-name/ (accessed on 1 April 2015).
4. World Economic Forum (2015). The global competitiveness report 2014–2015. Available at http://www3.weforum.org/docs/wef_globalcompetitivenessreport_2014-15.pdf (accessed on 30 June 2015).
5. *Times of India* (2015). Number of multi-millionaires growing the fastest in Pune. Retrieved from http://timesofindia.indiatimes.com/india/Number-of-multi-millionaires-growing-the-fastest-in-Pune/articleshow/46765616.cms (accessed on 1 April 2015).
6. *Economic Times* (2015). Publicly traded companies race to appoint women director on board ahead of April 1 deadline. Available at http://articles.economictimes.indiatimes.com/2015-04-01/news/60720046_1_directorship-women-directors-ireena gopal-vittal (accessed on 1 April 2015).
7. Singh, R.P. (2014). *Enterprise of the soul*. New Delhi : Penguin Books.
8. International Management Fund (2014). A New Multilateralism for the 21st Century: The Richard Dimbleby Lecture. Retrieved from http://www.imf.org/external/np/speeches/2014/020314.htm (accessed on 1 April 2015).
9. Collins, J.C. (2001). *Good to great: Why some companies make the leap and others don't*. New York, NY: Harper Business.
10. en.wikibooks.org (2015). Vuara/CHAPTER VI (MMY Gita). Retrieved from https://en.wikibooks.org/wiki/User:Vuara/CHAPTER_VI_(MMY_Gita) (accessed on 1 July 2015).
11. Goddard, D. (1956). *A Buddhist Bible*. London, UK: George, G Harrap.
12. poemhunter.com (2015). Invictus Poem by William Ernest Henley. Retrieved from http://www.poemhunter.com/poem/invictus/ (accessed on 1 July 2015).
13. Branden, N. (1999). *The art of living consciously: The power of awareness to transform everyday life*. Los Angeles, CA: Touchstone Books.

CHAPTER 1

Peaks and Valleys of Leadership

This chapter is divided into two sections:

- Section A: Peaks and Valleys of Leadership designed to portray the contours and valleys of leadership—toxic and virtuous
- Section B: Research Architecture used in this work

Section A: Peaks and Valleys of Leadership

INTRODUCTION

The multiple hues and facets of leadership ranging from the negative and toxic to the positive and virtuous, representing both the peaks and the valleys of leadership, have been highlighted in Part I. The dance of good vs. bad, virtuous vs. vicious, benevolent vs. harmful and angels vs. demons has been in existence through millennia in the minds of people. History is replete with examples of toxic leaders—Chengiz Khan, Niro, Marie Antoinette, Hitler, Stalin and many others—who unfortunately used power to conquer and inflict unimaginable tyranny and cruelty on the masses. There have also been stellar examples of great leaders (albeit few and far between)—Akbar, Ashoka, Julius Ceaser Augustus, Claudius, Chandragupta Maurya, Qinshihuang, Vikramaditya, to name a few—who demonstrated concern for the welfare of the people and worked tirelessly for the upliftment of humanity. In fact, the quest for leadership has been a perennial fascination through the ages. This can be noted across the ancient civilizations—Chinese, Babylonian, Egyptian, Greek and Indian. It is visible from the times of the Mahabharata to Moses to the Biblical period and in the Islamic period. Even today, the search for great leaders attracts the attention of scholars and researchers across numerous disciplines.

In the contemporary world, leaders such as Gandhi, Mandela and Martin Luther King have amply demonstrated the power of positivity in influencing the thinking of the masses and channelling the energy of people to build nations and create a new world order. In fact, the 20th century has been distinctive for a number of political leaders, who led their countries to independence and freedom, typically from the colonial rule of the British, French, Dutch, Germans and even Belgians. Leaders such as Gandhi, Mandela, George Washington, Abraham Lincoln, Thomas Jeffersen, Winston Churchill, Roosevelt, Charles de Gaulle and Eisenhower have amply demonstrated the power of positive value disposition and behaviours which have led to the betterment of the lives of millions. When we analyse leadership in the 20th century, we find that some of the greatest leaders were mostly political leaders, who combined their vision and concern for the larger populace with hard work, persistence and sacrifice to bring freedom from colonial rule. Gandhi was one of the earliest leaders to successfully liberate the people of India from the rule of the mighty British empire through non-violent means. Mandala freed South Africa by using a similar approach. Encouraged and inspired by these successes, leaders such as Dr K. Nkrumah in Ghana, Kenneth Kaunda in Zambia, Julius Nyerere in Tanzania and Patrice Lumumba in Congo walked the path of non-violence to attain freedom for their respective countries.[1] Abdel Nasser led the Egyptian Revolution in 1952 and freed Egypt from the tentacles of the reigning monarchy. In Asia, apart from India, Burma achieved its independence owing to the efforts of Aung San, who founded the Burmese Army. Tunku Abdul Rehman is the main architect of Malaysia; Mohd. Hatta was a central figure in Indonesia's fight for independence. In 1972, Mujibur Rehman liberated East Pakistan from the dictatorship of Yahya khan leading to the birth of a new nation re-christened as Bangladesh. Che Guevara and Jose Marti were the main leaders in the Cuban revolution, and Zapata, who is credited with starting the agrarian movement called Zapatismo, is also worshipped as the Mexican revolutionary war hero. In the annals of the histories of China and Russia, Mao and Lenin orchestrated the liberation of China and Russia, respectively, from the tyrannical rule of the Chinese emperors and Russian Czars.

The business world has also thrown up some great leaders, who built their organizations and thereby served society, such as Soichiro Honda, K. Matsushita, Akio Morita, Carlos Slim, Lou Gerstner, John Sculley, Bill Gates, Alfred Sloan, Carnegie, Gerald Ford, Lee Iacocca, Herb Kelleher, Stan Shih and Percy Barnevik to name a few. The Indian corporate sector also has some benevolent corporate giants to boast of, starting with Jamsetji Tata who had a vision and conviction that India could be a steel producer and thus the Tata Steel plant in Jamshedpur came into being. G.D. Birla not only ran a huge and powerful business empire, but also actively supported the struggle for freedom, besides making philanthropic contributions. In 1911, Sir Sorbji Pochkhanwala started India's first commercial bank that was wholly owned and run by Indians and thus the Central Bank of India was born. Other notable corporate leadership icons in India are J.R.D. Tata, Ratan Tata, Aditya Birla, A.M. Naik, Narayana Murthy, N. Vaghul, B.M. Munjal, Azim Premji, V. Kurien, Sunil Mittal, K.V. Kamath, Kiran Mazumdar Shaw and M. Damodaran, who are known and admired for the scale of their contributions towards building great organizations and assisting in national development.

The era of virtuous leaders, characterized not only by their focus on business but also by their concern for the well-being of people, seems to be on the wane. There are, however, a few notable exceptions—corporate leaders such as Bill Gates, Warren Buffet, George Soros, Azim Premji; musicians such as Bono and politicians such as Bill Clinton who have been engaged in social causes today with great vigour. In their new avatars as philanthropists and social activists, they are donating millions of dollars into the health, education and welfare of children and women in the most deprived parts of Africa and Asia. Buffet, the founder of Berkshire Hathaway, is well known for pledging to give away 99.00% of his personal wealth. He has popularized the 'Giving Pledge' to persuade the wealthiest in the world to make a commitment to give most of their wealth to philanthropic causes. Bill Clinton has been a forceful advocate of the fight against HIV/AIDS, malaria and tuberculosis and the need to stem greenhouse emissions. He has successfully persuaded billionaires, heads of state and others to declare their commitments to specific projects. George Soros has given away $8 billion dollars to causes related to human rights, education and public health. Tim Cook, the CEO of Apple Corporation, has recently given $800 million to some of the causes cited above. Bono has also been giving and simultaneously influencing the rich to help the poor people across the world. Such virtuous leaders—wealthy entrepreneurs turned philanthropists—are, however, in a miniscule minority.

The 'Giving Spirit' seems to be virtually absent among the majority of Indian corporate organizations. In the Indian context, philanthropy does not seem to keep pace with either the profits or the scale of the problem. There are innumerable accounts of the super-rich who have no qualms about the vulgar display and consumption of wealth with supreme unconcern for the deprived sections of society. Invariably, such corporate honchos are known to transact business through manipulation of state rules and processes in their favour by corrupting government functionaries and role holders. In other words, they are unabashed in their greedy use of public machinery as well as resources to generate wealth for themselves. This clearly reflects their unethical and exploitative mindset. It is no wonder, therefore, that the Indian government felt the need to bring in a legislation to ensure that a minimum 2% of net profit is spent on social development. Likewise, SEBI has framed stringent rules for promoting healthy and ethical corporate governance to prevent malpractices at the board level. Unfortunately, many independent directors on boards are a rubber stamp of the owners. The independent stance of the so-called 'Independent' directors more often than not exists only on paper. Our experience in many companies reveals that most CEOs are, in fact, not comfortable with questioning (though contributing) board members. CEOs prefer 'yes-men' to men and women with integrity, who will echo their predecided agenda and decisions. It is unfortunate that the board-level agenda in most organizations is unilaterally decided by the CEO, even without consultation with the independent directors (based on the experiences of the first two authors).

Globally, the first decade of the 2000s saw an alarming spate of corporate scandals wherein the top management, in collusion with their auditors, defrauded the public, investors and employees of billions of dollars. Amazingly enough, some of them such as Enron and Lehman Brothers enjoyed top-notch rating by magazines such as *Fortune* just prior to their debacle—*Fortune* magazine rated Enron as the most innovative company for six years and after this the downfall began. Lehman Brothers was ranked the number 1 'most' admired securities firm by *Fortune* magazine in 2007 only to melt down in 2008 and this firm dragged down many others along with it, inflicting a huge loss on individuals and organizations. The reverberations were experienced both in Asia and in Europe, illustrating the flip side of global interdependence. Today, many are tricksters, charlatans and thugs masquerading as leaders.

Rajat Gupta, the celebrated CEO at McKinsey & Co., has been jailed for the insider trading scam along with Raja Rathinam. Madoff's Ponzi Scheme tricked investors of $64.8 billion. Dennis Kozlowski, CEO, and Mark Swartz, CFO of Tyco, colluded and stole $600 million from the company. The accounting fraud which Arthur Anderson conducted at the behest of Enron (CEO Jeff Skilling and previous CEO Ken Lay) resulted in thousands of investors losing their life's savings as shareholders lost $74 billion. In 2002, WorldCom CEO, Bernie Ebbers, President Glanow and Chairman Leland of Freddie Mac, in 2005 AIG CEO, Hank Greenberg, and in 2008 the Lehman brothers were all guilty of accounting frauds worth billions.[2] Subsequent bankruptcies and disclosures resulted in losses in billions of dollars to thousands of investors along with huge job losses suffered by equally large numbers of people. The CEOs involved in the frauds were all imprisoned. Thus, it seems that even the celebrated leaders have feet of clay. They were toxic, over-ambitious, greedy and willing to go to any extent to maximize their wealth at the expense of all stakeholders. The heavy cost of their greed was borne by the public at large and the leaders themselves who lost everything and met dramatically tragic ends. It may be worthwhile mentioning that many cases have been reported in the newspapers, wherein the decline of performance of the organization was paralleled with the upward growth of CEO compensation, indicating the unethical approach and weak moral fibre of so-called leaders of corporations.

In India, although corruption has been very much part of the 'license-quota raj' of the ruling elite—bureaucrats, politicians and corporate executives—it was whispered about and speculated upon in a hush-hush manner in public life. The unholy nexus between the politician and the bureaucrat, as well as corporate leaders resulting in rampant corruption, has been an alarming trend in the last decade. It has become so all-pervasive in the recent past that there is a metaphorical avalanche of scams. Vijay Mallya, the flashy tycoon known for his penchant for the high-flying life, closed down Kingfisher Airlines and did not pay the staff for more than 18 months. Despite the vast personal wealth he enjoys, he continued to expect the government to bail out the beleaguered airline. He is known to have famously said that he would not sell the family silver to save Kingfisher. In 2013, the underhand dealings of the Augusta Westland chopper deal came into public light with Air Marshal S. Tyagi (Chief of Air Force) and Santosh Bagrodia (Former Union Minister) being named in the deal.

The Coalgate scandal—the arbitrary allocation of coal blocks to Public and Private Sector companies—came to light in 2013. Railgate revolved around a bribe being accepted by the nephew of the former Railway Minister, P.K. Bansal, and this also became a public news in 2013. The siphoning off of ₹750 crores in bribes and commissions by top officials of the BEML, in connection with import of Tatra Trucks emerged in 2011. In 2010, A. Raja, former Telecom Minister, was named for undercharging telecom companies in the allocation of 2G licenses for cellphone subscriptions. He was booked by the CBI and jailed subsequently. The CWG scam came to light in 2010 soon after the games were concluded. The Chairman of the organizing committee, Suresh Kalmadi, was the main accused and brought to himself and the country, worldwide shame. In 2009, the nation was rocked by the Satyam scandal, where the Founder and Chairman, Ramalingaraju, himself confessed to having inflated the balance sheet, in collusion with the auditors and the so-called 'eminent' board members such as Dr Ram Mohan Rao, former Dean of ISB and Dr Krishna Palepu, Professor Finance at Harvard. The other recent instances of corruption have been the Adarsh Housing Society Scam. The society was formed to house heroes and war widows of Operation Kargil. People who were allotted flats, however, consisted of high-profile politicians such as Ashok Chavan as well as some former army chiefs and key bureaucrats. The Bellary mining scam was yet another scam involving bribes being paid by the Reddy brothers to Yeddyurappa and family in exchange for mining licenses. In 2013, Saradha Chit Fund's Ponzi Scheme was exposed. Sahara's Subrata Ray is still in jail for defrauding millions of small-time investors. The term of the current government is no less rocky as La Mo Gate and the Vyapam scam hit the government.

Most of the above cases are related to either the defrauding of the exchequer or the cheating of the public by those holding high office in politics, government and corporate sector. It is hardly surprising, therefore, that there is a growing spectre of widespread cynicism infecting people in all walks of life. In fact, today, the term 'leader' is greeted more with contempt than with any positive feeling. Indians say that today there is no choice for the masses among politicians all of who appear to be the tarred with the same brush in their lust for self-aggrandizement regardless of which party they belong to. The latest example is that of the AAP which espoused great ideology, honesty and transparency, but demonstrated just the opposite behaviour. In most of the cases, this seems to cut across party lines, regardless of the ideology that politicians profess. In this morass of despondency, the emergence of Narendra Modi, the present Prime Minister of India, has been like a beacon of hope in the minds of many people. People have been moved by his larger vision, his concern for the well-being of the poorest of the poor and his faith in carrying everyone along, in addition to his thrust on economic and social development. However, one year after election, people are getting restless, wondering whether at all there is a convergence between promise and delivery, between what he says and what he does. In fact, the example of Modi as well as that of the AAP and Congress are making people, regardless of the section of society that they belong to, feel cynical about the possibility of actual action on the ground. In fact, they notice no difference among the parties, and consider them all to have a similar agenda of fooling the people, and holding on to power.

One wonders why it is that contemporary institutions and societies have failed to develop widely accepted, committed and virtuous leaders. Where are the leaders like Gandhi, Mandela, Roosevelt,

Jefferson, Charles de Gaulle, Martin Luther King, Jamsetji Tata, G.D. Birla, J.R.D. Tata, H.R. Nanda, Aditya Birla, Ratan Tata and Warren Buffer? Where are the leaders driven by a vision and a determination to transform the lives of others and create a better society? Where indeed are the leaders who care and focus on profit, people and planet? Where are those leaders embodying personal values of honesty and integrity, working not only for their *profit* but also for *People and Planet as well*? Today, the question continuously haunts us and partially in despair and partially in hope, we seek leaders who make their businesses socially responsible, who are concerned as to how their businesses impact the environment and who serve the community and help create a better world.

At this juncture, it may be worth highlighting the prevalent culture among Indian institutions and organizations. On the basis of our experiences of working as consultants and trainers for around 200 organizations and organizing numerous programmes for the bureaucracy, the following dominant patterns are observed:

1. Indian organizations and institutions are extremely hierarchical. The existing positional hierarchy has become embedded in the individual and collective mental architecture and is reflected every day in their conduct and behaviour. We have observed that in such contexts, who says what is more important, than what is being said. People overtly respect and pay attention to the chair and not to the individual.
2. There is a top-down approach in strategy crafting, where, unfortunately, the lower management is expected to solely comply and execute, as if they have no ideas of their own.
3. Unfortunately, the obnoxious Indian caste systems still pervade the interaction of the 'higher' echelons of the organization with the other 'lower' level functionaries. The caste system has been neatly adapted and reinterpreted in the organization in which top management are the Brahmanical thinkers, whereas the rest of the levels consist of the implementors. There is low degree of employee engagement, participation and involvement in decision-making. From the above discussion, it is clear that the common people at the

workplace are not valued, respected and their dignity is not honoured.

It is in this context that the present chapter has been written. This chapter seeks to examine the various shades of leadership, negative as well as positive, and its impact on individuals and organizations. It is presented in two parts:

- Part I: It deals with dark and toxic leadership.
- Part II: It presents the positive and virtuous leadership phenomenon.

PART I: DARK AND TOXIC LEADERSHIP PHENOMENON

In the modern period, interest in the scientific study of the dark leadership phenomenon accelerated in the aftermath of the World Wars and the struggle for conquest between the forces of democracy and autocracy. Work on dark leadership focuses on dark leaders in powerful positions who inflict serious psychological and emotional trauma among their subordinates and followers and bring irrevocable harm to the organization and society.

The dark side of leadership has been described using various semantics such as leadership derailment,[3] negative or evil leadership,[4] toxic leadership,[5] abusive leadership,[6] destructive leadership[7,8] and bad leadership.[9]

The leadership terms cited earlier constitute many dark leadership behaviours which have been examined in the literature. Some of the prominent Dark Leadership behaviours in the literature are hostility (verbal as well as non-verbal forms) ridiculing, undermining and yelling at subordinates;[10] unethical and unfavourable treatment of others, humiliation, sarcasm, threats and overworking an employee;[11] belittling the worth of subordinates, behaving in arbitrary ways, punishing, discouraging initiative and showing lack of consideration[12] and arrogance. Such leaders also use coercive power, bullying tactics, scolding and reprimanding.[13]

Antecedents of Dark and Toxic Leadership

Antecedents refer to the causal factors within the person—one's personality—leading to dark leadership behaviours. Hogan, Curphy and Hogan[14] proposed that certain personality traits such as extreme ambition or Machiavellianism lead to dark leadership. Machiavellianism is a personality trait characterized by shrewdness, manipulation and the use of any means to achieve one's political ends. High 'Machs' are politically oriented, seek control over followers, use tactics of impression management and avoid pursuit of organizational goals.[15,16] The underlying assumption is that the lust for power is the source of dark and toxic leadership. Kets de Vries[17] also suggested that dark and toxic leadership may result from an unresolved sense of self, an irrational idea of one's power and the fear of losing it.

Alongside the theme of power, the psychodynamic approach indicates that narcissism also leads to dark and toxic leadership.[18] Such leaders abuse power to achieve personal gain, often through unethical or even illegal manner to reinforce their self-image and gain more power.[19]

Narcissism is a personality disposition which includes grandiosity, arrogance, egotism, entitlement, weak sense of worth and occasionally hostility. In addition, hypersensitivity, anger, lack of empathy, amorality, irrationality, inflexibility and paranoia also define narcissistic leaders. The vision, plan and actions of narcissistic leaders are identical to their own psychological needs.[20] Narcissist leaders are more likely than others to engage in self-promotion and self-nomination due to their hunger for visibility and recognition.[21] They strongly suffer from the 'I' syndrome.

Lack of empathy is a characteristic hallmark of narcissistic leaders and it is clearly contrary to virtuous leadership.[22] Because narcissistic leaders lack empathy, unlike others they are more likely to make decisions guided by an idiosyncratic and self-interested view of the world. Finally, another trait shared by narcissistic leaders is paranoia[23] due to which they see enemies everywhere, and also they create enemies everywhere.[24] Although leaders are generally surrounded by sycophants, narcissistic leaders often distrust even those close to them and do not hesitate to even destroy their most loyal supporters. Rather than serving the organization, narcissistic leaders use all the resources available to them to attract the appreciation of others as a way of confirming their feelings of supremacy.[25] In sum, narcissistic leaders are principally motivated by their own egomaniacal needs and beliefs, superseding the needs and interests of the constituents and institutions that they lead, thus causing tremendous damage to the followers and organizations.

Consequences of Dark and Toxic Leader Behaviour

A great deal of research has brought out clearly that dark leadership has a deleterious impact at both the organizational and the individual levels. Some of the salient findings are currently presented in the following paragraphs.

Toxic Leaders and Outcomes at the Individual Level

1. Dark and toxic leadership results in low self-worth and reduced self-efficacy among subordinates.[26–29]
2. Toxic and dark leadership behaviours have been found to lead to poor work-related attitudes,[30,31] low commitment,[6] low work motivation[32] and greater job dissatisfaction[33] among subordinates.
3. Dark and toxic leader behaviours lead to psychological and emotional distress—anxiety, fear and distress among subordinates.[34–37] Toxic leadership is found to be positively related to negative affectivity.[33] Such behaviours by leaders have been found to result in reduced self-confidence and motivation.
4. The association of dark and toxic leader behaviour and higher stress levels among subordinates has been observed.[38–40] Anxiety and depression,[29] helplessness[41] and burnout[42,43] are the other known outcomes.
5. Dark and toxic leader behaviour results in emotional exhaustion among subordinates, as well as reduced emotional and coping capabilities.[44,45]
6. Negative relationship has been located between destructive leadership and subordinate performance.[30]

7. Toxic and dark leader behaviour harms the organization's bottom line and also its ability to attract ethical candidates.[46]

Toxic Leadership and Impact at the Organizational Level

1. Toxic and dark leaders tend to create a hostile work climate,[47] which leads to deviant behaviours such as sabotaging operations, withholding help, theft, insubordination and providing inaccurate and misleading information.[48–53]
2. Toxic organizations are created by toxic leaders. Toxic culture is characterized by social norms which legitimize toxic leadership as a means of exercising authority.[54] Toxic organizational culture generally originates from toxic leadership and is supported by toxic managers.
3. Destructive leadership and counterproductive work behaviour is also the prominent sign of a toxic organizational culture that is permissive of these types of negative behaviour. Toxic organizations are largely ineffective as well as destructive of its employees.[55,56] Consequently, a toxic work culture will lead to a detrimental impact on the psychological (e.g., stress and anxiety), sociological (e.g., negative impact on group interaction), as well as the physical well-being (e.g., asthma) of the employees.

On the basis of this review, it is apparent that dark and toxic leaders not only adversely affect individuals, but also disturb the psycho-socio-economic texture of the organization. They affect the organization's capability to innovate and excel, grow and compete and win the corporate Olympiad. It is no wonder that organizations, headed by toxic leaders, steeply go down the path towards destruction and even annihilation.

PART II: CHEMISTRY OF VIRTUOUS LEADERSHIP

In sharp contrast to the toxic leader discussed earlier, a virtuous leader has a positive impact on people owing to who he is, what he stands for, how he treats people, how he communicates and where he would like to take the organization. The entire edifice of leadership and its enormous impact on unleashing human potential in the organization is based on the premise of virtuous leadership.

Empirical research on positive leadership took off after the publication of the iconic book by Burns on transformational leadership.[57] In the middle of the 20th century, humanistic thinkers such as Chris Argyris,[58] McGregor,[59] Maslow,[60] Rogers,[61] Sullivan,[62] Erich Fromm,[63] Victor Frankl[64] and Charles Handy[65] greatly influenced our understanding of the best aspects of being a human. They considered humans to be essentially good and positive. McGregor[59] put forth the famous conceptualization of Theories X and Y, with the assumption of human nature as either 'negative' or 'positive' respectively. According to the theory X belief system, humans dislike working, avoid responsibility and need to be directed, have to be controlled, forced and threatened to deliver what is needed. They need to be supervised at every step, with controls put in place; they need to be enticed to produce results; otherwise, they have no ambition or incentive to work. Leaders with such a negative view of human nature therefore use toxic leadership behaviours to control and manage people. In contrast, the Theory Y model assumes that employees are happy to work, are self-motivated and creative and enjoy working with greater responsibility. It assumes that workers take responsibility and are motivated to fulfill the goals they are given; they seek responsibility and do not need much direction; they view work as a natural part of life and solve work problems imaginatively. Those leaders who have these positive assumptions about human nature use Theory Y styles characterized by trust in managing people.

Virtuous leaders generally operate by inspiring, uplifting their people and bringing out the best in them. According to Kelloway et al.,[66] positive leader behaviours trigger positive emotions among subordinates. It is based on the belief that positive leadership begets positive response from followers so that they give high quality results and perform their roles to the best of their ability, keeping both ethical considerations and multiple stakeholders in mind. Various terms have been used to describe positive leadership: ethical,[67] authentic,[68] inspirational,[69] transformational,[57] charismatic,[70] servant[71] and spiritual leadership.[72]

Leaders such as Mandela, Martin Luther King, Gandhi, Lincoln, Roosevelt, Charles De Gaulle and others mentioned earlier are shining examples of virtuous leadership. Positive and virtuous leadership constitutes a type of psychological and emotional relationship between the leaders and followers which is best exemplified in the behaviour of transformational leaders.[73]

The power of a positive leader lies in his influencing subordinates by building trust, commanding their respect through his integrity and credible behaviour and inspiring followers to achieve beyond expectations. A virtuous cycle gets created between the leaders and followers, reinforcing both and progressively increasing effective performance.

Transformational leadership[74–89] is the most researched type of positive and virtuous leadership. The transformational leader has been found to serve as an effective coach and mentor to his followers and provides them with the necessary support to accomplish their jobs.[90] Transformational leaders have been found to influence by communicating a vision for the group and motivating team members to work towards the collective vision. They also exert influence by expressing the confidence that their teams will achieve the goals.[91]

Another form of virtuous leadership is charismatic leadership. Charismatic leaders[92,93] influence the followers by empowering them, by using fluid speaking styles, through the power of clear articulation of strategic vision and by showing sensitivity to members' needs. Charismatic leaders influence by articulating a vision that relates followers' self-concept to their organizational roles.[94] According to Shamir,[70] by doing this, they arouse certain motives in followers, which may encourage subordinates to sacrifice self-interest for the larger collective goals. Charismatic leaders emphasize the collective goals and purpose to subordinates regularly, so that they are constantly reminded about the direction in which they are going.

Virtuous leaders influence primarily through the power of inspirational leadership.[95] They have powerful communication abilities and share the future vision in a way which inspires subordinates. Virtuous leaders also influence through their ethical behaviours.[96] They influence subordinates through effective two-way communication, both by expressing and by listening to others, reinforcement of ethical behaviours and ethical decision-making.[97] Ethical leaders have been found to respect their subordinates and consider their views while taking decisions.[98,99] Ethical leaders walk the talk and their behaviour is characterized by honesty, expressing care, making fair and balanced decisions, setting clear ethical standards, practicing what they preach and using reward and punishment to ensure that the standards are followed.

Virtuous leaders also influence through spiritual power. According to Fry,[72] spiritually inclined leaders subscribe to values, attitudes and behaviours that intrinsically motivate self and others. They create a vision with the aim of giving meaning and purpose to work, and of creating a work culture where leaders and followers have genuine care, concern, respect and appreciation for everyone. They give a perspective on life as essentially meaningful and the person as an entity who can make a difference.

The Servant Leader[100] influences by forming relationships with followers, empowering followers, serving followers and helping followers grow, succeed and behave ethically. Virtuous leadership behaviours clearly bring out the meaning of leadership as a type of relationship, which is highly interactive and reciprocal in nature. The above descriptions of virtuous leadership behaviour show that such leaders influence subordinates by

a. Being role models
b. Connecting and relating with people
c. Inspiring, energizing, envisioning and enabling
d. Creating meaning
e. Coaching and developing subordinate and
f. Being optimistic and courageous

Findings on the antecedents of virtuous leadership bring out that:

1. Positive leaders (ethical and authentic) have been found to be honest and humble.[101,102] Such leaders are sincere, modest, and full of integrity and are fair and equitable in the treatment of subordinates.

2. They are emotionally stable and characterized as calm, relaxed, consistent in their emotional expressions, and not likely to experience negative emotions frequently.[103] High emotional stability has been reported to be positively associated with leadership.[104] Emotional stability is an important predictor of virtuous leadership.[105]

3. Extroverts are more likely to be seen as leaders[106] by followers because of their self-confidence, initiative, communication and inclusive approach.

4. In group discussion contexts, extraverts have been normally found to emerge as group leaders.[107]

5. A strong relationship has been found between extraversion and charismatic and supportive leadership.[102]

6. Highly 'agreeable leaders are considerate, friendly, generous, helpful and willing to compromise their interests with others'. Agreeable people also have an optimistic view of human nature. They believe people are basically honest, decent and trustworthy. They have been found to be cooperative, gentle, kind, inclusive, promoting affiliation and avoiding conflict.[108,109] Owing to this aspect of their personality, they tend to promote cooperation and helpfulness among team members.[110] They also tend to be empathetic while delivering critical feedback, and encourage a friendly and fair work environment.[111] Agreeable leaders have been found to score high on idealized influence—subordinates attribution that the leader is charismatic, powerful and confident thus increasing their capability to influence subordinates.

7. Conscientious leaders clearly define role expectations and deliver reasonably on informal contracts.[112] They exhibit integrity and display more persistence in attainment of organizational goals. They achieve this by fostering a fair and just work climate.[113]

8. Virtuous leaders have been found to be high on 'openness to experience' trait.[114] They have also been found to cope well with organizational change.[115] Those who are high on 'openness to experience trait' are intellectually curious, appreciative of art and sensitive to beauty. They tend to be more aware of their feelings as compared to 'closed' people.

Impact of Virtuous Leaders on Individuals, Teams and Organizations

Substantial research has been conducted on the impact of positive and virtuous leadership at individual, team and organizational levels. The research findings bring out that:

- Transformational leadership impacts individual level performance.[89] It creates higher intrinsic motivation among followers as they start perceiving their work as more strategic and meaningful.
- It results in increased levels of self-worth which positively affects job performance.[116]
- It leads to better levels of task performance.[117,118]
- Transformational leaders motivate and inspire followers to engage in altruistic behaviour and to dedicate themselves to their jobs and organizations.[119–122]
- Transformational leadership is positively related to creative performance as transformational leaders encourage and intellectually stimulate followers to challenge the status quo, take risks and suggest innovative ideas.[84]
- Transformational leaders are able to achieve this by expressing confidence that teams will achieve their goals;[123] increasing followers' confidence and the intrinsic value of performance, which results in higher levels of motivation and performance.[124–129] Transformational leaders have been found to have a deep impact on followers, on teams and on organizations.[73]
- Virtuous leaders have an extraordinary impact on the organizational culture, on the way others interpret their circumstances and on their definition of well-being.[130,131] Leaders significantly affect organizational culture as they personally induce, develop and display positive emotions. Consequently, it results in positivity in followers and an increase in their organizational commitment.[132]
- Positive climate refers to a work environment in which positive emotions predominate over negative emotions.[133,134] Employees with optimistic attitudes and cheerful outlooks are

typical of positive culture; well-being predominates over distress and dissatisfaction. According to Mathieu and Zajac,[135] organizational performance is substantially and positively affected by a positive culture. A positive work culture has also been found to enhance productivity, creativity, decision making, social integration and pro-social behaviour.[136,137] Positive leaders facilitate positive energy—both by modelling positive energy themselves and by diagnosing and building positive energy networks among others, which in turn generates positive interpersonal relationships in organizations. Empirical studies also suggest that an organization's positive affective culture is positively associated with workforce performance,[138,139] higher levels of overall employee productivity and aggregate task performance.[140]

From the foregoing exposition, the following salient features of leadership both dark and positive emerge:

1. Toxic leadership is characterized by behaviours such as abusiveness and short-temper, arrogance, dishonesty, blaming others, creating insecurity, rudeness, favouritism, insensitivity, manipulative behaviour, ridiculing others, close mindedness, corruption and dishonesty.
2. The danger of toxic leadership lies in its negative outcomes on individuals, groups, organizations and society. Some of the key negative outcomes at the individual level are low self-worth, reduced self-efficacy, poor work-related attitudes, emotional exhaustion and high psychological distress among subordinates. These individual-level outcomes, in turn, lead to an increase in workplace deviance because of the prevalence of a hostile work climate, resulting in decreased organizational performance.
3. In contrast to toxic leadership, positive and virtuous leadership is characterized by behaviours such as performance-centric, respectful, empowering, openness, honesty, fairness, visionary, humility, approachable, courageous, equanimity and calmness, self-awareness, leading by example and mentoring others and so on.

4. Virtuous leaders are admired and appreciated because of their positive impact on individuals, groups and societies. Key positive outcomes are increased levels of self-worth and higher intrinsic motivation among followers, which in turn leads to extraordinary task achievement, creativity and performance.

The above findings are now presented schematically in Models 1.1 and 1.2.

MODEL 1.1

Toxic Behaviour Model—Antecedents and Outcomes

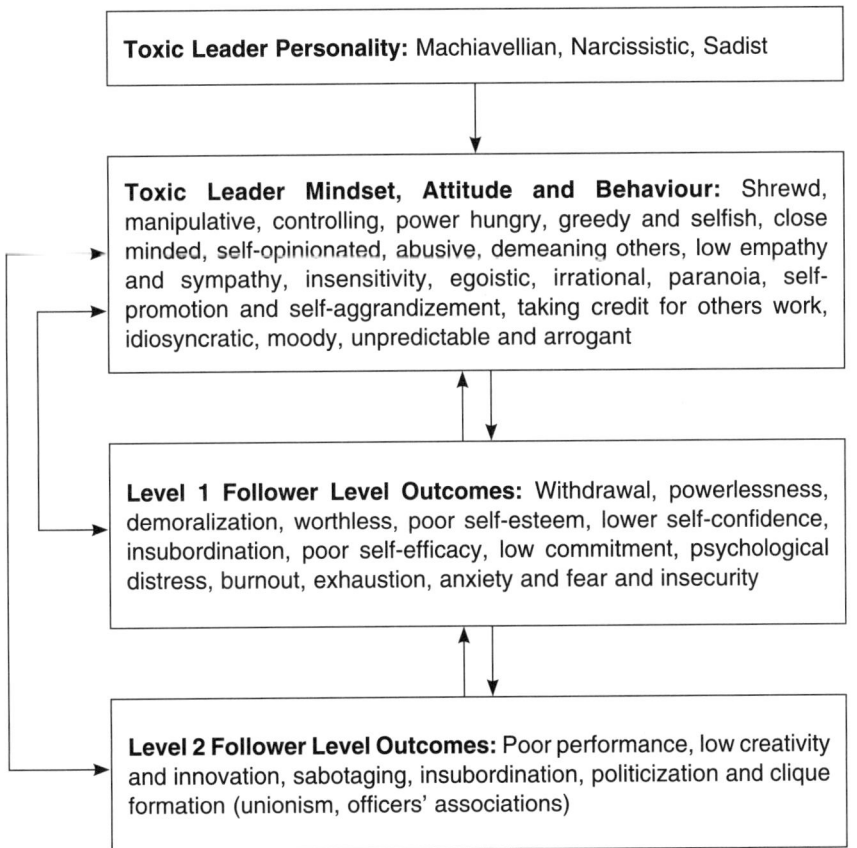

Toxic Leader Personality: Machiavellian, Narcissistic, Sadist

Toxic Leader Mindset, Attitude and Behaviour: Shrewd, manipulative, controlling, power hungry, greedy and selfish, close minded, self-opinionated, abusive, demeaning others, low empathy and sympathy, insensitivity, egoistic, irrational, paranoia, self-promotion and self-aggrandizement, taking credit for others work, idiosyncratic, moody, unpredictable and arrogant

Level 1 Follower Level Outcomes: Withdrawal, powerlessness, demoralization, worthless, poor self-esteem, lower self-confidence, insubordination, poor self-efficacy, low commitment, psychological distress, burnout, exhaustion, anxiety and fear and insecurity

Level 2 Follower Level Outcomes: Poor performance, low creativity and innovation, sabotaging, insubordination, politicization and clique formation (unionism, officers' associations)

MODEL 1.2

Virtuous Leadership Model: Antecedents and Outcomes

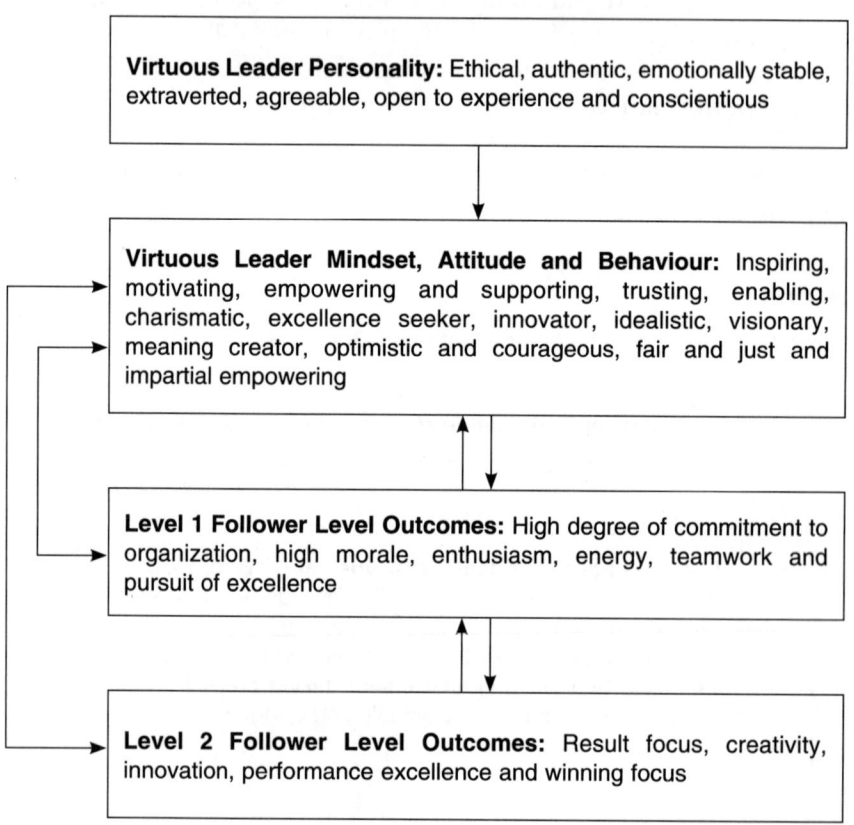

Model 1.1 depicts the personality traits of the toxic leader and their manifestation in the form of mindsets, attitudes and behaviour. The model also highlights impact on followers at two levels: Level 1, at the psychological level; and follower level outcomes, level 2, at the workplace.

Model 1.2 depicts the personality traits of virtuous leaders, their manifestations in mindsets, attitudes and behaviour. This is followed by the impact of virtuous leader behaviours at two levels: level 1 at the psychological level; and follower level outcomes level 2 at the workplace.

Section B: Research Architecture— Methodological Blueprint

OBJECTIVES OF THIS RESEARCH

The quality of any research is significantly influenced by the research architecture which is utilized. Needless to say, high-quality research architecture leads to dependable, valid and reliable research findings for evolving theoretical paradigms. Keeping these objectives in view, a suitable research design has been developed for the present work. We have utilized an eclectic approach using questionnaire, interview and secondary data sources for gathering information. Such an eclectic approach was, needless to say, adopted to overcome the inherent deficiency in each approach whether survey based or in-depth case based.

This research aims to study primarily the phenomenon of toxic leadership in the organizational context and its impact on subordinates' emotional distress, and coping mechanisms adopted by the followers of toxic leaders. In this work, independent variables such as personality, values and demographic factors were also utilized (see Tables A1.4–A1.6 for the details). Virtuous leader behaviours have also been studied to compare and contrast with toxic leader behaviour.

While studying the chemistry of toxic leaders as well as virtuous leaders, both survey and case methods were adopted.

PART I: CASE STUDIES TOXIC AND VIRTUOUS

Identification of Toxic Leaders

At the first stage, we could identify 15 toxic leaders on the basis of the feedback from various sources, as well as our own experience as consultants and trainers. In the second stage, we tried to find an adequate number of top- and senior-level respondents who were willing to share their experiences of working with such leaders. Our cut-off rate for the number of respondents speaking about the selected toxic leaders was 10. On the basis of this criterion, we could find only 11 leaders to study for this research.

Interviews were conducted (about 11 identified toxic leaders who were either CEOs or CMDs) with 110 senior-level executives (directors, vice presidents, executive directors and general managers) from the corporate sector who have worked with them. Since it was difficult to openly gather data on toxic leadership (owing to the sensitive nature of the issues under study), a purposive sampling approach was adopted.

Motivating people to talk was itself a big challenge. People spoke on condition of complete anonymity. There was clear fear of consequences among the respondents, if their names were to come to light in any way. Therefore, names and identities have not been divulged. Background information about the toxic leader under study has been deliberately kept vague to protect the identity of the leader under discussion

Identification of Virtuous Leaders

In the case of virtuous leaders, we studied five leadership cases on the basis of the extraordinary performances of the leaders in terms of company turnover, revenue growth, profits, culture shift, new strategies adopted and the impact that they could create at the institutional and national levels. In these cases, we kept 20 respondents per case as the cut-off to select a case. We were successful in identifying 20 respondents who were each willing to share their experiences of working with Major General Khurana, Mr Mallya and Mr Dubey. However, in the case of two leaders, R.V. Shahi and Vinod Rai, we could identify only around 10 respondents who were each willing to speak about their experiences of working with these leaders; hence, we reduced the cut-off number to 10 persons who had worked with them at different stages of their career. In the case of R.V. Shahi, we could get people who had worked with him in NTPC, BSES and Ministry of Power. In the case of Vinod Rai, we could identify ex-colleagues from the Kerala cadre, Ministry of Banking and Finance, CAG, CMDs who had worked with him while he was Secretary of the Department of Finance and three retired bureaucrats who had closely followed the saga of Vinod Rai's handling of various scams.

Interviews were conducted with 81 persons across the five cases. The respondents were selected by us through an unofficial process based on our own contacts in these organizations and not through the leaders themselves. This was done to bring a greater level of objectivity in the information for case writing.

Each interview lasted between one to two hours. Each interview opened with a broad question, 'Please share with us your experience of working with this leader.' Respondents were requested to give five adjectives to describe the leader. After that the interviewee was requested to explain the adjectives which they had given. As and when required, probe questions were asked: what, why and how?

To compress the time required to carry out data collection, both survey and interviews were carried out more or less concurrently.

Data Analyses

Interviews—both toxic and virtuous—were subjected to content analysis.[141,142] Two levels of thematic analysis were done. Related themes which we extracted in level 1 were further regrouped into level 2 of the data analysis and were then used for final case writing. It may be worthwhile mentioning that the entire research was conducted over three years, 2012–2015.

PART II: SURVEY-BASED RESEARCH

Seven scales have been used in the survey-based research. Three of these scales are either standard scales or modified scales designed to assess: (a) resilience, (b) personal values and (c) work locus of control. Since suitable scales were not available to assess emotional distress and coping, they were developed by the authors on the basis of an extensive literature review. Similarly, toxic and virtuous leadership scales have also been developed by the researchers based on an exhaustive literature review as well as focused group discussions. Psychometric properties of the scales are presented in Tables A1.2

to A1.6. The scale development for the leadership inventory including both toxic and virtuous leadership went through multiple stages, the details of which are given next.

Leadership Inventory (Toxic Leadership and Virtuous Leadership)

Phase 1: In the first phase, an extensive literature review was undertaken to identify the list of toxic and virtuous leader attributes. Through this process, 35 toxic leadership and 30 virtuous attributes were selected. Since there were many overlapping attributes, we went for phase two.

Phase 2: To validate the items in the second phase, a group of working managers ($N = 52$) were asked to indicate five behaviours of the leaders whom they despised and disliked working with. They were also asked to identify five attributes of leaders that they admired and felt excited to work with. The following instructions were given to the respondents at this stage:

> You might have worked with a leader whom you disliked and felt uncomfortable to work with. Keeping such a leader in view, kindly mention 10 words to describe the behaviors of that leader. Similarly, mention 10 words to describe the behavior of a leader whom you admired and liked to work with.

We selected only those 25 items from this list, where 75% of responses featured. In this process, we arrived at a pool of 25 items for toxic leadership. A similar approach was followed in generating a list of attributes of virtuous leaders. Through this process we arrived at 27 items regarding virtuous leaders.

Phase 3: To validate the items we discussed the same with experts consisting of 15 academicians and 15 HR heads. On the basis of their observations and comments, we could further reduce the number of items to 20 toxic and 20 virtuous leadership attributes, which were then adopted for the final data collection (refer to Table A1.1).

Pilot Testing of Toxic Leadership and Virtuous Leadership Inventory

In this study, toxic leadership has been operationalized in terms of leader values, attitude and behaviours which have an unpleasant demeaning and repulsive impact on the subordinates. Virtuous leadership has been operationalized in terms of those leader values, attitudes and behaviours which have a positive and inspiring impact on subordinates attracting them to work with such leaders.

The toxic leadership and virtuous leadership inventory was designed in such a way that respondents had to select 10 attributes out of 20 (from each list). At the pilot testing stage, 25 respondents were asked to identify 10 toxic leaders' attributes and then rate them on a five-point rating scale with 1 being to a minimum extent and 5 being to a maximum extent. A similar approach was adopted in the case of the virtuous leadership list as well.

While responding to the questionnaire, participants mentioned that they found it too difficult to rate each leadership attribute on a five-point scale. Perusal of the responses showed a uniform response pattern namely 5 on 5 in the majority of the responses. The mode of response was, therefore, modified and respondents were asked to select 10 leader behaviours. The same pattern was followed in the case of the virtuous leadership scale. This approach was finally adopted because the respondents found it too cumbersome and tedious to do both ranking and rating of the leader attributes.

Emotional Distress Inventory

Emotional distress is defined as mental distress or anxiety suffered as a response to a sudden, severe and saddening experience. It includes all highly unpleasant mental reactions. This inventory was developed by the researchers on the basis of extensive literature review. It consists of 18 items and all items are to be rated on a seven-point Likert scale, 1 being strongly disagree and 7 being strongly agree. This scale seeks to identify the type of emotional reactions that respondents experienced while working with a toxic leader (see Table A1.2 for details of the questionnaire and statistical properties).

Coping Inventory

Coping strategies refer to the specific efforts, both behavioural and psychological, that people employ to master, tolerate, reduce or minimize stressful events. This scale was also developed by the researchers on the basis of literature review. This scale attempts to identify the coping mechanisms used by followers while working with toxic leaders. This scale consists of 20 items, each to be rated on a seven-point Likert scale, 1 being never and 7 being always. (See Table A1.3 for details of the questionnaire and statistical properties.)

Resilience Scale

Resilience is the ability to bounce back and retain a sense of curiosity and hopefulness about the future in the face of adversity. Resilience has been assessed using a 12-item scale developed by Orioli, Trocki and Jones.[143] Respondents were asked to rate each of the items on a four-point scale with '1' being 'describe me not at all' and '4' being 'describe me very well'. (See Table A1.4 for details of the question- naire and statistical properties.)

Work Locus of Control Scale

Work locus of control refers to an individual's belief that work out- comes are controlled either by one's own actions—internal locus of control, or by factors beyond the individual's control—external locus of control. (See Table A1.5 for details of the questionnaire and statistical properties.) In our study, we have used work locus of control (WLOC) scale developed by Spector.[144] It consists of 16 items (8 for measuring internal WLOC and 8 for external WLOC) to be rated on a five-point Likert scale, 1 being least important and 5 being most important.

Personal Values Scale

Values are defined as beliefs and personal standards that guide indi- viduals to function in a society.[145] To understand the value system of the respondents, we have used a modified version of the Rokeach Value Survey (RVS). Our scale consists of 25 items, of which 16 items were taken from the RVS and 9 items were added by the researchers based on a survey of the literature. Respondents were asked to rate each of the items on a five-point scale with '1' being the least important and '5' being the most important. (See Table A1.6 for details of the questionnaire and statistical properties.)

Demographic Variables

Information about the respondents in terms of their age, gender, educational background, sector, work experience, years of experience in the present post, place of upbringing, type of family, birth order and nationality was also collected.

Sample Details: Questionnaire-based Research

The questionnaire was administered on a sample of heterogeneous middle level executives from various organizations. Table 1.1 provides the details. The sample consisted of middle-level executives who were requested to share their experiences of working with toxic and virtuous leaders.

Data Analysis

In the case of both toxic and virtuous leader scales, the item pool selected by the respondents on each scale was aggregated on the total sample through frequency distribution, and on the basis of this frequency, the items were ranked in order of priority separately for toxic and virtuous leaders. Since the data was not on a continuum, advanced statistical analysis could not be carried out. Hence, researchers used Spearman's coefficient of correlation and *t*-tests wherever relevant.

As far as the Likert scales were concerned, factor analysis and Cronbach alpha were worked out to assess the validity and reliability of the instruments. (See Tables A1.2–A1.6 for psychometric details.)

TABLE 1.1

Sample Details of Questionnaire-based Research

Sample classification	N	Percentage
Total sample	734	
International executives	164	22.34
Indian public sector executives	263	35.83
Indian private sector executives	307	41.82
Age		
Up to 30 years	268	36.51
31–45 years	233	31.74
46 years and above	233	31.74
Work experience		
Up to 5 years	250	34.06
6–15 years	154	20.98
16 years and above	330	44.95
Educational qualifications		
Graduation	342	46.59
Post-graduation	392	53.40
Gender		
Male	516	70.30
Female	218	29.70
Type of family		
Nuclear family	433	58.99
Joint family	301	41
Organizational sector		
Indian public sector executives	263	35.83
Indian private sector executives	307	41.82
Working industry		
Service industry	423	57.62
Manufacturing industry	311	42.37
Nationality		
International executives	164	22.34
Indian executives	570	77.65

Appendix

TABLE A1.1

Leadership Inventory
(Pilot Testing of Toxic Leadership and Virtuous Leadership)

Item no.	Toxic leadership attributes	Virtuous leadership attributes
1	Abusive	Demonstrate fairness in performance
2	Arrogant	Respectful about the dignity of others
3	Dishonest and lacked integrity	Humble and empowering
4	Blaming others	Good listener
5	Create insecurity among people	Provide clear sense of direction for performance
6	Ill-tempered	Ethical and honest
7	Manipulative and playing favourites	Dynamic and radiates positive energy
8	Insensitive to my feelings	Impartial
9	Demeaning others	Lead by example
10	Narcissist	Fast in making critical decisions
11	Play 'divide and rule'	Visionary
12	Power hungry	Kind hearted
13	Publicly ridiculed others	Approachable
14	Hypocrite	Courageous to take bold decisions
15	Rude	Respect people regardless of levels (non-hierarchical)
16	Self-opinionated and close minded	Cool and composed
17	Shared sensitive and personal information about others	Mentor and coach
18	Take credit of others works	Make people feel that they are valuable
19	Unreliable and untrustworthy	Man of words
20	Corrupt	Always remember person's name

TABLE A1.2

Emotional Distress Inventory

Items	Mean	SD	Corrected item—Total correlation	Give up/ despair	Anxious	Upset	Worth- lessness	Commu- nalities
1. Angry	5.12	1.48	0.435			0.827		0.692
2. Humiliated and insulted	4.75	1.67	0.596			0.719		0.639
3. Irritated	5.25	1.52	0.496			0.788		0.645
4. Insecure	4.30	1.73	0.591		0.783			0.680
5. Losing confidence in myself	3.68	1.85	0.604		0.826			0.691
6. Nervous	3.83	1.69	0.550		0.712			0.541
7. Shouting back	3.78	1.70	0.462				0.700	0.640
8. Unwanted	3.91	2.01	0.483				0.769	0.605
9. Alienated	3.93	1.68	0.653				0.725	0.616
10. Suffered with feeling of worthlessness	3.85	4.02	0.354				0.529	0.321

	Mean	SD				
11. Anxious	4.23	1.56	0.547		0.622	0.467
12. Deep sense of failure	3.53	1.71	0.622		0.669	0.594
13. Depressed and distressed	4.03	1.78	0.654	0.777		0.640
14. Detached from work	4.02	1.80	0.546	0.789		0.692
15. Frustrated	4.51	1.78	0.560	0.791		0.699
16. Helpless and hopeless	3.89	1.78	0.646	0.817		0.679
17. Ill-treated	4.50	1.69	0.575	0.600		0.503
18. Jittery	4.08	1.48	0.601	0.622		0.493

Cronbach's Alpha: 887
Extraction Method: Principal Component Analysis.
Rotation Method: Varimax with Kaiser Normalization.

TABLE A1.3

Coping Inventory

Items	Mean	SD	Corrected item—Total correlation	Avoidance	Approach	Assertive	Adaptive	Commu-nalities
1. Adapted with the leader's behaviour	3.16	1.48	0.155				0.746	0.609
2. Alienated and detached myself from the leader	3.37	1.55	0.520	0.727				0.564
3. Avoided any communication with him/her	3.24	1.63	0.556	0.777				0.632
4. Complained to the higher authority	2.17	1.48	0.486		0.728			0.585
5. Complained to the officers association	1.95	1.37	0.386		0.784			0.617
6. Considered it as a bad phase which would ultimately pass by	4.22	2.11	0.273				0.452	0.369
7. Did not share business related problems or opportunities with him	3.36	1.76	0.481	0.675				0.476
8. Silently disobeyed the leader's instructions	2.80	1.55	0.592	0.660				0.530
9. Exhibited lack of concern with organizational goals	2.44	1.61	0.527	0.598				0.484
10. Confronted with him/her and fought for my rights	3.12	1.57	0.460			0.579		0.540
11. Gossiped about the leader with others	2.80	1.65	0.536	0.450				0.403

Item							
12. Got into harsh arguments with the boss	2.31	1.39	0.540		0.514		0.455
13. Left the organization because of the leader	2.12	1.70	0.341		0.549		0.349
14. Tried to maintain positive relationship with the leader	4.02	1.57	0.056			0.648	0.575
15. Tried to maintain minimum relationship with the leader	3.56	1.64	0.433	0.640			0.480
16. Protested openly to the leader	2.61	1.51	0.484		0.584		0.530
17. Got furious but tried to compose myself for the right time to discuss	3.96	1.59	0.411			0.650	0.610
18. Tried to mobilize the opinion of others against the leaders	2.45	1.55	0.544		0.491		0.443
19. Was assertive and staunch in my opinion	3.76	1.56	0.397			0.768	0.638
20. Wrote anonymous letters to higher authority in the organization	1.44	1.10	0.401		0.743		0.562

Cronbach's Alpha: .844
Extraction Method: Principal Component Analysis.
Rotation Method: Varimax with Kaiser Normalization.

TABLE A1.4

Resilience Scale

Items	Mean	SD	Corrected item—Total correlation	Self regulation	Over-coming obstacles	Efficacy	Positive thinking	Commu-nalities
1. I can accomplish what I need to if I put my mind to it	3.65	0.64	0.197			0.700		0.511
2. I can bounce back after feeling disappointed	3.36	0.82	0.281			0.694		0.506
3. I can see the humorous side of situations	3.28	0.75	0.343			0.611		0.478
4. I decide certain problems are not worth worrying about	3.14	0.81	0.394			0.502		0.433
5. I find it easy to wait patiently when I need to	3.07	0.88	0.363	0.583				0.402
6. I know how to relax when tension builds up	2.93	0.80	0.388	0.814				0.687
7. I know how to satisfy all parts of myself	2.98	0.73	0.363	0.732				0.554
8. I often put things aside for a while to get a perspective on them	2.98	0.73	0.316				0.600	0.437

Item					
9. Obstacles or problems in my life have resulted in unexpected changes for the better	3.17	0.82	0.281		0.772	0.603
10. There is always more than one right answer	3.28	0.83	0.255		0.552	0.459
11. When I encounter a problem, I focus on what I can do to solve it	3.59	0.60	0.374	0.856		0.765
12. When something is not working I try to come up with an alternative plan	3.49	0.64	0.369	0.848		0.765

Cronbach Alpha: .690
Extraction Method: Principal Component Analysis.
Rotation Method: Varimax with Kaiser Normalization.

SOURCE: Orioli, Trocki and Jones (2000).[143]

TABLE A1.5

Work Locus of Control Scale

Items	Mean	SD	Corrected item—Total correlation
1. A job is what you make of it	1.99	0.87	0.300
2. On most jobs, people can pretty much accomplish whatever they set out to accomplish	2.31	0.87	0.320
3. If you know what you want out of a job, you can find a job that gives it to you	2.12	0.85	0.257
4. If employees are unhappy with a decision made by boss, they should do something about it	2.25	0.94	−0.001
5. Getting the job you want is mostly a matter of luck	2.74	1.11	0.473
6. Making money is primarily a matter of good fortune	2.63	1.07	0.416
7. Most people are capable of doing their jobs well if they make the effort	1.95	0.95	0.169
8. In order to get a really good job you need to have family members or friends in high places	2.12	1.09	0.429
9. Promotions are usually a matter of good fortune	2.40	0.99	0.491
10. When it comes to landing a really good job, whom you know is more important than what you know	2.47	1.07	0.431

Item			
11. Promotions are given to employees who perform well on the job	2.32	0.98	0.284
12. To make a lot of money you have to know the right people	2.75	1.11	0.256
13. It takes a lot of luck to be an outstanding employee on the most jobs	2.41	1.05	0.417
14. People who perform their jobs well generally get rewarded for it	2.35	0.97	0.315
15. Most employees have more influence on their supervisors than they think they do	2.78	0.93	0.048
16. The main difference between people who make a lot of money and people who make a little money is luck	2.29	0.99	0.382

Cronbach Alpha: .720

SOURCE: Spector (1988).[144]

TABLE A1.6

Personal Values Scale

Items	Mean	SD	Corrected item—Total correlation	Egalit-arian	Human-istic	Hedon-istic	Personal develop-ment	Pride	Material-istic	Commu-nalities
1. Money	3.56	0.77	0.206						0.777	0.618
2. Contribution to society	3.86	0.77	0.272				0.593			0.601
3. Opportunity to be creative	3.98	0.82	0.361				0.734			0.596
4. Opportunity for self-development	4.41	0.68	0.492				0.654			0.643
5. Opportunity to realize your potential	4.49	0.64	0.494				0.651			0.612
6. A comfortable life	3.88	0.90	0.364						0.605	0.623
7. An exciting life	3.87	0.97	0.389			0.532				0.507
8. A sense of accomplishment	4.33	0.78	0.458					0.705		0.608
9. Self-controlled	4.12	0.80	0.502	0.525						0.421
10. Equality	4.11	0.81	0.558	0.581						0.473
11. Family	4.42	0.76	0.443		0.714					0.603

	Mean	SD						
12. Freedom	4.28	0.78	0.553		0.588			0.563
13. Happiness	4.45	0.74	0.471		0.709			0.601
14. Status	3.77	0.94	0.431			0.723		0.632
15. Courageous	4.03	0.81	0.541	0.631				0.576
16. Responsible	4.37	0.69	0.463	0.550				0.530
17. Honesty	4.48	0.72	0.431		0.481			0.527
18. Pleasure	3.90	0.97	0.448			0.674		0.615
19. Salvation/Nirvana	3.66	1.12	0.399	0.507				0.420
20. Self-respect/dignity	4.37	0.79	0.436				.523	0.402
21. Social recognition	3.94	0.91	0.460			0.638		0.568
22. True friendship	4.23	0.85	0.490		0.452			0.496
23. Wisdom	4.34	0.73	0.586	0.593				0.513
24. Work Itself	3.99	0.87	0.494	0.563				0.447
25. Forgiving	4.01	0.88	0.460	0.629				0.496

Cronabach Alpha: .878
Extraction Method: Principal Component Analysis.
Rotation Method: Varimax with Kaiser Normalization.

REFERENCES

1. Kamerkar, M. (2015). Contribution of Gandhi's non-violence to world civilization. Retrieved from http://www.gandhi-manibhavan.org/activities/essay_worldcivil.htm (accessed on 15 July 2015).
2. Forbes (2015). The 10 Biggest Frauds in Recent U.S. History. Retrieved from http://www.forbes.com/pictures/efik45ekdjl/our-take-on-the-10-biggest-frauds-in-recent-u-s-history-2/ (accessed on 15 July 2015).
3. McCall, M.W., Jr. & Lombardo, M. M. (1983). *Off the track: Why and how successful executives get derailed.* Technical Report No. 21. Greensboro, NC: Center for Creative Leadership.
4. Conger, J.A. (1990). The dark side of leadership. *Organizational Dynamics, 19*(2), 44–55.
5. Lipman-Blumen, J. (2005). *The allure of toxic leaders. Why we follow destructive bosses and corrupt politicians—and how we can survive them.* Oxford: Oxford University Press.
6. Tepper, B.J. (2000). Consequences of abusive supervision. *Academy of Management Journal, 43*(2), 178–190.
7. Einarsen, S., Aasland, M.S., & Skogstad, A. (2007). Destructive leadership behaviour: A definition and conceptual model. *The Leadership Quarterly, 18*(3), 207–216.
8. Higgs, M.J. (2009). The good, the bad and the ugly: Leadership and narcissism. *Journal of Change Management, 9*(2), 165–178.
9. Benson, M., & Hogan, R. (2008). How dark side leadership personality destroys trust and degrades organisational effectiveness. *Organisations and People, 15*(3), 10–18.
10. Pelletier, K.L. (2010). Leader toxicity: An empirical investigation of toxic behavior and rhetoric. *Leadership, 6*(4) 373–389.
11. Djurkovic, N., McCormack, D., & Casimir, G. (2004). The physical and psychological effects of workplace bullying on intention to leave: A test of psychosomatic and disability hypotheses. *International Journal of Educational and Developmental Psychology, 3*(1), 35–47.
12. Ashforth, B.E. (1994). Petty tyranny in organizations. *Human Relations, 47*(7), 755–778.
13. Sims, R.L. (2002). Ethical rule breaking by employees: A test of social bonding theory. *Journal of Business Ethics, 40*(2), 101–109.
14. Hogan, R., Curphy, G.J., & Hogan, J. (1994). What we know about leadership: Effectiveness and personality. *American Psychologist, 49*(6), 493–504.
15. McHoskey, J.W. (1999). Machiavellianism, intrinsic versus extrinsic goals, and social interest: A self-determination theory analysis. *Motivation and Emotion, 23*(4), 267–283.
16. Becker, J.H.A., & O'Hair, H.D. (2007). Machiavellians' motives in organizational citizenship behavior. *Journal of Applied Communication Research, 35*(3), 246–267.
17. Kets de Vries, M.F.R. (1993). *Leaders, Fools and Imposters,* San Francisco, CA: Jossey-Bass.
18. Rosenthal, S.A., & Pittinsky, T.L. (2006). Narcissistic leadership. *The Leadership Quarterly, 17*(6), 617–633.
19. Kets de Vries, M.F.R. (2009). *Reflections on character and leadership.* West Sussex, UK: John Wiley & Sons.
20. Kets de Vries, M.F.R., & Miller, D. (1997). Narcissism and leadership: An object relations perspective. In R. P. Vecchio (Ed.), *Leadership: Understanding the dynamics of power and influence in organizations* (pp. 194–214), Notre dame: University of Notre Dame Press.
21. Hogan, R., Raskin, R., & Fazzini, D. (1990). The dark side of charisma. In K.E. Clark & M.B. Clarke (Eds), *Measures of Leadership,* (pp. 343–354), West Orange, NJ: Leadership Library of America.
22. White, R.K. (1991). Empathizing with Saddam Hussein. *Political Psychology, 12*(2), 291–308.
23. Sheng, M.M. (2001). Mao Zedong's narcissistic personality disorder and China's road to disaster. In O. Feldman & L.O. Valenty (Eds), *Profiling political leaders* (pp. 111–127). Westport, CT: Praeger.

24. Glad, B. (2002). Why tyrants go too far: Malignant narcissism and absolute power. *Political Psychology, 23*(1), 1–37.

25. Maccoby, M. (2007). *Narcissistic leaders: Who succeeds and who fails.* Boston, MA: Harvard Business School Press.

26. Kusy, M., & Holloway, E. (2009). *Toxic workplace: Managing toxic personalities.* San Francisco, CA: Jossey-Bass.

27. Baron, R. (1988). Negative effects of destructive criticism: Impact on conflict, self-efficacy, and task performance. *Journal of Applied Psychology, 73*(1), 199–207.

28. Burton, J., & Hoobler, J. (2006). Subordinate self-esteem and abusive supervision. *Journal of Managerial Issues, 18*(3), 340–355.

29. Duffy, M., Ganster, D., & Pagon, M. (2002). Social undermining in the workplace. *Academy of Management Journal, 45*(2), 331–351.

30. Aryee, S., Chen, Z.X., Sun, L.-Y., & Debrah, Y.A. (2007). Antecedents and outcomes of abusive supervision: Test of a trickle-down model. *Journal of Applied Psychology, 92*(1), 191–201.

31. Schat, A.C.H., Desmarais, S., & Kelloway, E.K. (2006). *Exposure to workplace aggression from multiple sources: Validation of a measure and test of a model.* Unpublished manuscript, McMaster University, Hamilton, Canada.

32. Elangovan, A.R., & Xie, J.L. (2000). Effects of perceived power of supervisor on subordinate work attitudes. *Leadership & Organization Development Journal, 21*(6), 319–328.

33. Tepper, B.J., Duffy, M.K., Hoonler, J., & Ensley, M.D. (2004). Moderators of the relationship between coworkers' organizational citizenship behavior and fellow employees' attitudes. *Journal of Applied Psychology, 89*(3), 455–465.

34. Richman, J.A., Flaherty, J.A., Rospenda, K.M., & Christensen, M. (1992). Mental health consequences and correlates of medical student abuse. *Journal of the American Medical Association, 267*(5), 692–694.

35. Rayner, C., & Cooper, C. (1997). Workplace bullying: Myth or reality—can we afford to ignore it? *Leadership and Organization Development Journal 18*(4), 211–214.

36. Harris, K.J., Kacmar, K.M., & Zivnuska, S. (2007). An investigation of abusive supervision as a predictor of performance and the meaning of work as a moderator of the relationship. *The Leadership Quarterly, 18*(3), 252–263.

37. Restubog, S., Scott, K., & Zagenczyk, T. (2011). When distress hits home: The role of contextual factors and psychological distress in predicting employees' responses to abusive supervision. *Journal of Applied Psychology, 96*(4), 713–729.

38. Chen, H., & Kao, H.S. (2009). Chinese paternalistic leadership and non-chinese subordinates' psychological health. *The International Journal of Human Resource Management, 20*(12), 2533–2546.

39. Hobman, E., Restubog, S., & Bordia, P. (2009). Abusive supervision in advising relationships: Investigating the role of social support. *Applied Psychology: An International Review, 58*(2), 233–256.

40. Burris, E.R., Detert, J.R., & Chiaburu, D.S. (2008). Quitting before leaving: The mediating effects of psychological attachment and detachment on voice. *Journal of Applied Psychology, 93*(6), 912–922.

41. Ashforth, B.E. (1997). Petty tyranny in organizations: A preliminary examination of antecedents and consequences. *Canadian Journal of Administrative Sciences, 14*(2), 126–140.

42. Harvey, P., Stoner, J., Hochwarter, W., & Kacmar, C. (2007). Coping with abusive bosses: The neutralizing effects of ingratiation and positive affect on negative employee outcomes. *The Leadership Quarterly, 18*(3), 264–280.

43. Wu, T., & Hu, C. (2009). Abusive supervision and employee emotional exhaustion: Dispositional antecedents and boundaries. *Group and Organization Management, 34*(1), 143–169.

44. Cropanzano, R., Rupp, D.E., & Byrne, Z.S. (2003). The relationship of emotional exhaustion to work attitudes, job performance, and organizational citizenship behaviors. *Journal of Applied Psychology, 88*(1), 160.

45. Kellerman, B. (2004). *Bad leadership: What it is, how it happens, why it matters.* Boston: Harvard Business School Press.

46. Sutton, R.I. (2007). *The no asshole rule: Building a civilized workplace and surviving one that isn't.* New York, NY: Warren Business Books.

47. Mawritz, M.B., Mayer, D.M., Hoobler, J.M., Wayne, S.J., & Marinova, S. (2012). A trickle-down model of abusive supervision. *Personnel Psychology, 65*(2), 325–357.

48. Robinson, S.L., & Bennett, R.J. (1995). A typology of deviant workplace behaviors: A multidimensional scaling study. *Academy of Management Journal, 38*(2), 555–572.

49. Bies, R.J., & Tripp, T.M. (1996). Beyond distrust: "Getting even" and the need for revenge. In R.M. Kramer & T.R. Tyler (Eds), *Trust in organizations: Frontiers of theory and research* (pp. 246–260). Thousand Oaks, CA: SAGE Publications.

50. Tripp, T.M., Bies, R.J., & Aquino, K. (2002). Poetic justice or petty jealousy? The aesthetics of revenge. *Organizational Behavior and Human Decision Processes, 89*(1), 966–984.

51. Mitchell, M.S., & Ambrose, M.L. (2007). Abusive supervision and workplace deviance and the moderating effects of negative reciprocity beliefs. *Journal of Applied Psychology, 92*(4), 1159–1168.

52. Tepper, B.J., Henle, C.A., Lambert, L.S., Giacalone, R.A., & Duffy, M.K. (2008). Abusive supervision and subordinates' organizational deviance. *Journal of Applied Psychology, 93*(4), 721–732.

53. Thau, S., Bennett, R.J., Mitchell, M.S., & Marrs, M.B. (2009). How management style moderates the relationship between abusive supervision and workplace deviance: An uncertainty management theory perspective. *Organizational Behavior and Human Decision Processes, 108*(1), 79–92.

54. Tepper, B.J. (2007). Abusive supervision in work organizations: review, synthesis, and research agenda. *Journal of Management 33*(3), 261–289.

55. Bacal, R. (2000). *Toxic organizations: Welcome to the fire of an unhealthy workplace.* Retrieved from http://work911.com/articles/toxicorgs.htm (accessed in 15 July 2015).

56. Dobrian, J. (1997). Match wits with the evil boss. *Getting Results for the Hands on Manager, 42*(11), 7.

57. Burns, J.M. (1978). *Leadership.* New York, NY: Harper & Row.

58. Argyris, C. (1957). *Personality and organization: The conflict between system and the individual.* New York, NY: Harper.

59. McGregor, D. (1960). *The human side of enterprise.* New York, NY: McGraw-Hill.

60. Maslow, A.H. (1954). *Motivation and personality.* New York, NY: Harper and Row.

61. Rogers, C. (1951). *Client-centered therapy: Its current practice, implications and theory.* London, UK: Constable.

62. Sullivan, H.S. (1953). *The interpersonal theory of psychiatry.* New York, NY: Norton

63. Fromm, E. (1941). *The forgotten language: An introduction to the understanding of dreams, fairy tales, and myths.* New York, NY: Rinehart and Co.

64. Frankl, V.E. (1959). *Man's search for meaning: An introduction to logotherapy.* Boston, MA: Beacon.

65. Handy, C. (1976). *Understanding organisations.* London, UK: Penguin Books.

66. Kelloway, E.K., Weigand, H., McKee, M.C., & Das, H. (2013). Positive leadership and employee well-being. *Journal of Leadership & Organizational Studies, 20*(1), 107–117.

67. Brown, M.E., Treviño, L.K., & Harrison, D.A. (2005). Ethical leadership: A social learning perspective for construct development and testing. *Organizational Behavior and Human Decision Processes, 92*(2), 117–134.

68. Avolio, B.J., Gardner, W.L., Walumbwa, F.O., Luthans, F., & May, D.R. (2004). Unlocking the mask: A look at the process by which authentic leaders impact follower attitudes and behaviors. *The Leadership Quarterly, 15*(6), 801–823.

69. Flynn, F.J., & Staw, B.M. (2004). Lend me your wallets: The effects of charismatic leadership on external support for an organization. *Strategic Management Journal, 25,* 309–330.

70. Shamir, B. (1991). Meaning, self and motivation in organizations. *Organization Studies, 12*(3), 405–424.

71. Greenleaf, R.K. (1996). *On becoming a servant-leader.* San Francisco, CA: Josey-Bass Publishers.

72. Fry, L.W. (2003). Toward a theory of spiritual leadership. *The Leadership Quarterly, 14*(6), 693–727.

73. Singh, P., & Bhandarker, A. (2012). *In search of change maestros.* New Delhi, India: SAGE Publications.

74. Conger, J. (1999). Charismatic and transformational leadership in organizations: An insider's perspective on these developing streams of research. *Leadership Quarterly, 10*(1), 145–179.

75. Judge, T.A., & Piccolo, R.F. (2004). Transformational and transactional leadership: A meta-analytic test of their relative validity. *Journal of Applied Psychology, 89*(5), 755–768.

76. Avolio, B.J., Bass, B.M., & Jung, D.I. (1999). Re-examining the components of transformational and transactional leadership using the multifactor leadership questionnaire. *Journal of Occupational and Organizational Psychology, 72*(4), 441–462.

77. Singh, P., & Bhandarker, A. (1989). Roadmap to transformational leadership. *IIMB Management Review, 11*(1), 39–50.

78. Carless, S.A. (1998). Assessing the discriminate validity of transformational leadership behavior as measured by the MLQ. *Journal of Occupational and Organizational Psychology, 71*(4), 353–358.

79. Tejeda, M.J., Scandura, T.A., & Pillai, R. (2001). The MLQ revisited: Psychometric properties and recommendations. *The Leadership Quarterly, 12*(1), 31–52.

80. Den Hartog, D.N., House, R.J., Hanges, P., Dorfman, P., & Ruiz-Quintanilla, A. (1999). Culture specific and cross-culturally endorsed implicit leadership theories: Are attributes of charismatic/transformational leadership universally endorsed? *Leadership Quarterly, 10*(2), 219–256.

81. Dvir, T., & Shamir, B. (2003). Follower developmental characteristics as predicting transformational leadership: A longitudinal field study. *The Leadership Quarterly, 14*(3), 327–344.

82. Jung, D.I., Chow, C., & Wu, A. (2003). The role of transformational leadership in enhancing organizational innovation: Hypotheses and some preliminary findings. *The Leadership Quarterly, 14*(4), 535–544.

83. Lim, B., & Ployhart, R.E. (2004). Transformational leadership: Relations to the five-factor model and team performance in typical and maximum contexts. *Journal of Applied Psychology, 89*(4), 610–621.

84. Shin, S., & Zhou, J. (2003). Transformational leadership, conservation, and creativity: Evidence from Korea. *Academy of Management Journal, 46*(6), 703–714.

85. Walumbwa, F.O., & Lawler, J.J. (2003). Building effective organizations: Transformational leadership, collectivist orientation, work-related attitudes, and withdrawal behaviors in three emerging economies. *International Journal of Human Resource Management, 14*(7), 1083–1101.

86. Podsakoff, P.M., MacKenzie, S.B., Morrman, R.H., & Fetter, R. (1990). Transformational leader behaviors and their effects on follower's trust in leader satisfaction, and organizational citizenship behaviors. *The Leadership Quarterly, 1*(1), 107–142.

87. Colbert, A.E., Kristof-Brown, A.L., Bradley, B.H., & Barrick, M.R. (2008). CEO transformational leadership: The role of goal importance congruence in top management teams. *Academy of Management Journal, 51*(1), 81–96.

88. Waldman, D.A., & Yammarino, F.J. (1999). CEO charismatic leadership: Levels-of-management and levels-of-analysis effects. *Academy of Management Review, 24*(2), 266–285.

89. Wang, G., Oh, I., Courtright, S.H., & Colbert, A.E. (2011). Transformational leadership and performance across criteria and levels: A meta-analytic review of 25 years of research. *Group & Organization Management, 36*(2), 223–270.

90. Howell, J.M., & Hall-Merenda, K.E. (1999). The ties that bind: The impact of leader–member exchange, transformational and transactional leadership, and distance on predicting follower performance. *Journal of Applied Psychology, 84*(5), 680–694.

91. Schaubroeck, J., Lam, S.K., & Cha, S.E. (2007). Embracing transformational leadership: Team values and the impact of leader behavior on team performance. *Journal of Applied Psychology, 92*(4), 1020–1030.

92. House, R.J. (1977). A 1976 theory of charismatic leadership. In J.G. Hunt & L.L. Larson (Eds), *Leadership: The cutting edge* (pp. 189–207). Carbondale: Southern Illinois: University Press.

93. Conger, J.A., & Kanungo, R. (1998). *Charismatic leadership in organizations.* Thousand Oaks, CA: SAGE Publications.

94. Galvin, B.M., Waldman, D.A., & Balthazard, P. (2010). Visionary communication qualities as mediators of the relationship between narcissism and attributions of leader charisma. *Personnel Psychology, 63*(3), 509–537.

95. Shamir, B., House, R.J., & Arthur, M.B. (1993). The motivational effects of charismatic leadership: A self-concept theory. *Organization Science, 4*(1), 1–17.

96. Brown, M.E., & Trevino, L.K. (2006). Ethical leadership: A review and future directions. *The Leadership Quarterly, 17*(6), 595–616.

97. Mayer, D.M., Aquino, K., Greenbaum, R.S., & Kuenzi, M. (2012). Who displays ethical leadership and why does it matter? An examination of antecedents and consequences of ethical leadership. *Academy of Management Journal, 55*(1), 151–171.

98. Detert, J.R., Treviño, L.K., Burris, E.R., & Andiappan, M. (2007). Managerial modes of influence and counter productivity in organizations: A longitudinal business-unit-level investigation. *Journal of Applied Psychology, 94*(2), 993–1005.

99. Kalshoven, K., Den Hartog, N., & Den Hoogh, A.H.B. (2011). Ethical leadership at work questionnaire (ELW): Development and validation of multi-dimensional measure. *Leadership Quarterly, 22*(1), 51–69.

100. Mayfield, J., & Mayfield, M. (2002). Leader communication strategies critical paths to improving employee commitment. *American Business Review, 20*(2), 89–94.

101. Ogunfowora, B., & Bourdage, J.S. (2014). Does Honesty-Humility influence evaluations of leadership emergence? The mediating role of moral disengagement. *Personality and Individual Differences, 56*(1), 95–99.

102. de Vries, R.E., Roe, R.A., & Taillieu, T.C.B. (1999). On charisma and need for leadership. *European Journal of Work and Organizational Psychology, 8*(1), 109–133.

103. Judge, T.A., & LePine, J.A. (2007). The bright and dark sides of personality: Implications for personnel selection in individual and team contexts. In J. Langan-Fox, C. Cooper, & R. Klimoski (Eds), Research companion to the dysfunctional workplace: Management challenges and symptoms (pp. 332–355). Cheltenham, UK: Edward Elgar Publishing.

104. Judge, T.A., Bono, J.E., Erez, A., & Locke, E.A. (2005). Core self-evaluations and job and life satisfaction: The role of self-concordance and goal attainment. *Journal of Applied Psychology, 90*(2), 257–268.

105. Northhouse, P.G. (1997). *Leadership: Theory and practice.* Thousand Oaks, CA: SAGE Publications.

106. Hogan, J., & Ones, D.S. (1997).Conscientiousness and integrity at work. In R. Hogan, J.A. Johnson, & S.R. Briggs (Eds), *Handbook of personality psychology* (pp. 849–870). San Diego, CA: Academic Press.

107. Judge, T.A., Bono, J.E., Ilies, R., & Gerhardt, M. (2002). Personality and leadership: A qualitative and quantitative review. *Journal of Applied Psychology, 87*(4), 765–780.

108. Graziano, W.G., & Eisenberg, N.H. (1997). Agreeableness: a dimension of personality. In R. Hogan, J. Johnston, & S. Briggs (Eds), *Handbook of personality psychology* (pp. 795–824). San Diego, CA: Academic Press.

109. Graziano, W.G., Jensen-Campbell, L.A., & Hair, E.C. (1996). Perceiving interpersonal conflict and reacting to it: The case for agreeableness. *Journal of Personality and Social Psychology, 70*(4), 820–835.

110. Hurtz, G.M., & Donovan, J.J. (2000). Personality and job performance: The big five revisited. *Journal of Applied Psychology, 85*(6), 869–879.

111. Mayer, D.M., Aquino, K., Greenbaum, R.L., & Kuenzi, M. (2008). *Who displays ethical leadership and why does it matter? An examination of antecedents and consequences of ethical leadership.* Presented at the 23rd Annual Meeting of the Society of Industrial and Organizational Psychology (SIOP), San Francisco, USA.

112. Bass, B.M. (1985). *Leadership and performance beyond expectations.* New York, NY: Free Press.

113. Mayer, D.M., Nishii, L.H., Schneider, B., & Goldstein, H.W. (2007). The precursors and products of fair climates: Group leader antecedents and employee attitudinal consequences. *Personnel Psychology, 60,* 929–963.

114. Judge, T.A., LePine, J.A., & Rich, B.L. (2006). Loving yourself abundantly: Relationship of the narcissistic personality to self- and other perceptions of workplace deviance, leadership, and task and contextual performance. *Journal of Applied Psychology, 91*(4), 762–776.

115. Judge, T.A., Thoresen, C.J., Pucik, V., & Welbourne, T.M. (1999). Managerial coping with organizational change: A dispositional perspective. *Journal of Applied Psychology, 84*(1), 107–122.

116. Bandura, A. (1986). *Social foundations of thought and action: A social cognitive theory.* Englewood Cliffs, NJ: Prentice- Hall, Inc.

117. Liao, H., & Chuang, A. (2007). Transforming service employees and climate: A multi-level multi-source examination of transformational leadership in building long-term service relationships. *Journal of Applied Psychology, 92*(4), 1006–1019.

118. McKenzie, S.B., Podsakoff, P.M., & Rich, G.R. (2001). Transformational and transactional leadership and salesperson performance. *Academy of Marketing Science Journal, 29*(2), 115–134.

119. Bass, B.M., & Avolio, B.J. (1993). Transformational leadership: A response to critiques. In M.M. Chemers & R. Ayman (Eds), *Leadership theory and research: Perspectives and directions* (pp. 49–80). San Diego, CA: Academic Press.

120. Kouzes, J.M., & Posner, B.Z. (2002). *The leadership challenge.* San Francisco, CA: Jossey-Bass.

121. Pillai, R., Schreisheim, C.A., & Williams, E.A. (1999). Fairness perceptions and trust as mediators for transformational leadership and transactional leadership: A two-sample study. *Journal of Management, 25*(6), 897–933.

122. Sosik, J.J. (2005). The role of personal values in the charismatic leadership of corporate managers: A model and preliminary field study. *Leadership Quarterly, 16*(2), 221–244.

123. Schaubroeck, J., Lam, S.K., & Cha, S.E. (2007). Embracing transformational leadership: Team values and the impact of leader behavior on team performance. *Journal of Applied Psychology, 92*(4), 1020–1030.

124. Avolio, B.J., & Yammarino, F.J. (2002). *Transformational and charismatic leadership: The road ahead.* New York, NY: Erlbaum.

125. Borman, W.C., & Motowidlo, S.J. (1993). Expanding the criterion domain to include elements of contextual performance. In N. Schmitt & W.C. Borman (Eds), *Personnel selection in organizations* (pp. 71–98). San Francisco, CA: Jossey-Bass.

126. Klein, K.J., Dansereau, F., & Hall, R.J. (1994). Levels issues in theory development, data collection, and analysis. *Academy of Management Review, 19*(2), 195–229.

127. Organ, D.W. (1988). *Organizational citizenship behavior: The good soldier syndrome.* Lexington, MA: Lexington Books.

128. Yammarino, F.J., Dionne, S.D., Chun, J.U., & Dansereau, F. (2005). Leadership and levels of analysis: A state-of-the-science review. *Leadership Quarterly, 16*(6), 879–919.

129. Zhu, W., Chew, I.K.H., & Spangler, W.D. (2005). CEO transformational leadership and organizational outcomes: The mediating role of human-capital-enhancing human resource management. *Leadership Quarterly, 16*(1), 39–52.

130. Diener, E. (1994). Assessing subjective well-being: Progress and opportunities. *Social Indicators Research, 31*(1), 103–157.

131. Fredrickson, B.L. (2003). Positive emotions and upward spirals in organizations. In K.S. Cameron, J.E. Dutton, & R.E. Quinn (Eds), *Positive organizational scholarship: Foundations of a new discipline* (pp. 163–175). San Francisco, CA: Berrett-Koehler.

132. Cameron K. (2012). *Positive leadership: Strategies for extraordinary performance.* San Francisco, CA: Berrett-Koehler.

133. Denison, D.R. (1996). What is the difference between organizational culture and organizational climate? A native's point of view on a decade of paradigm wars. *Academy of Management Review, 21*(3), 619–654.

134. Smidts, A., Pruyn, A.T.H., & van Riel, C.B.M. (2001). The impact of employee communication and perceived external prestige on organizational identification. *Academy of Management Journal, 44*(5), 1051–1062.

135. Mathieu, J., & Zajac, D. (1990). A review of meta-analysis of the antecedents, correlates and consequences of organizational commitment. *Psychological Bulletin, 108*(2), 171–194.

136. Bolino, M.C., Turnley, W.H., & Bloodgood, J.M. (2002). Citizenship behavior and the creation of social capital in organizations. *Academy of Management Review, 27*(4), 505–522.

137. Rhoades, L., & Eisenberger, R. (2002). Perceived organizational support: A review of the literature. *Journal of Applied Psychology, 87*(4), 698–714.

138. Scullen, S.E., Bergey, P.K., & Aiman-Smith, L. (2005). Forced distribution ranking systems and the improvement of workforce potential: A baseline simulation. *Personnel Psychology, 58*(1), 1–31.

139. Shaw, J.D., Gupta, N., & Delery, J.E. (2005). Alternative conceptualizations of the relationship between voluntary turnover and organizational performance. *Academy of Management Journal, 48*(1) 50–69.

140. Tsai, W.C., Chen, C.C., & Liu, H.L. (2007). Test of a model linking employee positive moods and task performance. *Journal of Applied Psychology, 92*(6), 1570–1583.

141. Krippendorff, K. (1980). *Content analysis: An introduction to its methodology.* Newbury Park, CA: SAGE Publications.

142. Neuendorf, K.A. (2002). *The content analysis guidebook.* Thousand Oaks, CA: SAGE Publications.

143. Orioli, E.M., Jones, T., & Trocki, K.H. (1999). *EQ Map technical manual.* San Francisco, CA: Q-Metrics.

144. Spector, P.E. (1988). Development of the work locus of control scale. *Journal of Occupational Psychology, 6*(4), 335–340.

145. Rokeach, M. (1973). *The nature of human values.* New York, NY: The Free Press.

CHAPTER 2

Toxic Leader Profile

INTRODUCTION

A striking takeaway from our counselling sessions with senior-level corporate executives was their deep appreciation for the strengths/weaknesses analysis and candid feedback on areas of improvement provided by us as a part of the counselling, coaching and mentoring sessions. In fact, over the years, we have been experiencing great demand for such sessions in the corporate world, both by individuals and by organizations. Such mentoring and feedback is highly valued in the context of the Indian organizational reality where authentic mentoring, counselling and feedback are virtually absent.

The harsh reality therefore is that people grow by rank in the organizational hierarchy but do not necessarily mature adequately with respect to their attitude and competencies. Unfortunately, people get into the self-attribution mode and start believing that their success and achievements are only due to their own capability and style, disregarding factors such as seniority, non-availability of competent persons at a given point in time in the organization, close proximity to the decision makers and other factors extraneous to their respective individual capabilities. In fact, this is the biggest unconscious conspiracy which many leaders suffer from. It would be worthwhile mentioning here that humans can only handle those forces which they are aware of. It is, however, well-nigh impossible for individuals to deal with the power of invisible forces which drive their behaviour.

It is because of this human incapability, to see themselves as others see them, that perceptions and data from others become crucial for sensitizing role holders to bring them on the path of reflection, growth and development. As mentioned earlier in the preface, it is no wonder that our efforts at coaching, mentoring and counselling are so highly appreciated. Many top level executives have expressed that this event (mentoring and counselling) has been a turning point in their life journey.

The present chapter is planned in this contextual framework and at the very least it will enable position holders to develop awareness and appreciation about their negative behavioural traits vis-à-vis unconscious trapping in toxic attitude. It will also provoke them to become aware of their own positive aspirations and ambitions which may have been hitherto dormant and thus not adequately acknowledged and utilized. Hopefully, this will provoke them to ponder over their own style and behaviour and generate in them the desire to take feedback from those close to them (not from sycophants!). These actions can help them embark on the path of positive attitudinal and behavioural change to become better human beings and better leaders, thereby moving forward on their journey of self-transformation.

There is a general tendency among thinkers and researchers to equate leadership with good leadership and hence bulk of the research and writing on the subject in the 20th century has focused on understanding and analysing characteristics of good leaders, their attributes and behaviour.[1-3] Virtuous leaders refer to those leaders who are able to positively influence and mobilize people towards achievement of organizational goals.[4,5]

Toxic leadership has been a common phenomenon recurring through the ages displayed by despots, tyrants and sadistic rulers. It appears that virtuous leaders—leaders with positive impact and benign approach—are quite rare. We were curious to understand toxic leaders and position holders in order to identify what behaviours are disliked and considered to have a negative impact by the individual employee. Another reason to focus on toxic leaders has been the fact that people learn as much from negative leaders—'what not to do', as they learn 'what to do' from virtuous leaders. In fact, metaphorically speaking, light shines much brighter when contrasted with darkness. Above all, there is the rising trend of research focus in the last decade (see Chapter 1) on trying to understand toxic leaders who negatively impact and damage both people organizations.[6–13] Although research output on toxic leadership exists, it is not of the same magnitude as virtuous leadership.

In the present chapter, our focus is on understanding the behaviours of toxic leaders holding powerful positions with power to affect the lives of a larger number of people and organizations. We have attempted to sketch the profile of toxic leaders in order to recognize them, and to identify their impact on others and understand the mechanisms adopted by 'victims' to cope with such leaders.

In this chapter, the focus will be on understanding such toxic behaviours as experienced and perceived by subordinates who are at the receiving end, since they are lower power holders. This chapter is divided into the following VII parts:

- Part I: Toxic Behaviours (Questionnaire Data)

    a. Overall analysis
    b. Self-level demographics: age, work experience, qualification, gender, family type
    c. Personality: resilience, work locus of control and values
    d. Organizational demographics: sector, industry type
    e. Nationality

- Part II: Demographics, Personality, Nationality and Emotional Distress

    a. Self-level demographics: age, work experience, qualification, gender, family type
    b. Personality: resilience, work locus of control and values
    c. Organizational sector, industry type
    d. Nationality.

- Part III: Demographics, Personality, Nationality and Coping Mechanisms

    a. Self-level demographics: age, work experience, qualification, gender, family type

b. Personality: resilience, work locus of control and values
c. Organizational sector, industry type
d. Nationality

- Part IV: Profiles of Toxic Leaders
- Part V: Analysis of the Toxic Leader Cases and Key Results
- Part VI: Toxic Leadership and Impact on Subordinates (Interview Data)
- Part VII: Overall Conclusions (Both Questionnaire and Interview Data)

PART I: OVERALL ANALYSIS OF TOXIC BEHAVIOUR

a. Overall Questionnaire Analysis

Analysis of Table 2.1 indicates that the 10 most toxic behaviours according to the sample are: arrogance, blaming others, self-opinionated and close minded, creating insecurity and favouritism, untrustworthy, abusive, ill-tempered, power hungry and hypocrite (their ranks being from 1 to 10). More than 52% of the sample has ranked the above 10 attributes as the most disliked behaviours of the toxic leaders. When we take 40% responses as the cut-off point, then from ranks 11 to 17 toxic leadership behaviours are featured. These attributes are: play divide and rule, dishonest and lacking in integrity, insensitive to others feelings, taking credit for others work, publicly ridiculing others, narcissistic and corrupt. The balance three items—rude, demeaning others, sharing sensitive and personal information about others—rank from 18 to 20. This table also shows that all the 20 characteristics are considered to be toxic by the respondents to varying degrees, since none have been excluded or dropped from the list.

TABLE 2.1

Toxic Leadership Attributes: Overall Frequency, Percentage and Rank

Toxic behaviours	Overall frequency (734)	%	Rank
Arrogant	525	71.5	1
Blaming others	498	67.8	2
Self-opinionated and close minded	456	62.1	3
Create insecurity among people	451	61.4	4
Manipulative and playing favourites	424	57.8	5
Unreliable and untrustworthy	421	57.4	6
Abusive	417	56.8	7
Ill-tempered	404	55	8
Power hungry	403	54.9	9
Hypocrite	385	52.5	10
Play 'divide and rule'	375	51.1	11
Dishonest and lacked integrity	365	49.7	12
Insensitive to my feelings	364	49.6	13
Take credit of others work	364	49.6	14
Publicly ridiculed others	354	48.2	15
Narcissist	323	44	16
Corrupt	311	42.4	17
Rude	237	32.3	18
Demeaning others	224	30.5	19
Shared sensitive and personal information about others	205	27.9	20

b. Toxic Leader Behaviours by Self-level Demographic Factors

Age

Table A2.1 (refer to Appendix) presents the 20 toxic attributes of leaders classified by the age of the respondents. As Table A2.1 brings out arrogance, blaming others, self-opinionated and creating insecurity among people emerged as top rank attributes regardless of age categories. Along with these similarities, two main differences in ranks are also clearly evident across the age groups. In less than 30 years age group, taking credit of others work (rank 6, 57.8%) and divide and rule (rank 9, 52.2%) are experienced to be more hurtful than abusive (rank 14, 47.8%) and ill-tempered (rank 10, 51.5%) which they experience to be less harmful as indicated by the ranks. Another important difference emerges in the priority given to toxic behaviours such as dishonest (rank 8, 54%) and insensitive to my feeling (rank 10, 53.2%), by the respondents belonging to the middle-age group of 31–45 years. On the other hand, favouritism (rank 15, 47.64%) and unreliable (rank 13, 51.07%) are probably/less disliked in the middle aged executives. Last, being rude, demeaning others, sharing sensitive and personal information about others are, relatively speaking, least disliked toxic leadership attributes across executives of all age groups. From the above analysis, we can say that there is a tremendous amount of similarity in the responses among the three age categories. This has been further validated by the correlation analysis (using Spearman rho) across the age groups. As the table indicates, all the rho values are significant at 0.01 level which clearly indicates significant homogeneity. In other words, there was no significant impact of age on the type of toxic leader behaviour that they dislike.

Work Experience

Table A2.2 presents the toxic attributes across the three work experience groups. Analysis of this table indicates that regardless of the level of work experience, arrogance and blaming others are the top two toxic behaviours of the leaders which are most disliked by everyone. Among other toxic behaviours taking credit of others work (rank 7, 57.6%) was considered to be more toxic by employees with less than five years work experience. Respondents with 6–15 years of work experience considered playing divide and rule (rank 6, 55.8%) and narcissism (rank 7, 53.9%) as more painful toxic behaviour. In contrast, they viewed favouritism (rank 16, 44.2%) and unreliable and untrustworthy behaviour (rank 17, 42.2%) as less toxic. Highly experienced executives with more than 16 years of work experience rated being unreliable and untrustworthy (rank 3, 64.2%) as more toxic than close-minded behaviour of leaders (rank 6, 60%). Last, demeaning others and sharing personal sensitive information are, relatively speaking, least toxic behaviours across all work experience groups. A glance at the overall rating pattern clearly brings out a high degree of similarity across all the categories of work experience. This has been further corroborated by the correlation analysis. All the rho values are significant. $P \geq 0.01$ level indicates convergence in the findings.

Educational Qualifications

Table A2.3 reports attributes as per the educational qualification of the respondents. Once again arrogance and blaming others are the two top-ranked toxic leadership behaviours. It is also evident from Table A2.3 that executives with postgraduate qualification rated taking credit of work done by others (rank 9, 53.57%) and playing divide and rule with the people (rank 10, 52.3%) as more negative behaviours than others. Last, being rude, demeaning others and sharing sensitive and personal information are the least negative toxic behaviours in both groups. Perusal of the overall pattern of rating by educational qualification again brings out high degree of convergence in the perceptual framework of the respondents. In this case also correlation value (rho) emerges as significant at $P \geq 0.01$ level.

Gender

Gender-wise analysis (Table A2.4) of the toxic behaviours again brings out a similar pattern. In other words, there are no significant differences evident between views of male and female regarding toxic leadership behaviours. As reported before, arrogance and blaming others are the two top most-hated toxic behaviours across gender categories. In this case, one noteworthy difference is the view regarding abusive behaviour. It is evident from Table A2.4 that male executives disliked abusive (rank 4, 60.4%) behaviour more while female executives considered it to be less disliked (rank 13, 48.1%). The correlation value comparing the two sets of ranks shows that both are significantly similar.

Family Type

Analysis of toxic behaviours by joint family versus nuclear family categories brings out that arrogance is considered the most toxic leadership attribute by respondents belonging to both nuclear and joint families. It is noteworthy that creating insecurity among employees is considered more toxic for employees belonging to nuclear family (rank 2, 67.4%) than employees belonging to joint family (rank 10, 52.8%). On the other hand, dishonesty and lacking integrity is rated more toxic by employees belonging to joint family (rank 8, 53.4%) than employees belonging to nuclear family (rank 14, 47.1%). The correlation value comparing the two sets of ranks shows that both are significantly similar (see Table A2.5).

c. Toxic Leader Behaviours by Personality

This part examines the ranks of toxic leadership attributes by two personality attributes—resilience and locus of control (internal locus of control and external locus of control).

Resilience

Table A2.6 reports the frequency, percentage and ranks on all the toxic attributes as per the resilience level of the respondents, that is, whether low or high. Perusal of this table brings out that arrogance and blaming others are considered to be most negative toxic leadership behaviour among executives, whether they have high or low resilience scores. Similarly, being rude and demeaning others are considered less negative among both sub-group of executives. Table A2.6 also indicates that the low resilience group rated ill-tempered (rank 5, 55.2%) behaviour of leaders as more toxic as compared with these in the high resilience group who gave it a much lower (rank 10, 54.7%) rank. On the other hand, the high resilience groups reported favouritism (rank 3, 62.2%) and playing divide and rule (rank 9, 58%) as more toxic than low resilience group (rank 7, 54% and 15, 45.2%). As pointed out in the previous tables, in this case also the news regarding toxic behaviour is significantly similar which is reflected by the correlational value. The correlation value comparing the two sets of ranks shows that both are significantly similar (see Table A2.6).

Work Locus of Control

Table A2.7 brings out the pattern of disliked toxic behaviours in two categories: internal locus of control and external locus of control. According to Table A2.7, arrogance and blaming others are considered to be the most toxic by executives with both high and low external locus of control. Similarly, being rude, demeaning others and sharing sensitive personal information are considered less negative among both sub-groups of executives. Table A2.7 also indicates that those with external locus of control rated insensitive to my feeling (rank 10, 52.5%) as more toxic than those with low external locus of control (rank 15, 46.8%). Lastly, respondents with internal locus of control rated dishonest (rank 9, 54.8%) as more toxic than respondents with external locus of control (rank 15, 44.4%). The correlation value comparing the two sets of ranks again shows that both are significantly similar (see Table A2.7).

Values

Table A2.8 (a, b and c) highlights the pattern of disliked leader behaviours across low versus high categories of six values—egalitarian, humanistic, hedonistic, personal development, pride and materialistic centricity. The results presented in these tables bring out a similar pattern, as brought out in the previous tables. Thus, regardless of the value the most hated toxic behaviours are abusive and arrogant behaviours. In other words, executives hate superiors characterized by abusive and arrogant styles; both of which hurt them the most. These tables also indicate overall homogeneity of pattern of response across the six value dispositions, indicating that regardless of value preference, the same set of toxic behaviours are disliked the most. The correlation analysis powerfully brings out that irrespective of categories the same sets of behaviours are most hated indicating significant similarity of response.

d. Toxic Leader Behaviour by Organizational Level Demographics

This part presents the findings on toxic behaviour as perceived the sample classified by organizational level categories: organizational sector and industry type.

Table A2.9 presents the perceived toxic leader behaviour across Indian public and private sectors. As usual, findings show that there is a significant similarity of bad leader behaviour regardless of sector, whether public or private. Again, arrogance is perceived to be the most-hated leaders' behaviour followed by blaming others and favouritism in both the groups. In contrast, taking credit of others' work is perceived as more toxic among Indian private sector executives (rank 8, 57.7%) than public sector executives (rank 15, 42.2%).

A similar pattern is observed in Table A2.10 wherein the ranking has been done across sectoral and manufacturing categories. Only being ill-tempered is considered as more negative in service sector (rank 7, 55.7%) than manufacturing sector (rank 11, 54%). Here, also, the correlation value is highly significant, indicating homogeneity in leader behaviour, notwithstanding the fact that the respondents are from manufacturing and service sector.

e. Toxic Leader Behaviours by Nationality

Table A2.11 depicts toxic leadership behaviour across Indian and international managerial groups. The prominent four toxic behaviours in both the groups are: arrogance, blaming others, self-opinionated and close-minded and creating insecurity among people. Manipulative and playing favourites (rank 3, 61.75%) and unreliable and untrustworthy (rank 6, 61.23%) are considered more toxic by Indian executives. In contrast, narcissism (rank 8, 52.4%), dishonesty (rank 9, 51.3%) and being corrupt (rank 10, 51.2%) are considered more toxic by international executives. Further analysis of this table indicates that there is a significant similarity in the views of managers regarding toxic leadership behaviours.

The picture which emerges from the analysis of Tables A2.1–A2.11 on toxic leadership attributes is given here.

- Arrogance has emerged as the single most repulsive and hated toxic leadership behaviour across all the variables chosen for the analyses.

- Arrogant behaviour is followed, more or less, by putting the blame on others, being close minded, creating insecurity, indulging in favouritism and being unreliable, as well as abusive and ill-tempered. These eight toxic behaviours are experienced to be most hurtful and painful.

- In fact, these toxic leader behaviours have been rated by more than 55% of the respondents.

- The responses have ranged from a minimum of 55% to a maximum of 71.5%.

- The overall analysis of these components reveals that toxic leaders are highly arrogant (that is they think too much of themselves, have an inflated ego and look down on others in public). They are self-opinionated and close-minded, believing that they are the paragon of all wisdom while others are ignorant. They are highly ill tempered and abusive with their junior colleagues and seem to derive sadistic pleasure in putting down others in public. They suffer from strong likes and dislikes and openly play favourites with those who are their sycophants. Through this process, they create a kitchen cabinet of sycophants, who wield extra power and who are many times perceived to be more powerful than the boss himself. They cannot be relied upon; people do not have faith in them and they trust no one. Perhaps this indicates their internal insecurity and constant need to be appreciated and validated.

PART II: IMPACT OF DEMOGRAPHIC AND PERSONALITY FACTORS ON EMOTIONAL DISTRESS

Scholars and thinkers in the field of management have all unequivocally emphasized the critical role which leaders play in shaping and architecting the destiny of their organizations, divisions and departments. Their attitude, style and behaviour have a profound impact on their followers leaders are capable of galvanizing exciting, creating purpose and meaning, in the minds of their team members, which enable the followers to passionately move towards the goal. Conversely, it has been found that, if leaders are toxic, narcissistic, ill tempered, dishonest, manipulative, non-appreciative of subordinates contribution, they create tremendous psychological trauma in the minds of their followers. It is in this perspective that this part has been written. This part examines the impact of toxic leaders on the emotional reactions of the followers and team members.

Table A2.12 reports the results of mean and standard deviation (SD) scores of emotional distress, characterized by giving up, feeling anxious, upset and worthless, experienced by subordinates working with toxic leaders. On a seven-point scale, the mean score is 4.12. Such emotional responses have a deleterious impact on follower's motivation, workplace attitude, commitment, creativity and innovation. It may also lead to lack of self-confidence, powerlessness, helplessness, meaninglessness and consequent alienation from the self and organizations. The major components of emotional distress are despair, anxiety, upset and worthlessness (refer to Table A1.2 of Chapter 1).

Examination of the overall emotional distress score across age categories (refer to Table A2.13) brings out that in all the three categories, higher emotional distress is experienced and this significantly varies by age categories. It is highest in the younger group (mean = 4.28, SD = 1.02) followed by the older group (mean = 4.12, SD = 1.27) and lastly by the middle-age group (mean = 3.95, SD = 1.21).

Table A2.14 presents the influence of work experience on emotional distress. The trend in the data demonstrated a similar pattern as in the previous table of age group. In this table also, work experience has a significant influence on emotional distress. Emotional distress is found to be highest in respondents with work experience up to five years (mean = 4.3, SD = 1.04). Analysis of educational qualifications and its impact on emotional distress reveals that it significantly affects emotional distress (refer to Table A2.15). Gender-wise analysis of emotional distress in response to toxic leaders clearly shows that, relatively speaking, females experience slightly more intense (though not significant) emotional distress as compared with their male counterparts.

Examination of family type and its impact on emotional distress reveals that executives who come from nuclear family backgrounds experience more emotional distress as compared with those from joint families. However, the difference is not significant (refer to Table A2.17). Table A2.18 examines the impact of resilience on levels of emotional distress triggered by toxic leader behaviour. Closer scrutiny of this table brings out that the intensity of resilience does not significantly impact levels of emotional distress. Impact of work locus of control on levels of experienced emotional distress has been presented in Table A2.19. This table clearly reveals the insignificant impact of work locus of control on emotional distress.

For examinations of impact of value system on emotional distress, refer to Table A2.20. Overall results indicate that hedonism does have a significant impact on emotional distress. Those who have low hedonism values feel more emotionally distressed, as compared with those with higher hedonism value. As per Table A2.21, an organizational sector does not have significant impact on emotional distress. Results also indicate that there is significant difference in emotional distress among service and manufacturing industries (refer to Table A2.22). Service-sector executives reported higher emotional distress in comparison with manufacturing-sector executives. Similarly, nationality also significantly impacts emotional distress (refer to Table A2.23). Indian executives reported significantly higher emotional distress than international working executives.

PART III: DEMOGRAPHIC, PERSONALITY AND NATIONALITY AND COPING MECHANISMS

This part focuses on findings regarding coping strategies utilized by subordinates working with toxic leaders.

In Table A2.24, impact of age on coping strategies used by subordinates is reported. The four coping strategies are: avoidance, approach, assertive and adaptive coping strategy. It is clearly evident from the obtained results that executives belonging to different age groups use significantly different coping strategies (refer to Table A2.24). Avoidance strategy is mostly used by younger age group (up to 30 years), approach strategy is least used by eldest employees who are more than 46 years of age. Similarly, assertive coping strategy is mostly used by younger employees and adaptive strategy is least used by middle-age executives (31–45 years). In Table A2.25, the impact of work experience on the four coping strategies has been reported. Results indicate the significant difference in use of coping strategies across three work experience groups: high, medium and low.

In Table A2.26, the impact of educational qualification, graduate and post graduate, on the four coping strategies—avoidance, approach, assertive and adaptive—has been depicted. Analysis of this table highlights that educational qualifications do have a significant impact on three coping strategies—escalating to higher level, assertiveness and adaptive. Respondents with post-graduate qualifications are found to be mostly using all the four strategies—avoidance, escalating to higher authority, assertive to handle such leaders. Table A2.27 provides insights into the coping mechanisms adopted by the male and female executives. The table shows that the usage of coping mechanisms used by females is significantly higher than that used by males, except in the case of adaptive coping strategy. The finding reveals that females resort to assertive as the first coping strategy followed by adaptive, then escalating to higher level and lastly avoidance. In the case of males, however, the most preferred strategy is adaptive followed by assertive, avoidance and lastly escalating to higher authority. It is very interesting to note that women tend to make greater efforts to assert—that is taking a strong stand—when faced with emotional conflicts. This explodes the myth that women at work are more submissive, harmony seekers and avoid confrontation.

Family structure and its impact on coping strategies are examined in Table A2.28. Perusal of this table reveals that family structure significantly influences avoidance and assertive coping strategies. Further analysis of this table shows that in the case of escalation to higher authority and adaptive coping mechanism, family structure does not have a significant influence. Relatively speaking, respondents from nuclear families use adaptive, assertive and avoidance strategies in that order as indicated by the higher mean scores. Respondents from nuclear families prefer to use adaptive as the first coping strategies, followed by assertive, avoidance and lastly escalating issues to the higher level.

In Table A2.29, the focus is on examining the coping strategies utilized by the high-resilience group vis-à-vis the low-resilience group. Analysis of this table brings out that resilience does not have significant degree of impact on type of coping strategies utilized, the only exception being escalating the issues to a higher level. Table A2.30 depicts the coping strategies by work locus of control. An examination of this table reveals that two of the coping strategies, avoidance and approach, are significantly influenced by work locus of control. In this table also, those with internal locus of control scores resort to strategies such as adaptive, assertive, avoidance and taking the issue to higher authorities in the organization.

Tables A2.31–A2.36 report the impact of values on coping strategy of the subordinates to deal with toxic leaders. The results reported in Table A2.31 clearly indicate that there is no impact of high or low egalitarian value on the use of coping strategy to deal with toxic leaders. According to Table A2.32, there is a significant difference in assertive coping between respondents with high and low humanistic values. Table A2.33 clearly depicts the significant impact of hedonistic value on avoidance and approach-coping strategies. An examination of Table A2.34 reveals that two of the coping strategies, avoidance and approach, are significantly influenced by personal development value. It is also clearly evident from Table A2.35 that pride does not have any impact on the use of coping strategy by subordinates. Lastly, materialistic value is found to have a significant impact on avoidance and approach-coping strategies (refer to Table A2.36).

Table A2.37 examines the coping strategies used by people across public and private sectors. This table depicts a significant impact of sectoral structure on coping strategies. Further analysis of this table reveals that executives in the private sector demonstrate greater propensity to sorting out conflicts, as indicated by the higher mean values in the private-sector group compared with the public-sector group.

Table A2.38 examines industry-wise (service and manufacturing) difference on coping strategies. Analysis of Table A2.38 brings out that avoidance and escalation strategies are significantly influenced by the industry sector. In the cases of assertive and adaptive approaches, the industry sector has no impact. The preferred coping strategies are adaptive followed by assertive. The least preferred strategy is found to be, escalation to higher levels.

Nationality and its impact on coping strategy is presented in Table A2.39. Analysis depicts that in the case of two coping strategies—avoidance and assertive—nationality significantly influences the coping strategies used. Indian executives tend to use avoidance and assertive strategy significantly more than the group of international executives. However, in the case of the other two coping strategies—escalating to higher level and adaptive—nationality does not have a significant influence. International executives in our sample used approach strategy more than Indian executives.

Conclusions

Examination of the emotional reaction to working with the chemistry of toxic leaders brings out the following salient features:

1. Age, work experience and educational qualification have significant impact on emotional distress.
2. Hedonism value significantly influences emotional distress.
3. Industry type and nationality significantly impact emotional distress.
4. Age, work experience and educational qualifications are found to significantly influence coping mechanisms such as being assertive, adaptive avoidance and escalating matters to a higher level.
5. Gender does have a significant influence on all the coping strategies.

6. Family structure significantly influences coping strategies in two cases, that is, avoidance and being assertive.
7. Personality attributes such as resilience have been found to be significant only on one attribute of coping, namely, escalating matters to higher level.
8. Work locus of control does have significant impact on two coping strategies, namely, avoidance and approach.
9. Ownership pattern, whether public or private, affects all the four coping strategies.
10. Industry sector, whether manufacturing or service, significantly influences two coping styles—avoidance and escalating problems to higher authorities. Nationality of the respondents significantly influences two coping strategies—avoidance and assertiveness.

PART IV: PROFILES OF TOXIC LEADERS

This section contains 11 cases on toxic leaders. The cases are regarding the heads of organizations across public sector, banking sector, Indian family-owned businesses and academic institutions. As mentioned earlier, we did an anthropological inquiry through our network of contacts to find out toxic leaders and ascertained the willingness of people to share their experiences of working with such leaders.

Each case has been presented here in order to bring out some of the unique nuances in the behaviours of the selected leaders. Names have been disguised since our objective is not to run down people; rather, it is to use this information to learn about toxic leadership phenomenon in the Indian context.

Case I: Mr A

Mr A had a highly successful career and rose to the level of CEO. He was known to be intellectually sharp and bright. However, wherever he worked, he would create tremendous hostility and discontent among the subordinates.

According to the 10 persons we interviewed, the following prominent behaviour patterns emerged:

- 'People in general were extremely scared of him' (10).
- 'You go with any great idea and he will ridicule it' (9). He would say, 'What a stupid idea' and bring out all the reasons, why it was a bad idea (5).
- He was totally contrarian in his thinking, 'if you say the sun rises in the east, he will make all efforts to prove that the sun rises in the west' (9). 'He tries to run down not only the idea but also the person in public'. It is the most humiliating experience (7). He used his intellectual power to prove others wrong. It was a past-time with him (2).
- He was extremely close minded (7). He hardly ever listened to anyone except his own favourites, whom he supported to the hilt, even if they did something wrong (5).
- 'He always gave the feeling that he is the paragon of all wisdom' (10).
- 'Highly arrogant person. He looked down on others and believed in one-upmanship' (10).
- He was always suspicious; he was a schemer and a sadist who enjoyed putting others in trouble (8).
- He believed in 'I'm OK, you are not OK' (7).
- He has a style of managing through 'Mooch and Pooch' (the boss is the one with the moustache while the subordinate wags his tail) (1).
- 'He enjoyed being flattered and patronized only those people who praised him' (7).
- Under his leadership, many mediocre officers got rewarded with promotions because they were his sycophants. Many high performers got sidelined because to him people did not matter unless they were his *chamchas* (5).
- He disliked people asking questions, because he thought of questions as criticism (4).
- 'He developed expertise in creating insecurity and shattering people's self-confidence' (5). One person who had worked very closely with him and who knew him personally said, 'He had a tremendous inferiority complex which he used to cover up by running down others and showing them to be fools'.

- 'He was moody and whimsical and people were scared to approach him as they were not sure of his state of mind' (6). Three of the persons who knew Mr A said that he was always like this, whimsical, rude, contrarian and over argumentative.
- He would constantly chase and monitor subordinates with the intent to criticize and punish. He would sometimes even push, shout and treat subordinates in a very inhuman way (7).
- Some of the persons said that his style affected their self-confidence (3); 'we began to doubt our own capabilities' (6). Through his body language he showed disdain (5). I used to feel it a burden to go to work (1). He used to create fear and insecurity (5). I felt that all my energy was sucked away (1).
- The quality of our work fell, people withdrew into a shell; no ideas were shared for fear that the boss might ridicule ideas (8).

The above quotes show that Mr A created powerlessness, shattered self-confidence, killed creative thinking, encouraged sycophancy and affected the collective morale of the organization. He was highly arrogant, used to put down people's ideas and humiliate them. He was extremely closed, encouraged sycophants and managed through fear. He was so much disliked in the organizations in which he worked, that once he left, he was never invited by anyone.

The above description reveals that Mr A is more of a Sadistic Tyrant.

Case II: Ms B

This is the profile of a woman toxic leader who went on to head a large Indian organization. She was known to be intellectually having cleared her college examinations with flying colours. While on a field posting as regional head, she failed miserably because she alienated most of the officers reporting to her and they withdrew into a shell and virtually stopped working (10).

People (10) whom we spoke to said the following about her conduct and behaviour as a leader:

- We were scared of her because she would shout and humiliate us in meetings (10).
- 'She always scolded people, using derogatory words such as fool, idiot, donkey, dumbass' (10).
- 'She has always been toxic irrespective of position she occupied' (5).
- 'She behaved as if she was the only superior brain in the country' (7).
- 'She never appreciated or praised anybody for good work, but certainly criticized people even for the smallest mistake' (10).
- 'She would exaggerate small errors far more than required' (6).
- 'Meetings would begin 5–6 hours late and then drag on without clear decisions and direction. All meetings with her were monologues; no one dared to speak before her' (8).
- Three of her team members said, 'she would not set clear expectations and key focus areas'. When plans were presented, she would disapprove of them without specifying the reason or suggesting a course of action. One draft would take 10–12 meetings to clear and by then the team lost all enthusiasm. Her directions at work were ambiguous and confusing and negatively affected the performance.
- 'She was very slow in disposing off files. We used to keep waiting for decisions which never came'. This slow decision making led to flight of customers (8).
- We, General Managers, would wait for hours to meet her only to be told to come the next day (9).
- 'It was very difficult to get an appointment with her' (10).
- Once she told me, 'I am busy now, I am going to Delhi tomorrow—come with all the files and meet me there'. 'I even went but all she did was make me wait and ultimately I had to go back empty handed'.
- 'She was highly political and managed to get the patronage from superiors' (7).
- 'She used to manipulate people putting one against the other and to create suspicion in people's minds' (7).
- 'She had little interaction with subordinates. Except for the selected few whom she liked, access to her was virtually blocked' (6).

- She managed by threat—officers were threatened with vigilance cases when she disagreed with certain decisions made by them (5).
- She would shout at people when things went wrong (6). When there were divergent views she would shout, threaten the concerned officers with transfers, to coerce them into submission. This blocked all upward information flow. A large number of charge sheets were given to many officers, for making decisions which she did not like (3).
- One of the senior-level officers gave an example from the past; he was in a meeting with her in her office, when one of the General Manager level officers (ex-boss of the narrator) walked in. 'My first instinct was to stand up and greet. She stopped me from doing so and insisted I continue to sit while my ex-boss was not even offered a seat. It was embarrassing for me and humiliating for my ex-boss. She liked doing such things'. She was vindictive and enjoyed humiliating people.
- According to one of the interviewees who knew her from her days as a management trainee, 'she treats her husband like a donkey and her son like a servant'.
- She provided no vision, no dream, had no courage and self-confidence, nor trust and faith in others (8).

From the above description, we can deduce that she was a Machiavellian Tyrant, who tried to manage by threat, intimidation and punishment. Her main objective was to dominate and control. It led to decision paralysis and created a culture of risk avoidance. She was highly moody and unpredictable. She seemed to be inhuman. She was highly political and survived through manipulation of the superiors.

Case III: Mr C

Mr C rose to the level of Secretary, Government of India and later on became the head of a regulatory body. Ten persons who worked with him said the following about his behaviour as the head of an institution:

- 'All his growth has been because of his expertise in playing political chess and a distinguished family background which gave him access to a good network' (9).
- 'He has been a ruthless politician. He has destroyed anyone who came in his path' (10).
- 'He does not spare even those who were his favourites, if he felt they were becoming too independent and not toeing his time' (4).
- 'He was a schemer and manipulator who knew how to put people against each other' (7).
- 'It was difficult to know what was operating in his mind'. 'His calm face covered his ruthless and selfish nature' (6).
- 'He was arrogant and felt that he was intellectually superior to others' (10).
- 'He was a true chameleon and could change colours to suit his goals' (6).
- 'He gave the slogan of cost cutting, but was lavish in fulfilling his own needs at the expense of the organization' (9).
- 'He was a hypocrite—had one set of rules for himself and another set for the rest' (6).
- 'He was publicly polite, but privately he was a highly scheming leader and ensured that power stayed in his hands in perpetuity' (7).
- 'His world view was political and competence had no role to play while giving recognition' (5).
- 'In meetings he would show off about his global connections and power by name dropping' (6).
- 'Most unreliable person … he can ditch you anytime' (8).
- 'He was a double faced snake.' What he meant he never said and what he said he never meant'. He always looked for 'yes' men (6).
- 'Deceived senior colleagues by misleading them and then getting them into trouble' (2).
- 'Highly selfish and manipulative' (9).
- He was a chronic liar who would twist the truth to suit his ends (2).

On the basis of the above responses, his entire profile can be captured in two words—Narcissistic and Machiavellian. Such behaviour drove away competent and capable professionals from the organization and brought down the institution which had a glorious past.

Case IV: Mr D

Mr D was the CEO of a large public sector organization with multiple plants in the manufacturing sector. As the CEO, he enjoyed plenty of power sufficient to make or destroy the organization. Some of the nuances of his behavioural profile are given below:

- 'He has been ruthlessly overambitious, capable of going to any extent to satisfy his ambition' (9).
- He wanted to prove to all that he was a very important and powerful man. He used to show his power by vetoing decisions of other high power holders (5).
- 'He demonstrated extremely poor people management skills'—for example, he would never offer a seat to colleagues visiting his office; (5) he would never greet them; (7) he used to shout at and ridicule juniors (5).
- He had the knack of creating enemies (8) by being rude (5); by showing no interest in others' problems (3); by saying no to all without giving a patient hearing (7).
- 'He used his position power to block many good initiatives of the company' (7).
- 'He kept trying to satisfy his ego by using his power to say no' (8).
- 'He made sure that people visited him in the office, with a request to clear pending files. At the same time, he would never visit any body's office' (6).
- 'He was a sadist and made sure that many of the benefits given to employees were gradually rolled back' (4).
- 'He never showed sympathy or empathy to others' (7).
- 'He was highly arrogant' (10).

- 'He was not bothered about the organization or how his action affected organizational results' (7).
- He used to proclaim that he was the only one who was interested in protecting the organization, while others were out to misuse organizational resources (6).
- He was ungrateful to even those who helped him in his career growth (5).
- He always spoke of 'I' and 'Me' (7).
- 'When he left the organization, people celebrated by distributing sweets' (10).

The above profile reveals that Mr D was highly egoistic, full of vanity and arrogance. He was hungry for ego massage; he was inhuman and showed highly unethical conduct at such a senior level. He was all about 'I' and 'Me'.

Case V: Mr E

Mr E is the scion of one of India's largest and successful family-owned businesses.

People whom we interviewed (10) made the following observations about his mindset and behaviour:

- 'He behaves like a despot, throwing his weight around, making people wait for hours, saying they are paid to wait' (10).
- He insults senior-level officers in front of the lowest level employees by making statements such as 'have you gone blind, can't you see?', 'have you gone mad, don't you even know this much' (8)?
- 'Don't quote me please, if I say that he is highly unethical. Whatever he has achieved has been done by buying off politicians'; bureaucrats and important functionaries in the country (1).
- 'He has been heard to say, it's your job to buy the politicians, and manage the bureaucrats, just see that company's interests are not affected' (2).

- 'He is highly arrogant and does not listen to people' (7). 'He was so arrogant that he never gave appointments for meetings when there was a request from his lieutenants'. I later came to know that he believes that it is his prerogative to decide to meet and not the other way round. He told his secretary 'let people know, I am the boss and I decide whom to meet and when to meet' (1).
- 'He is very greedy for profit making at any cost, even by hook or by crook' (5).
- 'He believes that every human being has a price and can be bought. We are treated like commodities, with little dignity. The compensation package at our level is the highest in the country. Two persons said we are paid not only for contribution, but also to stay on despite being badly treated by the boss'.
- 'In this organization, people are paid to spy on each other'. 'It is said that every key person has two others watching him and reporting his actions on a regular basis' (10).
- 'He believes that people are dispensable—use them and throw them' (8).
- 'Many highly competent persons joined and left in disgust because they were never respected, honoured and recognized' (7).
- 'He treats his deputies as if they are his personal servants' (6).
- 'He rarely asks people to sit before him. Only a select few have this honour' (5).
- 'His lavish lifestyle, homes, cars, expensive holidays, over the top weddings in the family, would put any king to shame' (6).
- 'He is always trying to prove how important he is, in running the country and in making policies' (5).

The above-cited behavioural profile brings out that this person has been highly unethical, having a profiteering motive, creating profit for himself through manipulation and politicking. He acts like a Maharajah, is insensitive towards his own people and manages by creating insecurity and pitting people one against the other. In sum, he appears to be an ego-centric despot.

Case VI: Mr F

Mr F had a reasonably successful career (in terms of rank) and ultimately reached the level of CEO of one of the top-ranking academic institutions. The interviewees made the following observations about his behaviour as a CEO not only with them individually but with most of the persons in the organization:

- One of the first statements made by him when he joined as the CEO was to say, 'Everything in the past is wrong. I have come here to set things right' (10).
- He was political from the beginning and created a kitchen cabinet of sycophants from the word go (7).
- He was accessible only to his yes men (10).
- He was a slave of the system mindlessly applying rules and regulations (10). 'He brought in high focus on processes and systems which are used to control rather than facilitate organizational excellence and growth' (6).
- 'He believed in high degree of centralization and insisted on approval for, spending even a few rupees' (9).
- 'Highly self-opinionated and close-minded never listened to anyone' (6).
- 'He would not hesitate to manipulate facts and data to serve his own interest' (3). 'He was corrupt and manipulated organizational systems to make money for himself' (10). 'He even manipulated rules to become CEO and kept other contestants out of the race' (4).
- 'He was a sadist and withdrew people's perks and benefits by bringing in new rules and frameworks which were not employee friendly' (7).
- He was highly arrogant and contemptuous about others (5).
- 'He was a man of strong likes and dislikes. He liked you only if you subjugated yourself to him'. 'He disliked everybody else' (10).
- 'He manipulated his own C.V. citing numerous achievements which the organizational members knew were fake' (5).
- 'He would not hesitate to manipulate facts and data to serve his own interest'. For example, he did not hesitate to take credit for other's work (5); he made all attempts to prove that

he is the boss (5); he was very rude with faculty and staff and did not allow them to sit down in his presence (5).

- 'He manipulated many female colleagues to file sexual harassment cases against those colleagues whom he wanted to punish' (8).
- 'He was very closed and believed that only he was blessed with superior wisdom' (7).
- 'He did not believe in teamwork and engagement and excluded most people from discussions' (10). He hardly ever called for faculty meetings and when he did so, he went on speaking (10).
- 'He was obstinate in decision making, and stuck to his decision even if it was not in the organizational interest' (6).
- 'He did not network at all and was disconnected not only from faculty and staff but also from alumni, corporate and ministry' (7).
- 'He was highly parochial and hired people from his own caste and community' (7).
- 'Whenever I met him I observed that he could not make eye contact. He used to gaze at an odd angle' (3). His body language indicated that he was trying to convey superiority, as if he was sitting on a high pedestal (3).
- 'He used power to control, not facilitate' (5).
- 'Highly self-opinionated and close-minded, never listened to anyone' (9).
- 'Perpetually boasting and showing off' (3). 'He would constantly boast, how superior he is compared with other directors in this country' (10).
- 'He was highly ungrateful to those who helped him grow (2); he let down those who groomed him' (6).
- Tried to undermine others to prop himself up (5).

From the above description, one may conclude that he was a sadist, greedy, focused on promoting his self-interest. He was highly egoistic, poor sensitivity, did not value people and manipulated and used them for his own benefit. He had no interest in organizational well-being and worked for his selfish and unethical agenda. This toxic leader appears to be an egocentric Machiavellian.

Case VII: Mr G

Mr G is the owner of a large conglomerate having multiple businesses and has achieved consistent success over the years. The business itself started really tiny and then grew into the giant that it is today. People said the following things about his general behaviour with the employees:

- He is extremely abrasive rude, non-trusting and impatient to get his own way (10).
- 'Totally drunk with power and thinks he can do anything to get his way' (7).
- In his dictionary there is no scope for accommodation—it's either my way or the high way (4).
- He is a despot and brooks no argument (1).
- 'Whimsical person, you never know what will make him react' (6).
- Many a time, we have seen him suddenly taking a strong liking for someone he meets once. The person is given a stupendous salary and brought in and praised to the skies. After a few months the same person is dubbed as useless and circumstances are created to ensure that he leaves (1).
- 'Scant respect for people. Does not hesitate to throw people out' (5).
- 'He avidly gathers information about key people and uses it to control them' (7).
- 'He uses unethical means to manage business' (3).
- He has proximity to political power which he uses to manipulate regulations in his favour (4).
- 'He does not hesitate to manipulate national resources to serve his own ends' (2).
- 'Too head strong, abusive and manipulative' (8).
- 'Encourages sycophants' (10).
- 'Does not trust anyone.... Not sure if he even trusts his own wife' (1).
- 'Highly egoistic and insensitive to others' (8).
- 'Rarely listens to others. Hearing what he wants to hear' (5).

- No respect and value for others, no empathy, tough attitude, manages through fear (1).
- Through such behaviour people's self-worth is destroyed. They go into a shell and withdraw. He wants to prove that the boss is always right (2).

From the above, one concludes that he is a despot with Hitlerian tendencies. He is egoistic, rude abrasive and greedy and insists on getting his own way.

Case VIII: Mr H

This is a company which was once reputed for its performance and capability to attract high-quality talent. Over a period, the company significantly decayed in terms of its profit, turnover and many other performance parameters. We spoke to 10 persons who had worked with the 'Owner–CEO' over a period of time.

While talking about the CEO, some of the following salient behaviours were highlighted:

- All the 10 whom we interviewed said 'he is a dictator'; 'no one can raise their voice before him'; 'highly arrogant'; 'thinks he is superior to us all'; he looks down condescendingly at others as if they were not worthy individuals who can be consulted or who had a useful point of view.
- 'Many times he behaves like an ego-maniac'. 'He is always surrounded by dopple gangers and sycophants' (8). 'The only way to relate with him is by becoming a sycophant. There is no other way' (5). Plenty of ego massage and praise are needed; saying yes sir, yes sir; 'you are great sir', this is what is encouraged here (6).
- 'Many people were willing to be in his good books by praising him'.
- In fact, there was fierce competition among the dopple gangers who worked against each other in a bid to become the closest one to the boss (1).

- He puts one divisional chief against the other and plays them against each other. Maybe, he thought it is safer for him to divide and rule (1).
- He had capable MDs but would make all the decisions himself. As one person said, 'why keep Alsatian dogs and become the guard dog yourself?'
- Although he can be quite charming and gentlemanly in general, but with his MDs he is rough and abrasive (8). He runs down the MDs in the presence of lower level functionaries from their divisions. Sometimes, he pours scorn at them, saying, 'don't you even know this much' (3)?
- He has an expert opinion on everything (3); he has even made the MDs miserable, before investors (1).
- Very whimsical, expects that other employees should not have anything better than him- whether it is a car or a house. If this actually happened, then the HR person is bound to lose his job (1). He expects that his car should move right in front; if someone else's car moves ahead of his car, that person would have problems in keeping his job (1).
- Insensitive about other feelings, yet he is quite touchy and sensitive about his own feelings (4).
- He would give an appointment for a meeting and then deliberately come late by 30 minutes just to prove the point that he was big boss (3).
- No one has the guts to express a different point of view and anyone who even tried has been ridiculed. In one or two cases, I have seen the person's career getting ruined (2).
- He conducts meetings like a despot; it is a one-way show with him giving a monologue and the others listening for hours (1).
- Favouritism is rampant. He behaves as if he was the 'Badshah' ruling his 'subjects' (5).
- Highly image conscious. He was more bothered that he should appear as a strong man in the public eye (4).
- Egocentric, self-centred, not inspirational, no concern for people, preached without practice; and very good at self-projection (5).

- He was so egoistic that he refused to seek help from his immediate lieutenants, fearing that it would ruin his image as a strong leader, even though the company was in trouble (5).
- He completely undermined the power and authority of the top management group. While dealing with unions and vendors, he would tell them to approach him directly by bypassing divisional heads.

These quotes bring out that Mr H was highly dictatorial and narcissistic.

Case IX: Mr I

This is the case of the CEO of one of the businesses of a large Indian conglomerate with a global presence. Interviewees (10) described their experiences with him as follows:

- Armed with an Ivey league degree, he believed that he was God's gift to the company (4). He thought no end of himself (4). He would not hesitate to publicly scold subordinates (4).
- Everyone said his style was arrogant. This was expressed as follows: He liked to prove that others were fools and that he 'knew it all'. 'He was highly self-opinionated and close minded' (10). 'He was haughty and made sure to convey that he was a cut above the rest' of us (7). 'He looked down at people, as if they were very inferior' (8). Most of the time he would say, 'you know nothing, I have seen the world, I know it all' and you better listen to me (7).
- 'He would rarely allow people to complete their sentences and would interrupt and speak' (6). He once told me, 'finish speaking in a few seconds. Why do you speak so much?' I was shocked because I was trying to deflect an imminent strike.
- He did not believe in sharing the agenda which he had for the division. As a result, no one was aware of the direction and plans for the future.

- He did not believe his people and suspected their motives (9).
- He was extremely moody and unpredictable (7).
- The interviewees (10) said that 'he never asked anyone to sit before him in his office'.
- He did not care about other's feelings. His clear focus was 'me' and 'mine' (6).
- He alienated the top brass of the company which in turn was reflected in low morale, lack of commitment and desire to quit the company at the first opportunity (7).
- Three of the subordinate officers confided that it took a long time to get an appointment with him. One person narrated his personal experience, 'I was trying to meet him for a few months and finally when I got the appointment, I went exactly at the appointed hour to his office'. I opened the door and to my utter amazement, he just gestured with his hands as if to say 'go away, don't disturb me, can't you see I am busy!' 'He did not even look up, much less apologize for not honouring the appointment'.
- 'He had mastered the art of managing his boss'; otherwise, there was no reason why he was allowed to stay on for years despite indifferent organizational performance.
- Working with such a leader had negative impact on the employees (10)—there was demoralization, reluctance to work with this boss; credibility down the line was hit; unhealthy relations were created.

The above exposition clearly brings out that Mr I was an ego-maniac submerged within himself. He was narcissistic, inaccessible, close-minded, busy proving his superiority, mistreating people, hurting their dignity and honour. He was committed to self rather than to the organization.

Case X: Mr J

This is the case of a person who had a matchless profile and academic credentials. He had an impeccable educational background having graduated from top institutions of the country and yet, he was asked to leave the organization. We talked to 10 academicians and administrators about the reason for his ouster.

Employees of the organization shared the following views about his behaviour and his subsequent ouster:

- All said that he was a narcissist of the first order—'he loved being in the media', 'if his photo was not there in the newspapers he would get restless'. Whenever he was called to preside over an event, howsoever insignificant, he would definitely go, so high was his need to be visible (8). One of them went to the extent of saying, 'even if he was invited for ribbon cutting in some nondescript place he would go'.
- 'He made tall statements in the media about the new ideas that he was bringing in to make the institution top class. However, he could not deliver on any of the promises' (2).
- Three of the persons said, 'we have not heard him speak good things about anyone'. He would typically say about other directors 'oh that fellow, useless, what does he know?'
- He was known to say, 'I am an honest man. I don't like to waste national resources. I don't travel by business class in flights; I don't stay at five-star hotels like the other directors.' On the other hand, these interviewees said that underneath these tall proclamations, we could see corrupt practices, be it in building construction, hiring of vendors or appointment of people—what was spent versus what was delivered there was a huge gap indicating that something was fishy. In all these matters, it was the director himself who played a key role and was an important beneficiary (7).
- His commitment to the institution was questioned (7) as he spent most of the time away from the institution without any specific reason. 'He is generally away on tour' (7); 'he stays only for two weeks in a month and the rest of the time he is away in his hometown' (5).
- One person said, 'what he meant he never said and what he said, he never meant'.
- Highly parochial; he made comments about the local people as untrustworthy—'they are not trustworthy; they can ditch you anytime' (3). This statement implied that most of the people on the campus were untrustworthy in his eyes.

- According to the professors, (3) 'He did not hire, high quality national level faculty', saying 'I want to groom younger faculty'. 'We don't need top quality faculty—what is the point of recruitment of such persons if they don't stay?'

In a nutshell, he was narcissistic, ceaselessly promoted himself by constantly trying to be in the media and by running down others. Besides, he was a corrupt man and shamelessly misused organizational resources for his personal benefit.

Case XI: Mr K

This is the profile of a CMD heading a public sector organization. The 10 interviewees said the following about him:

- 'In the first few months of joining the organization, he addressed us just once'. We felt that he was not interested in us (8).
- 'He did not speak clearly about his vision and direction for the organization. He typically sounded confused and speaking with him showed a lack of focus. For him position was more important than organizational performance, delivery and execution' (7).
- 'He was a cabin manager, and did not believe in mingling with people'. 'The fact of becoming CMD itself seems to have fully satisfied him'. He did not have the passion for achievement (7).
- One of the high-performing business heads said, 'initially I waited eagerly to hear his thoughts about where he wants to take the bank and what will be his approach'. Even a small signal from him would have been enough for us to work with zeal and energy.
- Another person said, 'he had no convictions and no concern about what was good for the organization'.
- A top-level officer said, 'he was unable to manage some of the board members who came with a clear agenda to pursue their

own personal gains. In fact, he could not handle the board and surrendered his powers to some of the board members who used to falsely mislead him about their proximity to the Government level power holders, which scared him into complying with them'. He did not have courage of convictions and therefore got easily bulldozed by some of the board members. He tried to placate them and helplessly gave in to their diktats, even though they harmed the interest of the organization.

- He wanted to have peace at any cost and compromised the interest of the organization. Through his style and weak moral fabric, he destroyed a good organization (5).

From the above, it can be concluded that he was survival centric, morally weak, mentally confused and greedy to stick to his position by placating others. In sum, he was a spineless and unethical survivor.

PART V: ANALYSIS OF THE TOXIC LEADER CASES AND KEY RESULTS

Content analysis[14,15] was carried out on the interview data to develop a comprehensive understanding regarding toxic leaders' behaviour which emerged in the cases presented above. Prominent thematic patterns which emerged from the qualitative analysis (content analysis) are presented in Table 2.2.

Analysis of Table 2.2 brings out that arrogance has emerged as the most cited (100%) toxic behaviour experienced by the senior and top-level executives in the present study. This is followed by egocentric behaviour, close-minded, ridiculing others and running them down, blatant pursuit of 'Me' centric agenda, playing favourites, abusive, untrustworthy, playing Machiavellian games, managing business through unethical, unscrupulous and corrupt practices. The above responses have featured in all the 11 cases in varying degree, ranging from 60% to 100%. In other words, these are the core attributes of toxic leaders in the Indian context.

TABLE 2.2

Toxic Behaviours from Interview Data*

	Frequency (*N* = 110)	Percentage	Rank
1. Arrogant	110	100.00	1
2. Ego centric and close minded	108	88.00	2
3. Publicly ridiculing and running down others	100	88.00	2
4. Me-centric narcissist	95	72.00	3
5. Playing favourites	88	72.00	3
6. Abusive	80	70.00	4
7. Untrustworthy	80	66.00	5
8. Machiavellian	75	66.00	5
9. Unethical: Dishonest, corrupt, lacking in integrity	70	60.00	5

* Interviews conducted about toxic CEOs.

PART VI: TOXIC LEADERSHIP AND IMPACT ON SUBORDINATES (INTERVIEW DATA)

At this stage, it may be worthwhile examining the impact of such toxic leaders on the respondents. On the basis of the content analysis of the interview responses, Table 2.3 has been constructed. Table 2.3 presents how the respondents felt while working with toxic leaders. Through content analysis of the interviews, we arrived at 10 disturbing reactions. Analysis of this table brings out that all the participants (100%) expressed the desire to quit the organization; they all (100%) suffered intense fear, anxiety and insecurity. Such reactions were subsequently followed by loss of self-confidence and self-worth, as well as feelings of powerlessness and helplessness, the percentages being 92% and 90%, respectively.

Powerlessness, helplessness and a sense of withdrawal have been reported by 90% of the respondents, whereas 88% of the respondents experienced lack of commitment and engagement to pursue

TABLE 2.3

Psycho-social Response to Toxic Leaders

	Frequency **N = 98**	**%**
1. Desire to quit	98	100
2. Fear, anxiety and insecurity	98	100
3. Loss of self-confidence and self-worth	90	92
4. Powerlessness and helplessness	88	90
5. Sense of withdrawal	88	90
6. Lack of passion and commitment to pursue organizational goal	86	88
7. Suspicion and low trust in others	79	80
8. Compliance	74	75
9. Disturbed family life	74	75
10. Risk avoidance and overcautious	69	70

organizational goals. In total, 80% respondents acknowledged that they experienced suspicion and low trust on others. Compliant behaviour was mentioned by 75% of the respondents and the same percentage also expressed that they suffered from disturbed family life. In total, 70% cited that they experienced high-risk avoidance and over-cautious behaviour rather than making efforts to confront the issue and handle the problem effectively (refer to Table 2.3).

PART VII: OVERALL CONCLUSIONS (BOTH QUESTIONNAIRE AND INTERVIEW DATA)

Comparison of the top 10 items arrived at using both questionnaire data and interview data brings out that seven of them are common in both the lists. In both the lists, items such as arrogance, manipulation, being critical, rude and abusing others feature very high. In other words, all the above attributes have featured prominently in the styles of the 11 toxic leader cases.

The expression of toxicity is more or less similar whether it is at the middle level or at the top level. The comparison, however, brings out that at the senior and top levels there is greater prevalence of indulging in dishonest and corrupt practices, 'me'-centric agenda (narcissistic), publicly ridiculing others and being rude and abusive—as compared with those at the middle level.

Toxic leaders have 'me' centric agenda, narcissistic orientation, and Machiavellian approach. They would be engrossed in ceaseless self-promotion and self-projection; use Machiavellian strategies such as manipulation, deception, divide and rule and putting one against the other. Such leaders destroy teamwork and collectivity and disempower people. Since the leader is arrogant, close-minded, creative ideas and solutions from the collective are totally killed. There would be a top-down autocratic, states-conscious approach in managing the business, without even basic levels of participation, involvement and engagement. Such organizations drive away capable people and are unable to attract high-quality talent down the line. Those who have no option but to stay in the organization will resort to survival-centric behaviours such as compliance, sycophancy and 'chamchagiri'. This is in stark contrast to practices of great organizations that practice, a bottom-up approach, web-centric and networking organizations, promoting R&D and innovation and putting customers and employees at the centre. Our findings regarding toxic leaders raise the question as to the capability of Indian organizations to compete, excel and grow globally. This is because in organizations headed by toxic leaders, humans are not treated with dignity, their talent is not well harnessed and their creativity is killed. In fact, there is unanimity that in this century, it is people power that will enable organizations to survive, grow, compete and win the global Olympiad. Drastic steps are needed in such organizations if they want to thrive, let alone compete globally.

It may be worthwhile asking a larger level question regarding the impact of such toxic styles on the (a) work culture, architecting corporate strategy, (b) connecting horizon with ground reality, (c) inspiring and motivating employees, for collective march to compete globally and deliver world-class performance. Toxic centric leadership style at the top level can be most damaging for the organization, leading it down the path of decay and destruction. Leaders with this profile would be devoid of futuristic vision; there would be heavy accent on short-term performance, many times crucifying the interest of the organization for the long run. They will be tempted to indulge in corrupt and dishonest practices, while transacting business and charting out the growth trajectory of the organization. They would not like to invest in R&D, the basic soul for ensuring competitive edge not only for today, but also for tomorrow. It is no wonder, therefore, that importing technology from the West, Japan, South Korea and even China has become a way of life, among most of the Indian corporations. It is equally true that such leaders resort to unethical practices such as buying politicians, bureaucrats, bankers, deceiving the customers which unfortunately has become a norm, as cited in the prologue—Satyam, Coalgate, Reliance Jio, Telecom, DLF, Unitech—to name a few.

Globally, it has been acknowledged that people power is the most critical differentiator for building competitive edge, pursuit of excellence and winning the corporate Olympiad. Other pillars of competitive edge, such as cost leadership, quality leadership, customer centricity and innovation, can provide only temporal competitive edge as these things can easily be learnt, adopted and imitated by competitors. It is only people power which cannot be imitated by the competitors. Great organizations are now positioning people power at the centre and growing and building them to harness their full talent and capability. Such strategies played a significant role in companies such as GE, IBM, L&T, Tatas, ABG, to name a few.

If people power is not effectively harnessed and utilized, then the result can be a culture of gossip mongering, politicking, game playing, pulling each other down, alienation, feeling of helplessness and meaninglessness. This becomes the surest path for organizational ruination.

Perusal of this chapter in a holistic and gestalt perspective brings out the following quintessential conclusions:

1. The most commonly experienced toxic leader behaviours are arrogance, putting the blame on others, self-opinionated and close-minded behaviours.
2. Narcissistic, sadist and Machiavellian behaviours are evident across middle- and senior-level leaders in organizations.
3. Top-level toxic leaders are more rude and abusive; they publicly humiliate others and believe in constant self-promotion

as compared with middle-level toxic leaders. One of the plausible explanations for toxic behaviour could be greater power at the top. They therefore feel invisible and feel that they can get away with anything they do, as there are no checks and balances at that level. Further, higher power holders (positionally speaking) suffer from illusions of superiority, which makes them feel that they have the license to misbehave with others. In fact, they feel that public humiliation, rudeness and abusiveness are ways of showing that they are the bosses. If we try to explain this from the psychoanalytic perspective, such people do not have well-evolved egos, probably suffer from insecurity and inferiority. Therefore, power is used as a powerful crutch and compensatory mechanism to feel superior to others. It is worthwhile mentioning here that, generally speaking, toxicity in a person may not be absolute. It may range from low to high. When it goes more towards the toxic end of the bipolar phenomenon, it starts hurting people, demoralizes, demotivates, disengages them and makes them want to quit the organization. Such leaders are reviled, disliked and hated. Likewise, virtuous behaviour also ranges from low to high and when it moves more towards the end of the pole, it makes people feel enthused and excited to work them. Such virtuous leaders thus become role models for others. They are liked and admired and people feel energized to work with them (virtuous leader phenomena are discussed in detail in Chapter 3).

4. Toxic leader behaviours have made Indian organizations, hotbeds of politics, game playing and one upmanship, thus harming the fabric of teamwork and collectivity.

5. At the middle level, executives cope with toxic leader behaviour by using styles of avoidance, approach, assertive and adaptive coping strategy, in that order.

6. While responding to the top-level toxic behaviour, senior people expressed the desire to leave the organizations, indulge into compliance-centric behaviour, demonstrating low commitment, passion and disengagement from the organization.

7. While responding to toxic leaders, middle-level executives expressed tremendous emotional distress.

Appendix

TABLE A2.1

Toxic Leadership Attributes by Age Categories: Frequency, Percentage and Ranks

S. no.	Toxic behaviours	Group 1			Group 2			Group 3		
		Age <30 years (268) frequency	%	Rank	Age 31–45 years (233) frequency	%	Rank	Age >46 years (233) frequency	%	Rank
2	Arrogant	193	72	1	161	69.1	2	171	73.3	1
4	Blaming others	189	70.5	2	166	71.2	1	143	61.3	4
16	Self-opinionated and close minded	167	62.3	4	149	63.9	4	140	60	5
5	Create insecurity among people	171	63.8	3	142	60.9	5	138	59.2	6
7	Manipulative and playing favourites	166	61.9	5	111	47.6	15	147	63	3
19	Unreliable and untrustworthy	152	56.7	7	119	51	13	150	64.3	2
1	Abusive	128	47.8	14	155	66.5	3	134	57.5	7
6	Ill-tempered	138	51.5	10	137	58.8	6	129	55.3	8
12	Power hungry	147	54.9	8	128	54.9	7	128	54.9	9

(Table A2.1 Contd)

(Table A2.1 Contd)

S. no.	Toxic behaviours	Group 1 Age <30 years (268) frequency	%	Rank	Group 2 Age 31–45 years (233) frequency	%	Rank	Group 3 Age >46 years (233) frequency	%	Rank
14	Hypocrite	133	49.6	11	124	53.2	9	128	54.9	10
11	Play 'divide and rule'	140	52.2	9	123	52.7	11	112	48	13
3	Dishonest and lacked integrity	117	43.7	15	126	54	8	122	52.3	11
8	Insensitive to my feelings	130	48.5	12	124	53.2	10	110	47.2	14
18	Take credit of others works	155	57.8	6	108	46.3	16	101	43.3	16
13	Publicly ridiculed others	130	48.5	13	106	45.4	17	118	50.6	12
10	Narcissist	110	41	16	117	50.2	14	96	41.2	17
20	Corrupt	88	32.8	18	121	51.9	12	102	43.7	15
15	Rude	64	23.9	20	90	38.6	18	83	35.6	18
9	Demeaning others	89	33.2	17	74	31.7	20	61	26.1	19
17	Shared sensitive and personal information about others	65	24.3	19	85	36.4	19	55	23.6	20

Rho values: Group 1 vs. 2 = .62**; Group 1 vs. 3 = .81**; Group 2 vs. 3 = .72**.
** indicates significant at .01 level.

TABLE A2.2

Toxic Leadership Attributes by Work Experience: Frequency, Percentage and Ranks

S. no	Toxic behaviours	Group 1 Work Exp <5 years (250)			Group 2 Work Exp 6–15 years (154)			Group 3 Work Exp >16 years (330)		
		frequency	%	Rank	frequency	%	Rank	frequency	%	Rank
2	Arrogant	191	76.4	1	100	64.9	2	234	70.9	1
4	Blaming others	174	69.6	2	96	62.3	3	228	69	2
16	Self-opinionated and close minded	152	60.8	5	106	68.8	1	198	60	6
5	Create insecurity among people	155	62	4	94	61	4	202	61.2	4
7	Manipulative and playing favourites	160	64	3	68	44.2	16	196	59.3	8
19	Unreliable and untrustworthy	144	57.6	6	65	42.2	17	212	64.2	3
1	Abusive	127	50.8	11	88	57.1	5	202	61.2	5
6	Ill-tempered	130	52	10	78	50.6	9	196	59.3	7

(Table A2.2 Contd)

(Table A2.2 Contd)

S. no.	Toxic behaviours	Group 1 Work Exp <5 years (250)			Group 2 Work Exp 6–15 years (154)			Group 3 Work Exp >16 years (330)		
		frequency	%	Rank	frequency	%	Rank	frequency	%	Rank
12	Power hungry	140	56	8	82	53.2	8	181	54.8	10
14	Hypocrite	131	52.4	9	70	45.5	15	184	55.7	9
11	Play 'divide and rule'	127	50.8	12	86	55.8	6	162	49	13
3	Dishonest and lacked integrity	112	44.8	15	75	48.7	12	178	53.9	11
8	Insensitive to my feelings	119	47.6	14	76	49.4	11	169	51.2	12
18	Take credit of others works	144	57.6	7	70	45.5	14	150	45.4	16
13	Publicly ridiculed others	120	48	13	73	47.4	13	161	48.7	14
10	Narcissist	97	38.8	16	83	53.9	7	143	43.3	17
20	Corrupt	76	30.4	18	77	50	10	158	47.8	15
15	Rude	57	22.8	20	62	40.3	18	118	35.7	18
9	Demeaning others	88	35.2	17	39	25.3	20	97	29.3	20
17	Shared sensitive and personal information about others	61	24.4	19	43	27.9	19	101	30	19

Rho: Group 1 vs. 2 = .52**; Group 1 vs. 3 = .84**; Group 2 vs. 3 = .62**.
** indicates significant at .01 level.

TABLE A2.3

Toxic Leadership Attributes by Educational Qualification: Frequency, Percentage and Ranks

S. no.	Toxic behaviours	Group 1			Group 2		
		Graduate (342) frequency	%	Rank	Post Graduate (392) frequency	%	Rank
2	Arrogant	226	66	2	299	76.2	1
4	Blaming others	242	70.7	1	256	65.3	2
16	Self-opinionated and close minded	209	61.1	3	247	63	4
5	Create insecurity among people	198	57.8	6	253	64.5	3
7	Manipulative and playing favourites	184	53.8	9	240	61.2	5
19	Unreliable and untrustworthy	197	57.6	7	224	57.1	6
1	Abusive	206	60.2	4	211	53.8	8
6	Ill-tempered	190	55.5	8	214	54.5	7
12	Power hungry	201	58.7	5	202	51.5	11

(Table A2.3 Contd)

(Table A2.3 Contd)

S. no.	Toxic behaviours	Group 1			Group 2		
		Graduate (342) frequency	%	Rank	Post Graduate (392) frequency	%	Rank
14	Hypocrite	183	53.5	10	202	51.5	12
11	Play 'divide and rule'	170	49.7	13	205	52.3	10
3	Dishonest and lacked integrity	175	51.1	11	190	48.4	14
8	Insensitive to my feelings	162	47.3	14	202	51.5	13
18	Take credit of others works	154	45	16	210	53.5	9
13	Publicly ridiculed others	173	50.5	12	181	46.1	16
10	Narcissist	134	39.1	17	189	48.2	15
20	Corrupt	159	46.4	15	152	38.7	17
15	Rude	105	30.7	19	132	33.6	18
9	Demeaning others	116	33.9	18	108	27.5	20
17	Shared sensitive and personal information about others	95	27.7	20	110	28	19

Rho: Group 1 vs. 2 = .86**.
** indicates significant at .01 level.

TABLE A2.4

Toxic Leadership Attributes by Gender: Frequency, Percentage and Ranks

S. no.	Toxic behaviours	Group 1			Group 2		
		Male (516) frequency	%	Rank	Female (218) frequency	%	Rank
2	Arrogant	374	72.4	1	151	69.2	1
4	Blaming others	355	68.7	2	143	65.6	2
16	Self-opinionated and close minded	323	62.5	3	133	61	4
5	Create insecurity among people	309	59.8	5	142	65.1	3
7	Manipulative and playing favourites	303	58.7	7	121	55.5	5
19	Unreliable and untrustworthy	308	59.6	6	113	51.8	6
1	Abusive	312	60.4	4	105	48.1	13
6	Ill-tempered	291	56.3	8	113	51.8	7
12	Power hungry	290	56.2	9	113	51.8	8

(Table A2.4 Contd)

(Table A2.4 Contd)

S. no.	Toxic behaviours	Group 1			Group 2		
		Male (516) frequency	%	Rank	Female (218) frequency	%	Rank
14	Hypocrite	274	53.1	10	111	50.9	9
11	Play 'divide and rule'	266	51.5	11	109	50	11
3	Dishonest and lacked integrity	256	49.6	13	109	50	12
8	Insensitive to my feelings	254	49.2	15	110	50.4	10
18	Take credit of others works	266	51.5	12	98	44.9	15
13	Publicly ridiculed others	255	49.4	14	99	45.4	14
10	Narcissist	228	44.1	16	95	43.5	16
20	Corrupt	218	42.2	17	93	42.6	17
15	Rude	167	32.3	18	70	32.1	18
9	Demeaning others	165	31.9	19	59	27.0	20
17	Shared sensitive and personal information about others	144	27.9	20	61	27.9	19

Rho: Group 1 vs. 2 = .90**.
** indicates significant at .01 level.

TABLE A2.5

Toxic Leadership Attributes by Family Type: Frequency, Percentage and Ranks

S. no.	Toxic behaviours	Group 1			Group 2		
		Nuclear family (433) frequency	%	Rank	Joint family (301) frequency	%	Rank
2	Arrogant	317	73.2	1	208	69.1	2
4	Blaming others	284	65.5	3	214	71	1
16	Self-opinionated and close minded	280	64.6	4	176	58.4	3
5	Create insecurity among people	292	67.4	2	159	52.8	10
7	Manipulative and playing favourites	251	57.9	5	173	57.4	5
19	Unreliable and untrustworthy	249	57.5	6	172	57.1	6
1	Abusive	241	55.6	8	176	58.4	4
6	Ill-tempered	240	55.4	9	164	54.4	7
12	Power hungry	243	56.1	7	160	53.1	9
14	Hypocrite	229	52.8	11	156	51.8	12

(Table A2.5 Contd)

(Table A2.5 Contd)

S. no.	Toxic behaviours	Group 1			Group 2		
		Nuclear family (433) frequency	%	Rank	Joint family (301) frequency	%	Rank
11	Play 'divide and rule'	232	53.5	10	143	47.5	15
3	Dishonest and lacked integrity	204	47.1	14	161	53.4	8
8	Insensitive to my feelings	228	52.6	12	136	45.1	16
18	Take credit of others works	216	49.8	13	148	49.1	13
13	Publicly ridiculed others	195	45	15	159	52.8	11
10	Narcissist	191	44.1	16	132	43.8	17
20	Corrupt	163	37.6	17	148	49.1	14
15	Rude	133	30.7	18	104	34.5	18
9	Demeaning others	124	28.6	19	100	33.2	19
17	Shared sensitive and personal information about others	110	25.4	20	95	31.5	20

Rho: Group 1 vs. 2 = .85**.
** indicates significant at .01 level.

TABLE A2.6

Toxic Leadership Attributes by Resilience: Frequency, Percentage and Ranks

S. no.	Toxic behaviours	Group 1			Group 2		
		Low resilience (400) frequency	%	Rank	High resilience (334) frequency	%	Rank
2	Arrogant	288	72	1	237	70.9	1
4	Blaming others	272	68	2	226	67.6	2
16	Self-opinionated and close minded	254	63.5	3	202	60.4	5
5	Create insecurity among people	244	61	4	207	61.9	4
7	Manipulative and playing favourites	216	54	7	208	62.2	3
19	Unreliable and untrustworthy	221	55.2	6	200	59.8	7
1	Abusive	215	53.7	8	202	60.4	6
6	Ill-tempered	221	55.2	5	183	54.7	10
12	Power hungry	209	52.2	9	194	58	8

(Table A2.6 Contd)

(Table A2.6 Contd)

S. no.	Toxic behaviours	Group 1			Group 2		
		Low resilience (400) frequency	%	Rank	High resilience (334) frequency	%	Rank
14	Hypocrite	206	51.5	10	179	53.5	11
11	Play 'divide and rule'	181	45.2	15	194	58	9
3	Dishonest and lacked integrity	188	47	13	177	52.9	12
8	Insensitive to my feelings	202	50.5	11	162	48.5	15
18	Take credit of others works	201	50.2	12	163	48.8	14
13	Publicly ridiculed others	182	45.5	14	172	51.4	13
10	Narcissist	180	45	16	143	42.8	17
20	Corrupt	167	41.7	17	144	43.1	16
15	Rude	130	32.5	18	107	32.0	18
9	Demeaning others	121	30.2	20	103	30.8	19
17	Shared sensitive and personal information about others	129	32.25	19	76	22.7545	20

Rho: Group 1 vs. 2 = .91**.
** indicates significant at .01 level.

TABLE A2.7

Toxic Leadership Attributes by Work Locus of Control (LOC): Frequency, Percentage and Ranks

S. no.	Toxic behaviours	Group 1			Group 2		
		Internal LOC (376) frequency	%	Rank	External LOC (358) frequency	%	Rank
2	Arrogant	265	70.5	1	260	72.6	1
4	Blaming others	260	69.1	2	238	66.5	2
16	Self-opinionated and close minded	237	63.0	3	219	61.2	4
5	Create insecurity among people	227	60.4	4	224	62.6	3
7	Manipulative and playing favourites	218	58.0	5	206	57.5	7
19	Unreliable and untrustworthy	214	56.9	6	207	57.8	6
1	Abusive	208	55.3	7	209	58.4	5
6	Ill-tempered	207	55.1	8	197	55.0	9
12	Power hungry	204	54.3	11	199	55.6	8

(Table A2.7 Contd)

(Table A2.7 Contd)

S. no.	Toxic behaviours	Group 1			Group 2		
		Internal LOC (376) frequency	%	Rank	External LOC (358) frequency	%	Rank
14	Hypocrite	206	54.8	10	179	50.0	13
11	Play 'divide and rule'	188	50.0	12	187	52.2	11
3	Dishonest and lacked integrity	206	54.8	9	159	44.4	15
8	Insensitive to my feelings	176	46.8	15	188	52.5	10
18	Take credit of others works	179	47.6	14	185	51.7	12
13	Publicly ridiculed others	187	49.7	13	167	46.6	14
10	Narcissist	169	44.9	17	154	43.0	16
20	Corrupt	176	46.8	16	135	37.7	17
15	Rude	123	32.7	18	114	31.8	19
9	Demeaning others	107	28.5	19	117	32.7	18
17	Shared sensitive and personal information about others	107	28.5	20	98	27.4	20

Rho: Group 1 vs. 2 = .92**.
** indicates significant at .01 level.

TABLE A2.8(a)

Toxic Leadership Attributes by Values (Egalitarian and Humanistic): Frequency, Percentage and Ranks

S. no.	Toxic behaviours	Group 1 Low egalitarian (421)			Group 2 High egalitarian (313)			Group 3 Low humanistic (398)			Group 4 High humanistic (336)		
		frequency	%	Rank	frequency	%	Rank	frequency	%	Rank	frequency	%	Rank
2	Arrogant	292	67.7	2	206	65.8	2	277	69.6	2	221	65.7	2
4	Blaming others	250	58	4	201	64.2	3	239	60	4	212	63.1	3
16	Self-opinionated and close minded	214	49.6	11	151	48.2	15	203	51	12	162	48.2	13
5	Create insecurity among people	249	57.7	5	175	55.9	8	219	55	8	205	61	4
7	Manipulative and playing favourites	224	51.9	9	193	61.6	5	220	55.2	7	197	58.6	6
19	Unreliable and untrustworthy	129	29.9	19	108	34.5	18	129	32.4	18	108	32.1	18
1	Abusive	306	71	1	219	69.9	1	289	72.6	1	236	70.2	1
6	Ill-tempered	226	52.4	8	177	56.5	7	209	52.5	10	194	57.7	7
12	Power hungry	215	49.8	10	160	51.1	12	202	50.7	13	173	51.4	10
14	Hypocrite	193	44.7	15	161	51.4	11	182	45.7	15	172	51.1	11

(Table A2.8(a) Contd)

(Table A2.8(a) Contd)

S. no.	Toxic behaviours	Group 1 Low egalitarian (421) frequency	%	Rank	Group 2 High egalitarian (313) frequency	%	Rank	Group 3 Low humanistic (398) frequency	%	Rank	Group 4 High humanistic (336) frequency	%	Rank
11	Play 'divide and rule'	208	48.2	13	156	49.8	14	203	51	11	161	47.9	15
3	Dishonest and lacked integrity	260	60.3	3	196	62.6	4	254	63.8	3	202	60.1	5
8	Insensitive to my feelings	232	53.8	7	172	54.9	10	222	55.7	6	182	54.1	9
18	Take credit of others works	131	30.3	18	93	29.7	19	127	31.9	19	97	28.8	19
13	Publicly ridiculed others	212	49.1	12	173	55.2	9	217	54.5	9	168	50	12
10	Narcissist	241	55.9	6	180	57.5	6	237	59.5	5	184	54.7	8
20	Corrupt	117	27.1	20	88	28.1	20	118	29.6	20	87	25.8	20
15	Rude	187	43.3	16	136	43.4	16	168	42.2	17	155	46.1	16
9	Demeaning others	207	48	14	157	50.1	13	202	50.7	14	162	48.2	14
17	Shared sensitive and personal information about others	177	41	17	134	42.8	17	174	43.7	16	137	40.7	17

Rho: Group 1 vs. 2 = .93**; Group 3 vs. 4: .92**.
** indicates significant at .01 level.

TABLE A2.8(b)

Toxic Leadership Attributes by Values (Hedonistic and Personal Development): Frequency, Percentage and Ranks

S. no.	Toxic behaviours	Group 5 Low hedonistic (356)			Group 6 High hedonistic (378)			Group 7 Low personal development (332)			Group 8 High personal development (402)		
		frequency	%	Rank	frequency	%	Rank	frequency	%	Rank	frequency	%	Rank
2	Arrogant	238	66.8	2	260	68.7	2	229	68.9	2	269	66.9	2
4	Blaming others	213	59.8	4	238	62.9	4	200	60.2	3	251	62.4	4
16	Self-opinionated and close minded	185	51.9	10	180	47.6	15	172	51.8	12	193	48	14
5	Create insecurity among people	199	55.9	8	225	59.5	5	190	57.2	6	234	58.2	7
7	Manipulative and playing favourites	201	56.4	6	216	57.1	8	182	54.8	8	235	58.4	6
19	Unreliable and untrustworthy	108	30.3	18	129	34.1	18	108	32.5	18	129	32	18
1	Abusive	258	72.4	1	267	70.6	1	246	74.1	1	279	69.4	1
6	Ill-tempered	178	50	12	225	59.5	6	178	53.6	9	225	55.9	8
12	Power hungry	184	51.6	11	191	50.5	13	156	46.9	14	219	54.4	9

(Table A2.8(b) Contd)

(Table A2.8(b) Contd)

S. no.	Toxic behaviours	Group 5 Low hedonistic (356)			Group 6 High hedonistic (378)			Group 7 Low personal development (332)			Group 8 High personal development (402)		
		frequency	%	Rank	frequency	%	Rank	frequency	%	Rank	frequency	%	Rank
14	Hypocrite	170	47.7	14	184	48.6	14	156	46.9	15	198	49.2	13
11	Play 'divide and rule'	171	48	13	193	51.0	12	175	52.7	10	189	47	15
3	Dishonest and lacked integrity	217	60.9	3	239	63.2	3	199	59.9	4	257	63.9	3
8	Insensitive to my feelings	204	57.3	5	200	52.9	10	195	58.7	5	209	51.9	11
18	Take credit of others works	107	30	20	117	30.9	19	103	31.0	19	121	30.1	19
13	Publicly ridiculed others	185	51.9	9	200	52.9	11	174	52.4	11	211	52.4	10
10	Narcissist	200	56.1	7	221	58.4	7	186	56.0	7	235	58.4	5
20	Corrupt	108	30.3	19	97	25.6	20	86	25.9	20	119	29.6	20
15	Rude	156	43.8	17	167	44.1	16	146	43.9	16	177	44	16
9	Demeaning others	160	44.9	15	204	53.9	9	159	47.8	13	205	51	12
17	Shared sensitive and personal information about others	157	44.1	16	154	40.7	17	136	40.9	17	175	43.5	17

Rho: Group 5 vs. 6 = .88**; Group 7 vs. 8 = .91**.
** indicates significant at .01 level.

TABLE A2.8(c)

Toxic Leadership Attributes by Values (Pride and Materialistic): Frequency, Percentage and Ranks

S. no.	Toxic behaviours	Group 9 Low pride (310)			Group 10 High pride (424)			Group 11 Low materialistic (367)			Group 12 High materialistic (367)		
		frequency	%	Rank	frequency	%	Rank	frequency	%	Rank	frequency	%	Rank
2	Arrogant	212	68.3	2	286	67.4	2	246	67	1	252	68.6	2
4	Blaming others	182	58.7	4	269	63.4	4	225	61.3	4	226	61.5	4
16	Self-opinionated and close minded	168	54.1	9	197	46.4	15	200	54.5	9	165	44.9	16
5	Create insecurity among people	168	54.1	8	256	60.3	5	206	56.1	7	218	59.4	5
7	Manipulative and playing favourites	171	55.1	6	246	58	6	216	58.8	6	201	54.7	7
19	Unreliable and untrustworthy	108	34.8	18	129	30.4	19	125	34	18	112	30.5	19
1	Abusive	217	70	1	308	72.6	1	243	66.2	2	282	76.8	1
6	Ill-tempered	167	53.8	10	236	55.6	8	191	52	11	212	57.7	6
12	Power hungry	159	51.2	12	216	50.9	13	183	49.8	13	192	52.3	12
14	Hypocrite	135	43.5	16	219	51.6	12	186	50.6	12	168	45.7	14

(Table A2.8(c) Contd)

(Table A2.8(c) Contd)

S. no.	Toxic behaviours	Group 9 Low pride (310)			Group 10 High pride (424)			Group 11 Low materialistic (367)			Group 12 High materialistic (367)		
		frequency	%	Rank	frequency	%	Rank	frequency	%	Rank	frequency	%	Rank
11	Play 'divide and rule'	143	46.1	15	221	52.1	11	170	46.3	15	194	52.8	11
3	Dishonest and lacked integrity	182	58.7	3	274	64.6	3	222	60.4	5	234	63.7	3
8	Insensitive to my feelings	169	54.2	7	235	55.2	9	204	55.5	8	200	54.5	8
18	Take credit of others works	93	30	19	131	30.9	18	109	29.7	19	115	31.3	18
13	Publicly ridiculed others	158	50.9	13	227	53.5	10	199	54.2	10	186	50.6	13
10	Narcissist	182	58.7	5	239	56.3	7	226	61.5	3	195	53.1	10
20	Corrupt	83	26.7	20	122	28.7	20	101	27.5	20	104	28.3	20
15	Rude	135	43.5	17	188	44.3	16	156	42.5	17	167	45.5	15
9	Demeaning others	162	52.2	11	202	47.6	14	167	45.5	16	197	53.6	9
17	Shared sensitive and personal information about others	155	50	14	156	36.7	17	178	48.5	14	133	36.2	17

Rho: Group 9 vs. 10 = .91**; Group 11 vs. 12 = .82**.
** indicates significant at .01 level.

TABLE A2.9

Toxic Leadership Attributes by Organizational Sector: Frequency, Percentage and Ranks

| S. no. | Toxic behaviours | Group 1 | | | Group 2 | | |
		Indian public sector executives (263) frequency	%	Rank	Indian private sector executives (307) frequency	%	Rank
2	Arrogant	187	71.1	1	226	73.6	1
4	Blaming others	179	68	2	215	70	2
16	Self-opinionated and close minded	151	57.4	8	201	65.5	4
5	Create insecurity among people	153	58.1	5	200	65.1	5
7	Manipulative and playing favourites	166	63.1	3	206	67.1	3
19	Unreliable and untrustworthy	157	59.7	4	192	62.5	6
1	Abusive	152	57.7	7	167	54.4	11
6	Ill-tempered	153	58.1	6	173	56.4	9
12	Power hungry	139	52.8	9	178	58	7

(Table A2.9 Contd)

(Table A2.9 Contd)

S. no.	Toxic behaviours	Group 1			Group 2		
		Indian public sector executives (263) frequency	%	Rank	Indian private sector executives (307) frequency	%	Rank
14	Hypocrite	136	51.7	10	167	54.4	12
11	Play 'divide and rule'	109	41.4	16	172	56	10
3	Dishonest and lacked integrity	135	51.3	11	146	47.6	15
8	Insensitive to my feelings	129	49	12	159	51.8	14
18	Take credit of others works	111	42.2	15	177	57.7	8
13	Publicly ridiculed others	121	46	13	161	52.4	13
10	Narcissist	99	37.6	17	138	45	16
20	Corrupt	118	44.8	14	109	35.5	18
15	Rude	86	32.7	18	91	29.6	20
9	Demeaning others	71	27	19	121	39.4	17
17	Shared sensitive and personal information about others	54	20.5	20	99	32.2	19

Rho: Group 1 vs. 2 = .86**.
** indicates significant at .01 level.

TABLE A2.10

Toxic Leadership Attributes by Industry Type: Frequency, Percentage and Ranks

S. no.	Toxic behaviours	Group 1			Group 2		
		Service (423) frequency	%	Rank	Manufac- turing (311) frequency	%	Rank
2	Arrogant	294	69.5	2	231	74.2	1
4	Blaming others	295	69.7	1	203	65.2	2
16	Self-opinionated and close minded	255	60.2	4	201	64.6	3
5	Create insecurity among people	266	62.8	3	185	59.4	5
7	Manipulative and playing favourites	237	56	6	187	60.1	4
19	Unreliable and untrustworthy	243	57.4	5	178	57.2	8
1	Abusive	234	55.3	8	183	58.8	6
6	Ill-tempered	236	55.7	7	168	54	11
12	Power hungry	224	52.9	9	179	57.5	7
14	Hypocrite	210	49.6	11	175	56.2	9

(Table A2.10 Contd)

(Table A2.10 Contd)

S. no.	Toxic behaviours	Group 1			Group 2		
		Service (423) frequency	%	Rank	Manufac-turing (311) frequency	%	Rank
11	Play 'divide and rule'	201	47.5	14	174	55.9	10
3	Dishonest and lacked integrity	205	48.4	13	160	51.4	13
8	Insensitive to my feelings	208	49.1	12	156	50.1	14
18	Take credit of others works	200	47.2	15	164	52.7	12
13	Publicly ridiculed others	215	50.8	10	139	44.6	16
10	Narcissist	185	43.7	16	138	44.3	17
20	Corrupt	168	39.7	17	143	45.9	15
15	Rude	122	28.8	18	115	36.9	18
9	Demeaning others	113	26.7	19	111	35.6	19
17	Shared sensitive and personal information about others	96	22.7	20	109	35	20

Rho: Group 1 vs. 2 = .91**.
** indicates significant at .01 level.

TABLE A2.11

Toxic Leadership Attributes by Nationality: Frequency, Percentage and Ranks

S. no.	Toxic behaviours	Group 1 International executives (164) frequency	%	Rank	Group 2 Indian executives (570) frequency	%	Rank
2	Arrogant	112	68.29	1	413	72.46	1
4	Blaming others	104	63.41	2	394	69.12	2
16	Self-opinionated and close minded	104	63.41	3	352	65.26	5
5	Create insecurity among people	98	59.76	4	353	61.93	4
7	Manipulative and playing favourites	52	31.71	18	372	61.75	3
19	Unreliable and untrustworthy	72	43.9	15	349	61.23	6
1	Abusive	98	59.76	5	319	57.19	8
6	Ill-tempered	78	47.56	12	326	55.96	7
12	Power hungry	86	52.44	7	317	55.61	9

(Table A2.11 Contd)

(Table A2.11 Contd)

S. no.	Toxic behaviours	Group 1 International executives (164)			Group 2 Indian executives (570)		
		frequency	%	Rank	frequency	%	Rank
14	Hypocrite	82	50	11	303	53.16	10
11	Play 'divide and rule'	94	57.32	6	281	50.53	14
3	Dishonest and lacked integrity	84	51.3	9	281	50.53	15
8	Insensitive to my feelings	76	46.34	13	288	49.47	11
18	Take credit of others works	76	46.34	14	288	49.3	12
13	Publicly ridiculed others	72	43.9	16	282	49.3	13
10	Narcissist	86	52.44	8	237	41.58	16
20	Corrupt	84	51.22	10	227	39.82	17
15	Rude	60	36.59	17	177	33.68	19
9	Demeaning others	32	19.51	20	192	31.05	18
17	Shared sensitive and personal information about others	52	31.71	19	153	26.84	20

Rho: Group 9 vs. 10 = .66**.
** indicates significant at .01 level.

TABLE A2.12

Descriptive Statistics

Variables	Mean	SD
Emotional Distress	4.12	1.17
Avoidance Coping Strategy	3.06	1.14
Approach Coping Strategy	2.15	0.98
Assertive Coping Strategy	3.59	1.22
Adaptive Coping Strategy	3.77	1.21
Resilience	3.63	0.46
Work Locus of Control	2.19	0.72
Egalitarian Value	3.89	1.01
Humanistic Value	4.20	1.03
Hedonistic Value	3.69	1.14
Personal Development Value	3.98	1.04
Pride Value	4.13	1.14
Materialistic Value	3.59	1.23

TABLE A2.13

F-test (Age as Independent Variable and Emotional Distress as Dependent Variable)

Variables	Groups	N	Mean	SD	F Value
Emotional Distress	Up to 30 years	268	4.28	1.02	
	31–45 years	233	3.95	1.21	4.95**
	46 years and above	233	4.12	1.27	

** indicates significant at .01 level.

TABLE A2.14

F-test (Work Experience as Independent Variable and Emotional Distress as Dependent Variable)

Variables	Groups	N	Mean	SD	F Value
Emotional Distress	Up to 5 years	250	4.3	1.04	
	6–15 years	154	3.98	1.16	4.39**
	16 years and above	330	4.06	1.25	

** indicates significant at .01 level.

TABLE A2.15

Independent Sample t-Test (Educational Qualification as Independent Variable and Emotional Distress as Dependent Variable)

Variables	Qualification	N	Mean	SD	t Value
Emotional Distress	Graduation	342	4.01	1.22	2.43**
	Post-graduation	392	4.22	1.12	

** indicates significant at .01 level.

TABLE A2.16

Independent Sample t-Test (Gender as Independent Variable and Emotional Distress as Dependent Variable)

Variables	Gender	N	Mean	SD	t Value
Emotional Distress	Male	516	4.08	1.16	1.72
	Female	218	4.24	1.20	

TABLE A2.17

Independent Sample t-Test (Family Type as Independent Variable and Emotional Distress as Dependent Variable)

Variables	Family type	N	Mean	SD	t Value
Emotional Distress	Nuclear Family	433	4.19	1.14	1.83
	Joint Family	301	4.03	1.22	

TABLE A2.18

Independent Sample *t*-Test (Resilience as Independent Variable and Emotional Distress as Dependent Variable)

Variables	Resilience	N	Mean	SD	t Value
Emotional Distress	Low Resilience	408	4.19	1.21	1.65
	High Resilience	326	4.05	1.13	

TABLE A2.19

Independent Sample *t*-Test (Work Locus of Control as Independent Variable and Emotional Distress as Dependent Variable)

Variables	Work locus of control	N	Mean	SD	t Value
Emotional Distress	Internal LOC	395	4.20	1.08	1.71
	External LOC	339	4.05	1.27	

TABLE A2.20

Independent Sample *t*-Test (Values as Independent Variable and Emotional Distress as Dependent Variable)

Variables	Egalitarian	N	Mean	SD	t Value
Emotional Distress	Low Egalitarian	374	4.20	1.23	1.79
	High Egalitarian	360	4.05	1.11	
Emotional Distress	Low Humanistic	429	4.18	1.20	1.47
	High Humanistic	305	4.05	1.14	
Emotional Distress	Low Hedonistic	378	4.22	1.20	2.19*
	High Hedonistic	356	4.03	1.14	
Emotional Distress	Low Personal Development	402	4.15	1.23	0.579
	High Personal Development	332	4.10	1.11	

(Table A2.20 Contd)

(Table A2.20 Contd)

Variables	Egalitarian	N	Mean	SD	t Value
Emotional Distress	Low Pride	424	4.14	1.15	0.44
	High Pride	310	4.10	1.21	
Emotional Distress	Low Materialistic	367	4.18	1.19	1.28
	High Materialistic	367	4.07	1.16	

* indicates significant at .05 level.

TABLE A2.21

Independent Sample t-Test (Organizational Sector as Independent Variable and Emotional Distress as Dependent Variable)

Variables	Organizational sector	N	Mean	SD	t Value
Emotional Distress	Public Sector	403	4.08	1.27	1.12
	Private Sector	331	4.18	1.06	

TABLE A2.22

Independent Sample t-Test (Industry Type as Independent Variable and Emotional Distress as Dependent Variable)

Variables	Industry type	N	Mean	SD	t Value
Emotional Distress	Service Sector	423	4.25	1.09	3.26**
	Manufacturing Sector	311	3.96	1.26	

** indicates significant at .01 level.

TABLE A2.23

Independent Sample t-Test (Nationality Type as Independent Variable and Emotional Distress as Dependent Variable)

Variables	Nationality	N	Mean	SD	t Value
Emotional Distress Total	International Executives	164	3.86	1.31	3.38**
	Indian Executives	570	4.21	1.12	

** indicates significant at .01 level.

TABLE A2.24

F-Test (Age as Independent Variable and Coping Strategy as Dependent Variable)

Variables	Groups	N	Mean	SD	F Value
Avoidance Coping Strategy	Up to 30 years	268	3.66	1.21	
	31–45 years	233	2.65	0.85	68.76**
	46 years and above	233	2.80	1.05	
Approach Coping Strategy	Up to 30 years	268	2.46	1.15	
	31–45 years	233	2.07	0.79	24.62**
	46 years and above	233	1.88	0.87	
Assertive Coping Strategy	Up to 30 years	268	3.95	1.23	
	31–45 years	233	3.20	1.08	24.41**
	46 years and above	233	3.57	1.23	
Adaptive Coping Strategy	Up to 30 years	268	3.98	1.33	
	31–45 years	233	3.57	1.19	7.47**
	46 years and above	233	3.73	1.06	

** indicates significant at .01 level.

TABLE A2.25

F-Test (Work Experience as Independent Variable and Coping Strategy as Dependent Variable)

Variables	Groups	N	Mean	SD	F Value
Avoidance Coping Strategy	Up to 5 years	250	3.66	1.18	
	6–15 years	154	2.96	1.02	63.75**
	16 years and above	330	2.67	0.98	
Approach Coping Strategy	Up to 5 years	250	2.43	1.10	
	6–15 years	154	2.23	0.99	22.32**
	16 years and above	330	1.90	0.82	
Assertive Coping Strategy	Up to 5 years	250	3.90	1.26	
	6–15 years	154	3.42	1.19	12.39**
	16 years and above	330	3.44	1.17	

(Table A2.25 Contd)

(Table A2.25 Contd)

Variables	Groups	N	Mean	SD	F Value
Adaptive Coping Strategy	Up to 5 years	250	3.99	1.34	7.13**
	6–15 years	154	3.78	1.29	
	16 years and above	330	3.61	1.05	

** indicates significant at .01 level.

TABLE A2.26

Independent Sample *t*-Test (Educational Qualification as Independent Variable and Coping Strategy as Dependent Variable)

Variables	Qualification	N	Mean	SD	t Value
Avoidance Coping Strategy	Graduation	342	2.76	0.90	7.02
	Post-graduation	392	3.34	1.27	
Approach Coping Strategy	Graduation	342	2.03	0.87	3.09**
	Post-graduation	392	2.26	1.07	
Assertive Coping Strategy	Graduation	342	3.19	1.09	8.62**
	Post-graduation	392	3.94	1.23	
Adaptive Coping Strategy	Graduation	342	3.50	1.15	5.88**
	Post-graduation	392	4.01	1.22	

** indicates significant at .01 level.

TABLE A2.27

Independent Sample *t*-Test (Gender as Independent Variable and Coping Strategy as Dependent Variable)

Variables	Gender	N	Mean	SD	t Value
Avoidance Coping Strategy	Male	516	2.95	1.12	4.43**
	Female	218	3.35	1.16	
Approach Coping Strategy	Male	516	2.07	0.96	3.46**
	Female	218	2.34	1.03	
Assertive Coping Strategy	Male	516	3.46	1.17	4.31**
	Female	218	3.89	1.30	
Adaptive Coping Strategy	Male	516	3.73	1.21	1.46
	Female	218	3.87	1.23	

** indicates significant at .01 level.

TABLE A2.28

Independent Sample *t*-Test (Family Type as Independent Variable and Coping Strategy as Dependent Variable)

Variables	Family type	N	Mean	SD	t Value
Avoidance Coping Strategy	Nuclear Family	433	3.17	1.17	2.90**
	Joint Family	301	2.92	1.10	
Approach Coping Strategy	Nuclear Family	433	2.15	0.97	.06
	Joint Family	301	2.15	1.01	
Assertive Coping Strategy	Nuclear Family	433	3.69	1.22	2.53**
	Joint Family	301	3.45	1.22	
Adaptive Coping Strategy	Nuclear Family	433	3.81	1.18	1.03
	Joint Family	301	3.72	1.27	

** indicates significant at .01 level.

TABLE A2.29

Independent Sample *t*-Test (Resilience as Independent Variable and Coping Strategy as Dependent Variable)

Variables	Resilience total	N	Mean	SD	t Value
Avoidance Coping Strategy	Low Resilience	408	3.01	1.11	1.50
	High Resilience	326	3.14	1.19	
Approach Coping Strategy	Low Resilience	408	2.06	0.92	2.79**
	High Resilience	326	2.26	1.06	
Assertive Coping Strategy	Low Resilience	408	3.64	1.23	1.23
	High Resilience	326	3.53	1.22	
Adaptive Coping Strategy	Low Resilience	408	3.82	1.20	1.21
	High Resilience	326	3.71	1.23	

** indicates significant at .01 level.

TABLE A2.30

Independent Sample t-Test (Work Locus of Control as Independent Variable and Coping Strategy as Dependent Variable)

Variables	Work locus of control	N	Mean	SD	t Value
Avoidance Coping Strategy	Internal LOC	395	3.22	1.14	3.99**
	External LOC	339	2.89	1.13	
Approach Coping Strategy	Internal LOC	395	2.25	1.04	2.96**
	External LOC	339	2.03	0.92	
Assertive Coping Strategy	Internal LOC	395	3.62	1.28	0.570
	External LOC	339	3.56	1.16	
Adaptive Coping Strategy	Internal LOC	395	3.82	1.26	0.991
	External LOC	339	3.73	1.17	

** indicates significant at .01 level.

TABLE A2.31

Independent Sample t-Test (Egalitarian as Independent Variable and Coping Strategy as Dependent Variable)

Variables	Egalitarian	N	Mean	SD	t Value
Avoidance Coping Strategy	High Egalitarian	374	2.99	1.11	1.79
	Low Egalitarian	360	3.14	1.18	
Approach Coping Strategy	High Egalitarian	374	2.13	0.98	0.633
	Low Egalitarian	360	2.17	1.00	
Assertive Coping Strategy	High Egalitarian	374	3.57	1.22	0.530
	Low Egalitarian	360	3.61	1.24	
Adaptive Coping Strategy	High Egalitarian	374	3.75	1.34	0.031
	Low Egalitarian	360	3.80	1.07	

TABLE A2.32

Independent Sample *t*-Test (Humanistic as Independent Variable and Coping Strategy as Dependent Variable)

Variables	Humanistic	N	Mean	SD	*t* Value
Avoidance Coping Strategy	Low Humanistic	429	3.05	1.17	0.514
	High Humanistic	305	3.09	1.12	
Approach Coping Strategy	Low Humanistic	429	2.11	1.00	1.20
	High Humanistic	305	2.20	0.97	
Assertive Coping Strategy	Low Humanistic	429	3.69	1.24	2.57**
	High Humanistic	305	3.45	1.19	
Adaptive Coping Strategy	Low Humanistic	429	3.80	1.25	0.715
	High Humanistic	305	3.73	1.17	

** indicates significant at .01 level.

TABLE A2.33

Independent Sample *t*-Test (Hedonistic as Independent Variable and Coping Strategy as Dependent Variable)

Variables	Hedonistic	N	Mean	SD	*t* Value
Avoidance Coping Strategy	Low Hedonistic	378	3.19	1.23	3.09**
	High Hedonistic	356	2.93	1.04	
Approach Coping Strategy	Low Hedonistic	378	2.26	1.04	3.20**
	High Hedonistic	356	2.03	0.92	
Assertive Coping Strategy	Low Hedonistic	378	3.67	1.28	1.73
	High Hedonistic	356	3.51	1.15	
Adaptive Coping Strategy	Low Hedonistic	378	3.73	1.27	1.08
	High Hedonistic	356	3.82	1.16	

** indicates significant at .01 level.

TABLE A2.34

Independent Sample *t*-Test (Personal Development as Independent Variable and Coping Strategy as Dependent Variable)

Variables	Personal development	N	Mean	SD	t Value
Avoidance Coping Strategy	Low Personal Development	402	2.96	1.13	2.75**
	High Personal Development	332	3.19	1.16	
Approach Coping Strategy	Low Personal Development	402	2.08	0.95	2.15*
	High Personal Development	332	2.24	1.03	
Assertive Coping Strategy	Low Personal Development	402	3.56	1.25	0.767
	High Personal Development	332	3.63	1.19	
Adaptive Coping Strategy	Low Personal Development	402	3.73	1.24	0.981
	High Personal Development	332	3.82	1.19	

* indicates significant at .05 level; ** indicates significant at .01 level.

TABLE A2.35

Independent Sample *t*-Test (Pride as Independent Variable and Coping Strategy as Dependent Variable)

Variables	Pride	N	Mean	SD	t Value
Avoidance Coping Strategy	Low Pride	424	3.04	1.18	0.723
	High Pride	310	3.10	1.10	
Approach Coping Strategy	Low Pride	424	2.09	0.97	1.84
	High Pride	310	2.23	1.02	
Assertive Coping Strategy	Low Pride	424	3.66	1.19	0.477
	High Pride	310	3.50	1.27	
Adaptive Coping Strategy	Low Pride	424	3.81	1.14	0.422
	High Pride	310	3.72	1.31	

TABLE A2.36

Independent Sample *t*-Test (Materialistic as Independent Variable and Coping Strategy as Dependent Variable)

Variables	Materialistic	N	Mean	SD	t Value
Avoidance Coping Strategy	Low Materialistic	367	3.20	1.17	3.14**
	High Materialistic	367	2.93	1.11	
Approach Coping Strategy	Low Materialistic	367	2.26	0.99	2.86**
	High Materialistic	367	2.06	0.98	
Assertive Coping Strategy	Low Materialistic	367	3.65	1.18	1.34
	High Materialistic	367	3.53	1.27	
Adaptive Coping Strategy	Low Materialistic	367	3.79	1.24	.485
	High Materialistic	367	3.75	1.19	

** indicates significant at .01 level.

TABLE A2.37

Independent Sample *t*-Test (Organizational Sector as Independent Variable and Coping Strategy as Dependent Variable)

Variables	Organizational sector	N	Mean	SD	t Value
Avoidance Coping Strategy	Public Sector	403	2.85	0.95	5.79**
	Private Sector	331	3.33	1.30	
Approach Coping Strategy	Public Sector	403	2.06	0.90	2.82**
	Private Sector	331	2.26	1.08	
Assertive Coping Strategy	Public Sector	403	3.43	1.20	4.01**
	Private Sector	331	3.79	1.23	
Adaptive Coping Strategy	Public Sector	403	3.68	1.18	2.31**
	Private Sector	331	3.89	1.25	

** indicates significant at .01 level.

TABLE A2.38

Independent Sample *t*-Test (Industry Type as Independent Variable and Coping Strategy as Dependent Variable)

Variables	Industry type	N	Mean	SD	t Value
Avoidance Coping Strategy	Service Sector	423	3.29	1.14	6.37**
	Manufacturing Sector	311	2.76	1.09	
Approach Coping Strategy	Service Sector	423	2.26	1.01	3.38**
	Manufacturing Sector	311	2.01	0.94	
Assertive Coping Strategy	Service Sector	423	3.61	1.21	0.602
	Manufacturing Sector	311	3.56	1.25	
Adaptive Coping Strategy	Service Sector	423	3.84	1.33	1.69
	Manufacturing Sector	311	3.68	1.04	

** indicates significant at .01 level.

TABLE A2.39

Independent Sample *t*-Test (Nationality as Independent Variable and Coping Strategy as Dependent Variable)

Variables	Nationality	N	Mean	SD	t Value
Avoidance Coping Strategy	International Executives	164	2.86	0.97	2.58**
	Indian Executives	570	3.13	1.19	
Approach Coping Strategy	International Executives	164	2.28	1.00	1.84
	Indian Executives	570	2.12	0.98	
Assertive Coping Strategy	International Executives	164	3.21	1.22	4.61**
	Indian Executives	570	3.70	1.21	
Adaptive Coping Strategy	International Executives	164	3.74	1.41	.416
	Indian Executives	570	3.78	1.16	

** indicates significant at .01 level.

REFERENCES

1. Avolio, B.J., Gardner, W.L., Walumbwa, F.O., Luthans, F., & May, D.R. (2004). Unlocking the mask: A look at the process by which authentic leaders impact follower attitudes and behaviors. *The Leadership Quarterly, 15*(6), 801–823.
2. Gardner, W.L., Cogliser, C.C., Davis, K.M., & Dickens, M.P. (2011). Authentic leadership: A review of literature and research agenda. *The Leadership Quarterly, 22*(6), 1120–1145.
3. Judge, T.A., & Piccolo, R.F. (2004). Transformational and transactional leadership: A meta-analytic test of their relative validity. *Journal of Applied Psychology, 89*(5), 755–768.
4. Kouzes, J.M., & Posner, B.Z. (2002). *The leadership challenge.* San Francisco, CA: Jossey-Bass.
5. Yammarino, F.J., Dionne, S.D., Chun, J.U., & Dansereau, F. (2005). Leadership and levels of analysis: A state-of-the-science review. *Leadership Quarterly, 16*(6), 879–919.
6. Levinson, H. (1972). *Organizational diagnosis.* Cambridge, MA: Harvard University Press.
7. Levinson, H. (1976). *Psychological man.* Boston, MA: Levinson Institute.
8. Lowman, R. (Ed.) (2002). *Handbook of organizational consulting psychology.* San Francisco, CA: Jossey-Bass.
9. Frost, P. (2003). *Toxic emotions at work.* Boston, MA: Harvard Business School Press.
10. Kellerman, B. (2004). *Bad leadership: What it is, how it happens, why it matters.* Boston, MA: Harvard Business School Press.
11. Lubit, R. (2004). *Coping with toxic managers, subordinates and other difficult people.* Englewood Cliffs, NJ: Prentice Hall Financial Times.
12. Fox, S., & Spector, P. (2005), *Counterproductive work behaviour: Investigations of actors and targets.* Washington, DC: American Psychological Association.
13. Zaleznik, A. (2009). *Executive's guide to understanding people: How freudian theory can turn good executives into better leaders.* New York, NY: Palgrave Macmillan.
14. Krippendorff, K. (1980). *Content analysis: An introduction to its methodology.* Newbury Park, CA: SAGE Publications.
15. Neuendorf, K.A. (2002). *The content analysis guidebook.* Thousand Oaks, CA: SAGE Publications.

CHAPTER **3**

Virtuous Leadership

Historanicsidatsfmi time to time virtuous leaders have
emerged and made epochal contributions to building and
shaping human civilizations.

They could guide the collective human consciousness towards
the larger purpose and meaning of life. Thinkers and philosophers
such as Patanjali, Nagarjuna, Confucius, Chanakya, Cicero, Lao Tzu,
Buddha, Socrates, Plato, Aristotle, Guru Nanak and many others
enlightened and showed people the art of living consciously. Those
who took inspiration from such thinkers and followed the path
shown by them lead the life of fully functioning and self-actualizing
humans.

Luminaries in the field of science and technology, such as
Thomas Edison, Albert Einstein, Galileo, Leonardo Da Vinci,
Aryabhatta, Isaac Newton, C.V. Raman, M.S. Swaminathan,
V. Kurien, Tim Berners Lee, Charles Babbage, Norman Borlaug,
Jonas Salk, James Watson, Francis Crick, Louis Pasteur, Alexander
Graham Bell, Alexander Fleming, Walter Fiers to name a few,
through their continued efforts could transform the quality of
human living, significantly bringing down poverty and hunger,
reducing mortality rates, improving human longevity as well as
heightening connectivity. Political thinkers and revolutionaries such
as Gandhi, Mandela, Marx, Mao, Lenin, Martin Luther King and
other ushered in a new dawn of freedom and democracy by liberat-
ing people from the shackles of tyrannical rule.

Corporate leaders such as Morita, G.D. Birla, J.R.D. Tata, Andy Grove, Bill Gates, Jack Welch, Steve Jobs taught new ways of creating wealth through their entrepreneurial zeal, path-finding approach, connecting horizon with ground, integrating thought with action, creating the future in the present, etc., and in turn elevating living standards of large numbers of people. They focused not only on creation of wealth for the owners but also on taking care of stakeholders' interests. They valued human dignity by being respectful, ethical, sensitive about human feelings, transparent in their practices and egalitarian. Through such an approach, these leaders successfully galvanized, motivated and inspired organizational members to give their best.

In addition, they could also build organizations geared towards growth with sustainability and taking care of multiple stakeholders. We can conclude from the foregoing exposition that leaders from different walks of life have been powerful engines for change and transformation in society. In the management field there has been an endless debate, discussion and research, on the beliefs, values, mindsets, attitudes and behaviour which make one a great leader. The present chapter purports to explore the leadership profile in the corporate world which makes a person inspiring, transforming and admired as a role model.

At this juncture, it would be highly relevant to view the leader–subordinate relationship, using the prism of the leader constituency model. The success of a virtuous leader lies in his capability to feel the pulse of expectations of the members of his constituency and attempting to meet the same. Needless to say, the success of the virtuous leader lies in this, because the fulcrum of good leadership is centred in the convergence between expectations of constituency members and style of the leaders.

The raison d'être behind studying virtuous leaders' profile lies in the fact that this book purports to map out the odyssey from toxic to virtuous leadership. It is hoped that this approach will enable role holders to find out where they stand—towards the toxic or transformational end of the leadership continuum.

This chapter focuses on findings on virtuous leadership. It is divided into four parts:

- Part I: Findings from the questionnaire data—Virtuous leadership attributes

- Part II: Virtuous leader behaviours by self-level, personality and organizational level demographic factors
- Part III: Case studies of virtuous leaders
- Part IV: Comparison of findings from questionnaire and interview data

PART I: FINDINGS FROM THE QUESTIONNAIRE DATA—VIRTUOUS LEADERSHIP ATTRIBUTES

Table 3.1 highlights the salient behaviours displayed by virtuous leaders. Perusal of this table reveals that virtuous leaders demonstrate behaviours such as being humble and empowering, respecting the dignity of others, being a good listener, providing clear sense of direction for performance and approachable. These attributes are ranked from 1 to 5, respectively. This pattern clearly indicates that virtuous leaders influence subordinates through unpretentiousness and empowering behaviour, respecting the dignity of others, listening intently, through their approachability along with bringing clear sense of direction for performance. In other words, they powerfully integrate human skills with focus on performance outcomes.

The above-mentioned approach enables leaders to galvanize and motivate subordinates towards performance excellence. Needless to say, such a behavioural disposition generates the feeling, enthusiasm and passionate desire to work with such leaders. More than 65% of the respondents have selected these attributes as those which they consider important virtuous leader behaviours.

More than 50% of the sample have rated the following items as the next most important cluster of virtuous leaders behaviours— being ethical and honest, dynamic and radiating positive energy, making people feel they are valuable, mentoring and coaching, demonstrate fairness in working, leading by example and impartial. They are ranked from 6 to 12. Again, in this cluster, virtuous leaders seamlessly combine interpersonal skills along with demanding contributions. The third category of important items (rated by 44% to 49% of the respondents) constitutes leadership behaviours such as visionary, courage to make bold decisions, speedy in making critical decisions, respecting people regardless of level, kind-hearted and

TABLE 3.1

Virtuous Leadership Attributes: Overall Frequency, Percentage and Ranks

Item no.	Virtuous leadership behaviours	Overall (734) frequency	%	Rank
3	Humble and empowering	595	81	1
2	Respectful about the dignity of others	590	80.3	2
4	Good listener	537	73.1	3
5	Provide clear sense of direction for performance	483	65.8	4
13	Approachable	471	64.1	5
6	Ethical and honest	463	63	6
7	Dynamic and radiates positive energy	431	58.7	7
18	Make people feel that they are valuable	424	57.7	8
17	Mentor and coach	417	56.8	9
1	Demonstrate fairness in working	401	54.6	10
9	Lead by example	400	54.5	11
8	Impartial	388	52.8	12
11	Visionary	357	48.6	13
14	Courageous to take bold decisions	343	46.7	14
10	Fast in making critical decisions	335	45.6	15
15	Respect people regardless of levels (non-hierarchical)	324	44.1	16
12	Kind hearted and supportive	320	43.6	17
16	Cool and composed	270	36.7	18
19	Man of words	227	30.9	19
20	Always remember person's name	186	25.3	20

supportive. Further analysis of this table indicates the very fact that the previously cited virtuous leader behaviours are mentioned by more than 40% of the sample, indicates that all of them are considered important by subordinates.

PART II: VIRTUOUS LEADER BEHAVIOURS BY SELF-LEVEL, PERSONALITY AND ORGANIZATIONAL LEVEL DEMOGRAPHIC FACTORS

Tables A3.1 to A3.5 examine the impact of self-level demographic variables such as age, work experience, qualification, gender and family background on the preferred virtuous leader behaviours. Analysis of these tables brings out significant convergence in the preference for virtuous leaders behaviours. This is regardless of self-level variables mentioned previously.

Table A3.1 presents 20 virtuous leadership attributes classified as per the age of the respondents. As Table A3.1 indicates kind-hearted and supportive (rank 9, 53.3%) leader behaviours are experienced as more virtuous in the younger group, less than 30 years of age. The group in the next age category (31–45 years) rated making people feel that they are valuable (rank 4, 72.1%) as a more important attribute of virtuous leadership as compared with the other groups. Lastly, respondents from higher-age group (greater than 46 years) rated being ethical and honest as one of the most preferred virtuous leadership attributes (rank 2, 76%).

As per Table A3.2 kind-hearted and supportive leader behaviours (rank 9, 54%) are more preferred by respondents with work experience up to 5 years than respondents with work experience of more than 16 years (rank 17, 36.36%). Respondents with 6–15 years of work experience rated mentor and coach (rank 5, 59%) among the top virtuous attributes. Lastly, respondents with work experience more than 16 years rated being ethical and honest (rank 3, 75.76%) as one of the most important leadership attributes than respondents with less work experience.

It is also evident from Table A3.3 that executives with postgraduate qualification rated leading by example (rank 9, 55.8%) as a more preferred attribute than graduate respondents (rank 12, 52.9%). Graduate respondents rated mentoring and coaching behaviour (rank 7, 61.1%) as a more important virtuous leadership attribute than postgraduate respondents (rank 12, 53%).

Table A3.4 indicates that male respondents rated being ethical and honest (rank 4, 68.2%) and demonstrate fairness in working (rank 8, 59.7%) as more preferred leadership attribute than female respondents. On the other hand, female respondents rated make people feel that they are valuable (rank 6. 60.5%) as a more important leadership attribute than male respondents. It is clearly evident from Table A3.5 that respondents belonging to nuclear family rated approachable (rank 4, 67.8%) and dynamic and radiates positive energy (rank 6, 61.8%) as more virtuous leadership attributes than respondents belonging to joint family. On the other hand, respondents belonging to joint family rated mentor and coach (rank 6, 62.1%) higher than respondents belonging to nuclear family (rank 11, 53.1%).

Tables A3.6 to A3.8 present the responses across personality variables such as resilience, locus of control and values. Findings from these tables yet again indicate that there is a strong convergence of the responses regarding preferred virtuous leader behaviour, which appears to cut across the personality variables of the respondents. Tables A3.9 to A3.11 present the preferred virtuous leader behaviours categorized by demographic variables such as industry sector (public or private) industry type (manufacturing or service) and nationality. Findings from these tables clearly demonstrate that these demographic variables also do not make any significant difference to the perceptual framework of respondents regarding virtuous leader behaviour.

It is also evident from Table A3.9 that being ethical and honest (rank 3, 69.5%) and demonstrate fairness in working (rank 7, 59.3%) is rated higher as a preferred virtuous leadership attribute among Indian public sector respondents. On the other hand, Indian private sector respondents rated being mentor and coach (rank 6, 67.1%) and making people feel they are valuable (rank 8, 60.9%) as a more important virtuous leadership attribute. Table A3.10 suggests that respondents belonging to service sector rated virtuous leadership attributes such as making people feel they are valuable (rank 6, 58.6%), being mentor and coach (rank 7, 52.9%) and lead by example (rank 8, 52.9%) higher than respondents belonging to service sector. Being ethical and honest (rank 3, 72.6%) and demonstrate fairness in working (rank 5, 68.8%) are more preferred virtuous leadership attributes according to manufacturing sector respondents. Lastly, as per Table A3.11, international executives rated making people feel they are valuable (rank 4, 70.7%) and visionary (rank 8, 58.5%) as more preferred virtuous leadership attributes than Indian executives. Indian executives, on the other hand, rated approachable (rank 5, 67.1%) and dynamic and radiates positive energy (rank 7, 62.9%) highly in terms of preferred virtuous leadership attributes than international executives.

On the basis of the above analysis, the following salient conclusions are evident:

1. Virtuous leaders demonstrate sensitivity and respect for people. They are courageous, humanist and ethical in their dealing with people.
2. Virtuous leaders focus on performance excellence which is the litmus test for outstanding leadership. In other words, it appears from the above that there is a need to combine human sensitivity along with performance centricity.
3. The very fact that there is significant similarity in the preferential framework of respondents across all demographic variables brings out that there is universality regarding what constitutes virtuous leader behaviour.
4. The biggest implication from the above cited findings is that those desirous of becoming virtuous leaders must demonstrate humanistic approach, sensitivity to people, humility, ethical behaviour and performance focus. They must also groom and build people, led by example, along with being visionary and courageous.

PART III: CASE STUDIES OF VIRTUOUS LEADERS

This part presents five case studies of virtuous leaders in the following order:

1. Vinod Rai, the Unassuming Crusader
2. R.V. Shahi, Towards the Next Orbit
3. Major General D.N. Khurana, Change Master
4. M.D. Mallya, Towards the Next Curve
5. R.K. Dubey, Connecting Horizon with Ground Realities

Case I: Vinod Rai, the Unassuming Crusader

ACHIEVEMENTS AND CONTRIBUTIONS

The Indian bureaucratic labyrinth is so complex and gargantuan that many of those who join the service with great scholastic capability and laudable goals get sucked into the swirling vortex of complexities. Very few bureaucratic role holders have been able to go against the tide, confront multifarious forces and vested interests and leave a lasting imprint at the national level. Vinod Rai is one of a handful of such individuals who stands tall among the bureaucrats of the last decade with his zeal, passion and unwavering commitment to the national cause. He is in the league of other noteworthy change masters such as Chaturvedi and T.N. Sheshan who left an indelible mark at the national level.

Vinod Rai is one of the rare idealist and courageous officers filled with the dream to do good. Wherever he served he strived to make a difference. When he was the District Magistrate in Trissur district, he did so much work for developing the district that he was given the honorific title as the second Shaktan Tamburan, the first one being the prince himself.

When he was in Kerala State Cooperative Marketing Federation (KSCMF) he could bring the disparate spice and cashew traders together—900 primary agriculture credit cooperatives and as a result KSCMF became the largest exporter of pepper from India. The bigger impact which he could make was when he was in the Ministry of Finance and introduced the insurance reforms and framed the new pension scheme.

It was, however, his stint as the CAG which brought him into the limelight at the national level. Through the exposes on the 2G, 3G, Coal Scam and others (see Appendix I.1 for details), a deep impact was made on the collective consciousness of the nation. His performance and development orientation is most visible in the thrust given to performance audit function in the CAG office. Although this 'result-focused' audit—different from compliance audit and financial audit—focuses on outcomes of government projects, it was not much liked by the government which felt that it was infringing on the government's turf.

In order to map the persona, profile and leadership style of Mr V. Rai, we interviewed two IAS officers, three officers from CAG, two ex-CMDs from the banking sector and two IAS officers who were his former colleagues in the Ministry of Finance and two ex-secretaries, Government of India. Three ex-Secretaries, Government of India, were interviewed to find out how they perceived his handling of the various scams unearthed during his tenure as CAG. It was also done to find how people perceived his skill and acumen, as well as his strategic thinking and facing and handling of issues before the JPC and PAC. (See Appendix I.2 for the details.) In sum, it can be concluded that Vinod Rai has been a master at combining both ends and means equally focusing on both process and results.

THE PRESENT CASE

The present case sketches the profile, competencies and capabilities of Vinod Rai, the leader, which enabled him take up causes and work for the greater good. He is deeply respected and highly admired across the country for his courage to speak out and expose corruption under the previous government. He is the man who could change the collective conscience of the nation and instil pride among the idealists of the country, in the scam-filled era prevalent a few years ago.

On the basis of content analysis of around 20 hours of in-depth interviews with the selected individuals mentioned earlier, we have identified the following themes of his leadership as perceived by the interviewees:

1. Ethical
2. Balanced Leader
3. Courageous
4. People Leader
5. Result Orientation
6. Humble
7. Consensus Builder

8. Constituency Management
9. Visionary Strategist
10. Radar-like Mindset
11. Managing Complexity and Conflicts

1. Ethical

Vinod Rai has earned an enviable reputation as an ethical leader. Everyone (11) said that he was a man of integrity, scrupulously honest, upright, highly ethical, and above all true to the various roles that he had to play during different stages of his career (1). All the persons (10) we talked to said they were not surprised by the stand he took as the CAG. 'Once he takes up a just cause he does not give up'. 'Even if a powerful minister tries to brush it aside, he will try again and again to persuade' (3). 'He never condoned unfair decisions' (7); 'for a noble cause he can go to any extent' (3); 'his strong ethical orientation was clubbed with objectivity' (6).

'He goes the extra mile to solve genuine problems. In fact, he would create a process using the learning from that problem so that the problem is not repeated in the future' (3).

He was ethical to the organization and whichever assignment he took up, he quickly became a part of the place and worked within the organizational setup and hierarchy. He always said 'we', never said 'I'. (8) There were no games, no politics and no attempts at destruction of existing systems and structures (1); 'while in the CAG, he strengthened the existing systems such as the Audit Advisory Board' (3); 'the board was in existence, but in his tenure it was given a boost. In a similar vein, the performance audit system was introduced by Vinod Rai's predecessor, but it was he who gave it a heavy emphasis' (3).

According to one of his colleagues from the Kerala cadre, because he did not tamper with existing systems, he was acceptable even to various political parties. His colleagues (3) from the IAS said that they feel proud of the way he fought for a larger cause.

During the virulent attacks on him around the telecom scam, there were rigorous efforts made to find out dirt against him, but they hardly found anything. This further established what those close to him had known along—that he was highly ethical. He did not encourage sycophants and had no favourites (6); he was fair in dealing with all of us (5).

His credibility as an upright, honest and ethical officer was further strengthened by the manner in which he discharged his role as CAG, exposing even the ruling party and thereby doing a service to the nation.

2. Balanced

One of the major secrets of Vinod Rai's success in managing his team, handling conflicts, dealing with various stakeholders, as well as solving ticklish problems has been his balanced personality.

Most interviewees (8) spoke about his balanced personality in the following way:

'He is very balanced and stable personality'. 'I have never seen him lose his temper, or raise his voice'; 'calm and composed'; 'peaceful and steady mind'; 'never agitated, always cool and calm'; 'he has no emotional ups and downs'. 'Very balanced'; 'very clear-headed person'; 'even if he feels for someone it does not affect his decision making'; 'always objective in his decision-making'. He possessed rugged and robust common sense, an uncommon ability which helped him in many difficult situations.

'He treated everyone in the same positive and pleasant way regardless of hierarchy. He did now show strong dislikes or strong likes towards anyone'. In fact, our CAG interactions showed that many officers felt that they were close to him and were special to him and this further reinforces the point about treating everyone equally as mentioned above.

A second aspect which was brought out through the interviews (6) was his mastery over self, which projected him as a balanced leader—'He could speak the toughest things very mildly'; when he was being verbally attacked in the JPC hearings, he did not react. According to his ex-colleagues from the CAG office, 'he continued to speak in a mild manner'; 'even in the most tense situations he would joke'.

Another aspect of balance which emerged from the interviews was his time management. Most of the persons (8) we interviewed mentioned that he was self-disciplined and managed his time very well; he could find time for work, sports, hobbies and family. The most evolved indicator of balance which he showed was to conduct himself with dignity in difficult situations.

In sum, it is his balanced and healthy personality which makes him acceptable to all and in turn they are readily influenced by his thoughts and actions.

3. Courageous

Mr Vinod Rai has been a courageous person, according to everyone we talked to. They expressed their view as follows:

'Man of exemplary courage'. 'He is not afraid of anything'. 'He has the spirit of a warrior'.

According to one of his former colleagues, even as a young trainee officer in Nagaland, he single handedly retrieved the dead body of his district collector, who had been killed by militants. The body was left in our isolated place and no one was willing to go fearing a threat to their lives. It was he who had the courage to go ahead and bring the body.

'He does not get intimidated by any problem you take to him'. 'Like a good fighter in the ring, he sizes up the problem carefully and quickly and tackles the problem'.

He was courageous in dealing with ministers too; 'he used to put his point of view to the minister. If he disagreed, he did not give up. He pursued, until the problem was justly solved'.

An insight into his thought process is evident in the following view shared by one of his colleagues known to him for many years: 'while solving problems he kept the larger public good in mind and was not very bookish in applying rules. He stood by his core principle that integrity should never be compromised. I think this gave him inner strength and courage'.

Even during his days in Kerala, his ex-colleagues from the Kerala cadre said that he never feared the displeasure of his minister. He was straightforward and would advise the minister against certain decisions, explaining why it was a bad decision administratively.

Everyone admired the manner in which Vinod Rai dealt with the PAC and JPC and said this in the following manner:

He never showed any fear while facing the JPC; he has been a fighter; he has been bold, courageous and fearless'; 'even before the PAC, he would make his points although in a polite manner'. 'People sweat and panic when they have to face JPC or PAC, but he came out with flying colours'. 'He spoke the truth with great power'; 'very sure of himself'; 'once he was clear on the case and the facts, he would just go ahead and make a decision without bothering about people accusing him'.

'His advice to his people shared by his ex-colleagues from the CAG (3) is very revealing of his courageous and idealistic nature—make a difference; own up what goes wrong'; face what comes; focus on the next steps; reveal his inner belief system when dealing with problems, difficulties and even adversities.

In an attempt to explain the inner person driving Vinod Rai's behaviour, people said, 'he is a man of tremendous inner strength' (11); he knows who he is (7); he was very honest and that is why he could take a strong stand on the various scams (10); he is religious and that is why he does not get perturbed (3). In sum, the adage 'what (is it) that courage can't do?' has been aptly illustrated by the leadership style of Vinod Rai.

4. Mentor People and People Leader

One of the greatest qualities exhibited by Vinod Rai has been his very strong connect with people and concern for them (8). This extended beyond his own team, his department, his organization and even those operating outside the organization.

The interviewees had very positive feelings about his connect with people (9) and expressed this as follows.

Very helpful person ... he goes out of his way to help out; 'He is one of the most affable persons I have met. He brings out the best in people'. 'He was highly accessible to all officers'; 'had no hang ups of walking into our offices if needed'; 'he was able to relate to people at any level'. 'He was highly regarded and accepted because of his helpful nature'. 'He has a Karna-like willingness to help people. Once you share with him your problem and ask for help, then your problem becomes his problem. He takes great care to do his best to help you' (1).

One of his ex-colleagues shared a very revealing story from more than 10 years ago, 'On one occasion when a serious error occurred on a budget speech, due to computer glitches 15 years ago, I decided to type a note and hand over to the CM taking the blame for it. Rai Sir came to know and tried to reassure me. I was still troubled and went over to the minister's residence to hand over the letter owing responsibility for the fiasco. The Minister laughed out loud, saying, Vinod Rai had just come and taken the entire blame on himself. This indicates how much he stood up for and protected his own team members'.

As a boss he appreciated good work in the CAG. He would write many sentences of appreciation on some of the completed reports much to the surprise and delight as they said (3), a rare phenomenon. As a boss he was nurturing and guiding more like a parental figure (7).

He was also caring about people when they had personal problems as indicated by the following examples:

One of the ex-colleagues shared, 'My father was not well and I was going through a bad time'.

'Vinod Rai came to know about this through a friend, and came to my office to comfort me'.

Another officer said, 'He had a simple strategy of leading people—it is your duty to motivate your team and get the best out of them. You stand by them in their moments of sorrow and trials, you rejoice with them when they are happy'.

A third important aspect which emerged from the interviews was his style of mentoring and grooming people: 'He has been a fantastic mentor' (8); 'even in the CAG, he never interfered with the working of junior level officers' (4); in the Telecom case and the coal case, when the matters reached his level Vinod Rai stood by his people. 'I was convinced that they were a fine group of highly trained officers'. As was his nature he protected his team. Although three to four of the concerned officers used to go for the JPC hearing, he himself took all the questions on behalf of the team. He took full ownership and responsibility for the reports.

As the CAG, he was accepted very well because he became part of the organization and did not stand apart from it as an IAS officer. 'We felt he was a part of us. This is rare'.

A fourth aspect of people leadership that was visible in his approach has been his empathy and developmental orientation as a boss. This was expressed as follows (7):

Many of us in CAG felt that we were his favourites and that we were special that is how he made everyone feel; when you talk to him you feel that he is completely with you; when a mistake was committed he never dwelt on it or expressed anger or focused on finding faults. He would say OK, how can we solve it! What should we do? And he would help us find a solution, 'he never used position power, always used personal power to get things done'; 'he was very fair'; 'he believed in developing people; he inspired all of us, worked with all of us and communicated with all of us; he connected with everyone. His style has been described as was guided autonomy' (1).

During the commonwealth games investigation while he was CAG he addressed the team of 150 officers involved in this work and inspired them to such a level that 'we felt we were on a mission' (3). The deadlines were accepted and the target of 3 months was achieved. People worked day and night to meet the target (3).

'He never made us feel small' (3); he used to appreciate our work so much that our self-esteem considerably improved (3).

When his successor was being sworn in there was a large distinguished gathering across political parties and the services apart from the offices of the CAG office. When Vinod Rai walked in, it was observed that all the officers (300) stood up out of respect for him, something which they did not do for any other dignitaries including ministers. Some of the IAS officers we talked to (3) said that it is to his credit that during the troubled period while he was CAG, not a single person from the organization leaked stories, made false allegations or tried to mislead. Everyone was solidly with him. This is indeed a great indication of the commitment and ownership of the team.

The ultimate testimony was paid, when one of his former colleagues said, 'If I get a boss like Vinod Rai, I can work in the Andamans or Siachen'. Another from the CAG said, 'I felt blessed to work in such close proximity with him for so long'.

In sum, he connected with people by interacting with them, listening to them and socializing with them, He earned their respect by helping, by providing them space to develop and by inspiring them.

5. Result Orientation

Vinod Rai was driven by the need to deliver outcomes. Almost everyone highlighted this aspect of his working style. People expressed this as follows:

In all his assignments, results mattered to him. He was an unorthodox thinker, and this helped solve many problems successfully. In his quest to solve problems, he adopted a practical and pragmatic stance for the larger public good, rather than following the rules to the 't'. He did not view rules as an end in themselves.

His focus was on work. He did not get into other matters. One of the ex-colleagues expressed this aspect as, 'I found him to be a Karma Yogi, working for the larger cause and nobler goals with detached approach'.

His emphasis on performance audit while in the CAG was responsible for throwing up huge losses to the exchequer, emanating from the government auctioning spectrum cheap to the Telecom operators. His mindset is evident in his advice to his team members, 'if you shut a door on someone, always open a window if you are convinced about the outcomes being worthwhile'.

It is this approach to solve problems and deliver results which is another hallmark of his leadership in the bureaucracy.

6. Humble

All the persons we talked to said that Vinod Rai was a humble person and a humble leader. This has been described in various ways as follows:

'I have known him for more than 20 years. Every time I meet him, he is the same person—friendly, open, humorous and unassuming. Nothing has changed him'. 'He avoids pomp and show. He could have easily commanded this when he went on his regular temple visits. He never misused his position and went like a common man'. 'He is a peculiar combination of sophistication and refinement and when he meets you, he makes you feel more important'. 'He never brags. He never narrates tall tales of his exploits, something many people like to do…'. 'Uses the "I" word very rarely'. 'Humble yet dignified'. 'His humility was seen in his humor'. Sometimes, he would say 'I am basically a gardener' (which is one of his hobbies). The fact that he could laugh at himself is one of the indicators of his humility combined with a clear sense of what he stands for.

Referring to the faceoff between the CAG and the government, one of the interviewees who knew him well said, 'Knowing him closely I don't think that he himself thought that he was standing up to the government, or daring them when the scams were uncovered. Many people in his position would have cultivated the image of a crusader or an activist. He would have felt that he did what needed to be done. No gloating, but a sense that it was a karma that had to be fulfilled, because it was entrusted to him by the creator'. His humility is perhaps best illustrated in his statement, 'I regularly visit temples to thank god and not to ask for anything; it gives me peace of mind to go to a temple'. This statement reflects an element of contentment, gratitude and satisfaction, and reveals a person who is not mired in endless greed and discontent.

7. Participative and Consensus Building Leader

Vinod Rai has been lauded by most interviewees (8) as the leader with an involving and consensus building approach. This has been expressed in different ways as follows:

> 'Sir encouraged people to speak out'.
> 'Ready to listen to people's views'.
> 'He expected others to speak frankly rather than beat around the bush'.
> 'We had complete freedom to speak out even if he did not like our point of view'.
> 'Did not stop others from expressing their views'.
> 'He listened intently and spoke logically'.
> 'Even officers' two-three levels down did not hesitate to express their views'.
> 'He encouraged discussions'.
> 'He was egalitarian and believed in discussions'.

On occasion he is known to have told his next level officers, 'you don't have to route every file upwards through me'. If it is not related to me, you can send it directly to the minister (2). 'He allowed subordinates full autonomy in functioning to develop their capabilities' (6). 'Encouraged people to take initiative' (8).

The above reveals a style which liberates people to express and speak out, share their views and ideas, develop themselves, as well as arrive at agreement on a course of action. Above all, this approach led people to own the work and give it their best. In sum, Vinod Rai has demonstrated the powerful wisdom that any battle can be fought only through the power of people and team.

8. Constituency Management

Mr Rai was outstanding at managing both the internal and the external constituencies. Through the power of his connect with his own people as well as his result focus, achievements and personal image as an upright officer, he successfully established positive image and high credibility within the organization that he worked with— whether in the government departments, or in the Kerala State Marketing Federation, or the Department of Finance or the CAG.

According to his ex-colleagues from the Kerala cadre, he earned the trust of ministers while he was in Kerala, because of his apolitical approach to his work; he could deal with ministers across the ideological opinion. Most of the interviewees (8) brought out that he believed in connecting with the public, the customers, opinion makers and the end users wherever he was posted. This was evident in the manner in which he was able to bring together 900 odd small pepper cooperatives together under one large umbrella cooperative. This was also visible in the manner in which the actively invited feedback from the opinion makers on various issues (through the Advisory Board Mechanism) whether on water pollution, or energy or the environment while he was the CAG. According to some of the officers (3) in the CAG, 'he had close relationships in the Finance Ministry. He would get very valuable information through his networks, which was very useful for us in our working'. 'He had a powerful network and therefore we got plenty of information from everywhere and this helped us a lot in our work; 'He cultivated people all over'; nothing misses his mind. He knows what's happening where ... gets information from multiple sources.

The fact that when he took over as the CAG, he went to the Planning Commission and projected the work of the CAG, indicates his style of reaching out to important constituencies. Under him efforts were made to make the audit reports more attractive and reader friendly so that they could reach the general public. His constituency management has another important aspect, namely his helpful nature. Hence, it is not at all surprising that through this approach he could create a widespread network which in turn came to his aid, when needed. The strength and power of leaders depends on how intimately and closely they relate to both external and internal constituencies. Vinod Rai has amply demonstrated this through his style.

9. Visionary Strategist

All the interviewees said the following about Vinod Rai:

- 'Vinod Rai was a visionary and strategic leader. He has been very strategic in his moves'. He could see much ahead and anticipate outcomes of decisions up to two to three levels. He was able to visualize requirements 5 or 10 years ahead ... for example the likely changes in treasury management. People in the Finance Ministry were trained in advance for this purpose on the latest available technology.
- As a strategic mind, he was unorthodox in his thinking. He was a maverick. He could think differently. People said he had a solution for every problem. He had great presence of mind.

Most of the interviewees (8) also indicated his holistic and big picture-thinking ability as follows:

- He would visualize outcomes of decisions and prepare for various likely outcomes. He was a big picture thinker—could connect things with the larger realities. He had multilayered thinking capability. He goes beyond data while analysing a problem. He had an anticipating mind. He could think of tomorrow today. He had a great sense of timing.

The observation made by one of the ex-bureaucrats, 'Must have been an excellent chess player' speaks volumes of his strategic thinking capability, knowing what to say when; the right time to make the moves, how to checkmate and neutralize, how to anticipate and act accordingly and so on.

The manner in which he convinced and persuaded one of the ministers in the Kerala government while he was Finance Secretary is an eye opener in this regard. The issue was regarding the transfers of staff in the department. The union leaders went to the minister and got an order issued saying that transfer orders can be issued directly without the concerned officer's involvement so that they get the power to do as they pleased. When Vinod Rai came to know, he went up to the minister and said, 'I don't have any objection, but tomorrow if he finds you inconvenient and goes directly to the Chief Minister and get an order against you will you agree?' As a result of this intervention, the minister was convinced and the order was subsequently dropped.

His strategic thinking and presence of mind was visible in the answers he gave to the tough questions thrown by the JPC which consisted of a high-powered member team of distinguished members from the Rajya Sabha—Jaswant Singh, Yashwant Sinha, SS Ahluwalia, Gurudas Dasgupta, Sitaram Yechury, Manish Tiwari, P.C. Chacko, T.R. Balu, Ravi Shanker Prasad and Sharad Yadav. Full list appended at the end of this case study.

In sum, Vinod Rai begins with the end in mind and prepares for tomorrow today.

10. Radar-like Mindset

Vinod Rai has been a leader with a radar-like mindset, keeping track of things, finding ground-level information as and when needed, in order to make informed and correct decisions.

Most of the interviewees who worked closely with him (7) said he was alert and had strong grasp on information. 'He was alert and observant'. 'A very intense listener who could quickly size up a situation'. He believes in power of information to make an informed decision. 'I don't know from where, he would bring us information, relevant to our working'. 'He had a vast network all over, through which he got information'. 'He is very open minded'. 'He is a good learner and 360° information seeker'.

His advice to his team members while in the CAG provides an insight regarding this capability. He used to tell us, 'you have to keep your eyes and ears open; and get more and more feedback'. This sums up his radar-like mindset and it contributed significantly to his decision making, problem solving and staying ahead of the curve.

11. Managing Complexities and Conflicts

According to all the interviewees, Vinod Rai has the remarkable capability to coolly manage in situations characterized by complexity and conflicts. One of his ex-deputies gave the example of an MLA whose proposal he had rejected while he was in Kerala. The man was irritated and in protest continued to sit in his office. Just before leaving office in the evening the officer reminded the MLA that he should leave the office and in a lighter vein also said he should leave else he might get locked in. The MLA took offense and created a fuss, saying that he was being threatened with a lock-up. As the mis-understanding increased tempers began to run high and the officer was in a fix as to the next course of action. Someone from his office had informed Mr Vinod Rai. 'A few minutes later Rai walked into my office and asked me about a file (fictitious)'. He turned casually, looked at the angry MLA and said, 'why are you sitting here. Let's have a cup of tea in my office'. This timely gesture defused the situation for both the officer and the poor MLA who was looking for a way to exit without losing face.

The major event where his remarkable skills came into play was in facing the JPC constituted to examine the allegations coming from the CAG reports. He presented the case coolly and calmly before heavy weights such as Dr Murli Manohar Joshi and others (see Appendix I.2). According to his colleagues, he was composed, never showed 'any fear despite the harsh criticism and personal attacks which he had to face'. The prime reason for this was a state-ment given by one of his former colleagues who upon retirement disputed the statement made by the CAG, saying that the losses to the exchequer were highly exaggerated. He did this despite the fact that while in service he had himself signed the report accepting the findings. His ex IAS colleagues said that they were very scared for him; however, he stood like a rock, bold and courageous.

Some of the characteristics which people saw in that period reflect what helped him—'he was highly strategic and planned how to argue the case'. He knew how to handle the JPC. 'He had great presence of mind'. 'He made his harsh points very politely'. 'He did not show any fear, and he presented the case, logically, calmly, with facts and data'.

Describing his style before the JPC, his ex CAG colleagues (3) said, 'he sometimes spoke very tough; he answered every question'; 'he never got agitated, he was always cool and calm'; 'he explained complex things in a simple way'. The manner in which he spoke, neither friendly nor insulting or getting agitated himself, despite all provocation was something to learn from, said these colleagues. He was probably able to do this because of his sheer objectivity, utter honesty and strategic mindset and the intention behind his speech and actions. In his words, 'these cases were not brought up by us as a vendetta of any kind. In the process of regular audit work, the auditors stumble upon these cases and they got escalated to higher levels until it reached the CAG. 'When I saw it I knew it was a can of worm which I could not ignore'. As all the people we talked to said, 'once he takes up an issue, he does not leave until it is resolved'.

There was a complex matter involving one of the IAS officers, a conniving insider who as a vendetta complained to the chief minister (CM) against him, making false allegations, although the real reason was that the officer was refusing to collude and oblige him. There was a hot exchange of words and the CM wanted to suspend the officer. Vinod Rai walked in; 'he had soothing and calming effect on the CM'. Rai explained to him calmly how unfair it would be to suspend the officer. After hearing his explanation, the CM was convinced and retracted his plan.

VINOD RAI: THE PERSON

After going through long sittings trying to grasp the inner world of Mr Vinod Rai by interviewing him as well as getting a 360° feedback about him, we have been able to conclude the following about him as a person, his philosophy and value systems:

He comes across as a karma yogi meaningfully engaging himself in the work without too much attachment to the rewards. He considers karma as his dharma and therefore is a truly actualizing leader. Mr Rai is a powerful symbiosis of being ethical, courageous and bold and fearlessly standing up for the right cause. He has tremendous faith and believes that without faith nothing can be done and with it everything is possible. He believes that connectedness is the soul of leadership. The more one connects the more power he gets; power from people, power from external constituency members and power from other environmental forces. He is a maverick and a strategist who has developed the fine art of managing complexity and conflict.

He follows 360° information search with powerful alert antenna and radar-like mindset. Mr Rai is a humanist, demonstrating enormous sensitivity to people along with being objective. He believes that battles can be won only through the power of people. In other words, he comes across as a kaleidoscopic team builder. He has beautifully combined with intellectual, emotional and spiritual quotient.

Mr Vinod Rai is both highly spiritual and religious person. He has immense faith in the Almighty. He believes that god guides destiny and gives peace of mind. He is courageous and in speaking the truth ensures that the message is given without becoming rude, uncouth or unpleasant. This emanates from his belief that truth ultimately triumphs. He deeply admires Abraham Lincoln for his capability to deliver against all odds. His admires Krishna and Arjuna from the Mahabharata—Krishna for his wisdom and strategic thinking and Arjuna for his valour and relentless search for excellence.

He is a firm believer that it is through people that excellence can be achieved. He is meticulous and a perfection seeker. He is futuristic and planned. While he has a global world view, at the same time he is a hard-core nationalist with patriotic fervour. He is an eternal optimist, who always looks at the bright side of things and believes in moving ahead leaving the turbulence behind. He is a compassionate leader and has always sought to uplift people and work for development.

APPENDIX I.1: AUDITED CASES OF MR VINOD RAI AS CAG

During his tenure as CAG, Vinod Rai successfully led several audits and unearthed various scams worth lakhs of crores of rupees. The details of the major scams are given as follows:

a. 2G Saga

1. Highlighting of Change of Terms of Reference based on letter written by Dayanidhi Maran, then Telecom Minister to Prime Minister, ensuring the spectrum pricing to be removed from terms of reference of the GoM.
2. The formula applied for computing the loss was used after great deliberation and a logical understanding of tax laws in India and abroad. Mathematical or econometric models are premised on certain assumptions, and hence vulnerable to criticism, and so the modelling methodology was dropped. Thus, it was decided to use data and other indicators which were already in public domain.
3. The computed and presented loss of ₹176,739 [lac] crores was vetted and deliberated at all levels, and processes were followed to a 'T'. This was to ensure immense scrutiny which the report was bound to undergo, and so CAG and his officers left nothing to chance.

   a. Using price offered by S Tel as an indicator of the market valuation of 6.2 MHz of 2G spectrum at that time, value for all 122 licenses worked out to be 65,725 crores and adding ₹24,591 crores as the value of the licenses for the new technology, the total amount came to be ₹90,316 crores (against ₹9,013 crores collected by DoT).
   b. Calculating the loss at 3G rates, the value for all the licenses worked out to be ₹111,511 crores. The value of dual technology and spectrum beyond the contracted quantity was added to it, and the total value came out to be ₹176,379 crores.

(Pioneer report on 15 February 2014 validated CAG stand, when it reported, 'Former CAG Vinod Rai and his team had the last laugh on Thursday when the ten-day-long 2G Spectrum auction ended by fetching ₹61,162 crores to the public exchequer'.)

b. Commonwealth Games

1. The IOA bid in May 2003 estimated an all-inclusive cost of ₹1200 crores. Against this, budget estimate in 2010 was ₹18,532 crores (this too after excluding DMRC, DIAL and likes).
2. The revenue projection went up from ₹900 crores in March 2007 to ₹1780 crores in July 2008, without any basis for this change (actual revenue realized was ₹173.96 crores).
3. Scholarship revenue was projected at ₹960 crores (actual realization was ₹375 crores, and two-third of this was contributed by PSUs after a special Government directive).
4. Organizations had projected ₹300 crores from donations/raffle (actual realization was ₹0.99 crores).
5. Organizing Committee was responsible for tendering the catering services in Games village as well as various sporting venues. The processing of the contracts meandered, taking over 14 months. First tender was cancelled and re-tendering happened in 2010, and in the process transparency, quality and economy were the casualties.

An article in *Hindustan Times* summed up the situation: 'In a report submitted to Centre in July 2009, the CAG had said, "There was a need to rethink the governance model for the Games Project."'

c. Coal Block Allocation

1. In India, power producers bought coal from one of three sources:

a. Import (average price of import from Indonesia for 2001–2011 was ₹3678/ton, and Indonesia supplies most of our coal supplies).

b. E-Auction by Northern Coalfields Limited (average price for 2001–2011 was ₹2387/ton).

c. CIL (which is regularly audited by CAG, and so its accounts and other details can be taken as authentic). Average sales price of all grades of coal sold by CIL was found to be ₹1028/ton, and this was the most conservative one too.

2. Even going by the cost of production of coal by CIL, the average cost came out to be ₹583 per ton. There was an added financing cost of ₹100–150 per ton. Taking financing cost to be ₹150, there was profit of ₹295 (1028 – 583 – 150) per ton. Multiplying this by extractable coal reserves (6282 million tonnes), the financial gain figure of ₹1.85 lakh crores was achieved, and certainly a part of this would have been garnered by the government, had the auctions been carried out.

10 January 2014 Newspaper headlines summed it up 'Government admits to irregularities in Coal Block allocation. Allotments were made in good faith, but could have been done in better way, Attorney General tells Supreme Court'.

d. Gas Exploration Case

1. At the time of this audit, there were 14 auditors working in the supreme audit authority of Oman and its oil exploration agency.

2. CAG observed, 'As regards the adverse impact of the Profit Sharing Mechanism in protecting Government of India's share (linked to the IM) designed in the late 1990s, there does seem to be enough ground to re-visit the formula'.

e. Civil Aviation

1. Having purchased aircrafts at the rate of ₹1300 crores per aircraft, what was the reason for selling them at ₹427 crores per aircraft to Etihad Airways within five years of the delivery, was the first question asked?

2. At the behest of the ministry, the initial proposal to buy 28 aircrafts was modified to 50 aircrafts (increasing the cost of purchase from $1104 million to $6149 million).

   a. The planning commission noted that assumptions regarding traffic projections were risky and the upgradation was ambitious. It also felt that the airline's projected increase in its market share from 19% to 30% was not backed by any strategy.

   b. Department of Expenditure in Ministry of Finance observed that argument of enhancement of capacity leading to increase in market share was not an assumption which had been substantiated. They stated that Purely Supply Side response would run into huge demand side risk.

3. However, the Ministry of Civil Aviation stuck to their viewpoint and persuasion, Public Investment Board gave a clearance to the proposal worth ₹38,000 crores (market share for Air India had oscillated between 19.5% and 19.4% during 1999–2004).

4. During negotiations, the seat capacity of the long-range and extended-range aircraft were reduced by 28 and 38 seats respectively, with the Air India board not even being aware of the same.

5. Finally, the eGoM made its recommendation to the Prime Minister on 24 December 2005 and 30 December 2005, PMO conveyed its acceptance of purchase of 68 aircrafts to the ministry of Civil Aviation and on the same day, Air India signed its agreement with Boeing.

6. Decisions impacting the commercial viability were ministry-driven, there was seemingly scant regard for cost-benefit

analysis, the board was kept in dark at crucial junctures and there was lack of accountability in entire decision-making process.

Newspaper report summed the outcome and subsequent sale of aircrafts to Etihad airways as 'Five Aircrafts at the Cost of One' by Air India.

With regard to flying rights,

1. During 2003–2004, Air Emirates had a capacity entitlement of 10,400 seats per week and was landing at six Indian cities. In 2008–2009, their cities of call increased to 14 and capacity entitlement was increased to 54,200 seats per week. (This despite that Indian carriers were utilizing only 30% of capacity negotiated for them, while the foreign carriers were utilizing 65% of the capacity.)

2. In February–March 2008, Dubai Civil Aviation Authority (CAA) wrote to engage in bilateral talks for reviewing and enhancing the existing entitlements. Despite the protest of Air India, negotiations were carried and it was decided to increase capacity through [increase] exchange of letters. In the same meeting, Dubai CAA also agreed to 'Change of Gauge' for Indian Carriers, which meant Indian Carriers could alter the size and frequency of their aircraft to meet traffic requirement. No sooner had the Dubai CAA delegation returned to their country, they expressed their inability to honour the 'Change of Gauge' for Indian carriers due to 'Infrastructure Constraints at Dubai Airport' and the same would be revisited at a later date. Till 2012, the Indian Carriers did not get permission, while Emirates was further allotted two more ports of call. By 2009, it was 14 ports for Emirates, nothing additional for Air India.

3. A detailed analysis by CAG revealed that [for] 59% of the 2.3 million inward and 3.9 million outward passengers which Emirates carried [s]were sixth freedom passengers.

Business Standard summed it well saying 'Sixth Freedom chokes Air India'.

Steps Taken to Shift CAG Functioning in Terms of Culture, Mindset and Styles

1. Accountants under Vinod Rai did auditing for the United Nations, Food & Agriculture Organization, World Food Program, and International Atomic Energy Agency (IAEA) and World Intellectual Property Organization.
2. The audits underwent a cultural change as a result of positive reporting: From being fault finders who were often wiser in hindsight to starting the process of recognizing and reporting good practices observed during an audit.
3. Secondly, to ensure widespread dissemination of audit observations the salient observations of the reports were docketed into small booklets (referred to as 'Noddy Books') and shared with various stake-holders including media, legislators, students, NGOs, citizen groups.
4. Thirdly, the packaging of the reports was improved to be easily comprehensible and reader friendly.
5. For the first time, for deeper insight and more widespread coverage of social sector issues, Social Audit concept was launched, and credible citizen groups' working in specific areas were requested to help. This helped in better outreach of the works and helps engage with the stakeholders in a better manner.
6. Benchmarking of best practices with supreme audit organizations in different geographies was carried out, and the same was implemented in the country while ensuring that the human capital at CAG office was professionally outstanding and equipped with latest trends in public auditing.

Source: Rai, V. (2014). *Not just an accountant—Diary of the nation's conscience keeper.* New Delhi: Rupa Publications.

APPENDIX I.2

Composition of JPC

Shri P.C. Chacko—*Chairman*
MEMBERS
Lok Sabha
2. Shri V. Aruna Kumar 3. Shri Ijyaraj Singh 4. Shri Jai Prakash Agarwal 5. Shri Deepender Singh Hooda 6. Shri Bhakta Charan Das 7. Dr. Nirmal Khatri 8. Sardar Partap Singh Bajwa 9. Shri T.R. Baalu 10. Shri Kalyan Banerjee 11. Shri Jaswant Singh 12. Shri Yashwant Sinha 13. Shri Harin Pathak 14. Shri Gopinath Munde 15. Shri Sharad Yadav 16. Shri Dara Singh Chauhan 17. Shri Shailendra Kumar 18. Shri Gurudas Dasgupta 19. Shri Arjun Charan Sethi 20. Dr M. Thambidurai
Rajya Sabha
21. Shri Ananda Bhaskar Rapolu 22. Shri P. Bhattacharya 23. Shri Praveen Rashtrapal 24. Dr Ashok S. Ganguly 25. Dr Yogendra P. Trivedi 26. Shri Dharmendra Pradhan 27. Shri Ravi Shankar Prasad 28. Shri Ramchandra Prasad Singh 29. Shri Satish Chandra Misra 30. Shri Sitaram Yechuri

---

Case II: R.V. Shahi, Towards the Next Orbit

ACHIEVEMENTS AND CONTRIBUTIONS

Presently: Chairman and Managing Director, Energy Infratech Pvt. Limited, an Engineering and Project Development Consulting Company; Chairman, Advisory Board of Indian Energy Exchange; Chairman, Adani Power Advisory Board; Central Advisory Committee of Central Electricity Regulatory Commission; Energy Advisor, South

Asia, World Bank; Chairman, Task Force, Rajasthan Power Sector; Member Convener, Power Advisory Group, Ministry of Power.

Secretary to the Government of India, Ministry of Power (April 2002–January 2007): top most position at official level in the Power Ministry. Besides being responsible for the entire Indian Power Sector (168,000 MW capacity including captive plants), as Secretary, he was directly responsible for the Central Public Sector Undertakings, namely, National Thermal Power Corporation (NTPC), Power Grid Corporation of India Ltd, National Hydroelectric Power Corporation, Satluj Jal Vidyut Nigam Ltd, Tehri Hydro Development Corporation, Power Finance Corporation, Rural Electrification Corporation, Bhakra Beas Management Board and Damodar Valley Corporation. He was also President of the Governing Council of Central Power Research Institute (Government of India), Chairman of the Executive Committee of Bureau of Energy Efficiency and Chairman of the Governing Council of National Power Training Institute (Government of India), having five large Training Institutes in various parts of the country.

During the five-year tenure as Secretary to the Government of India, Ministry of Power, the Indian electricity sector witnessed a major restructuring of the power industry through formulation and implementation of several legislative and policy initiatives aimed at the creation of a competitive market structure. These include Electricity Act (2003), National Electricity Policy (2005), Electricity Tariff Policy (2006) and Accelerated Power Development Reform Programme (2002) aimed at Distribution Reform. Setting and Operationalizing of Bureau of Energy Efficiency under Energy Conservation Act (2001), Rural Electrification Policy (2005), Ultra Mega Power Project Policy (2006), Merchant Power Plant Policy (2006). 50,000 MW Hydroelectric Initiative (2003), 100,000 MW Thermal Project Initiative (2004). Setting up and operationalizing Appellate Tribunal for Electricity (2005).

Chairman and Managing Director of BSES Ltd, a professionally managed company under the control of financial institutions (1994–2002): During this period the company was transformed from a small distribution utility to a multi-unit fully integrated power utility having generation, transmission and distribution. He was directly involved in Privatization and Acquisition of Distribution Companies in the States of Orissa and Delhi.

National Thermal Power Corporation (NTPC) holding various positions between 1978 and 1994. These included General Manager in charge of Dadri Power Project; Executive Director in charge of Southern Region of NTPC; and finally Member on the Board of Directors of NTPC In-charge of Operations, R&D and Commercial functions. Prior to this, he worked for over 10 years (1967–1978) with Hindustan Steel Ltd/Steel Authority of India in Industrial Engineering—final post—Joint Chief (Industrial Engineering).

The present case sketches the profile, competencies and capabilities of R.V. Shahi, the Leader, which enabled him to strive throughout his life, to move relentlessly from one orbit to the next. He is a man who is known, admired and respected for his unique and significant contributions in every position that he occupied as a leader and therefore considered a role model by anyone who came in contact with him (for details regarding his awards, publications and educational qualifications, refer to Appendix II.1). He is the man who could create a new landscape in the Indian power sector and is considered to be a tall bureaucrat among his peers (for details regarding policy initiatives in power sector under him and their impact, refer to Appendices II.2 and II.3).

THE PRESENT CASE

We conducted extensive interviews with 10 individuals (three ministry, five NTPC, two BSES) who worked closely with Mr Shahi while he was in the NTPC, BSES and Ministry of Power. Before mapping his virtuous qualities as a leader, we are very briefly highlighting here his career trajectory, which will serve as a backdrop to understand and appreciate his contributions as a leader.

Based on content analysis of the 20 hours of in-depth interviews with various persons ranging from Directors, CMDs and Secretaries, Government of India as well as Mr Shahi, we have identified the following themes of his leadership as perceived by the interviewees:

1. Himalayan Vision with Oceanic Depth
2. Binocular Vision with Microscopic Details
3. Constituency Management

4. Entrepreneurial Path Breaker
5. Radar like Mindset
6. Global Perspective
7. Ethical
8. Humble and Unpretentious
9. Olympian
10. People Developer and Team Builder
11. Leading by Example

1. Himalayan Vision with Oceanic Depth

All the persons we interviewed for this work extolled Mr Shahi's far-sightedness and long-term perspective along with his capability to move from narrow and solo role definition to a more holistic thinking. This was described by people as follows:

He is far-sighted, a person who always looked beyond the horizon. He had the ability to look at the big picture and had a strategic vision. He never missed the wood for the trees. He had dreams of creating a SAARC grid and brought unlimited power supply to the entire region—India, Pakistan, Bangladesh, Nepal, Bhutan and Sri Lanka.

His role and power thus did not govern his vision, dream and the larger goal. He would think beyond the role and position assigned to him for, e.g., as G.M. he thought like a Director, as Director he thought like CMD, as CMD he thought for the country, as Secretary he thought for the globe (5). He had earned a great reputation as a leader in the power sector, owing to successful turnarounds of plants at Unchahar, Badarpur and BSES, carried out under his leadership.

When he became Secretary Power he got a wide canvas on which to 'dream and do'. His achievements and contributions have been substantial. This fact is noteworthy as previous policies in the power sector had, for decades, not delivered to any visible extent.

To appreciate Mr Shahi's contribution, it is important to revisit the Indian Power Scenario in the early 2000s. There was a huge gap between demand and supply of power. The sector was riddled with loss-making SEBs, illiquid power generators like NTPC, NHPC and a gargantuan demand for giant sized, infrastructure which the government simply could not fund owing to scarcity of resources.

In the same period, NTPC collection had dropped to 75% of bill. Practically, whole of internal resource (profit and depreciation) was receivable. Similar was the situation in other public sector companies in power, and coal. Above all, banks and private sector did not show any interest and enthusiasm in investing in the power sector. In fact, by 2002 they had virtually abandoned this sector.

It is interesting to note that despite the dire circumstances, which would have discouraged many successful leaders, Mr Shahi accepted the offer to become Secretary Power without hesitation—this despite the salary being one-fifth of what he was getting as CMD BSES. According to Mr Shahi, he accepted the offer because it provided him with the rare opportunity to turn around the sector, to make a difference at the national level, to unshackle this industry and to enhance electricity supply to the whole country, the basic requirement for industrialization and quality of living. This vision is mammoth in terms of scale and size as well as impact. He was well aware of the apparently impossible challenges before him and yet he dared to dream big. We have, therefore, conceptualized this category of his leadership as Himalayan Vision with oceanic depth.

2. Binocular Vision with Microscopic Details

This category highlights two kinds of leadership abilities of Mr Shahi—the ability to not only take a broad sweep view of what lay ahead but also realize the same. Embedded within this ability are qualities like capability to look ahead, anticipate future trends, not only dream big, but have a grip on ground-level issues as well as build agreement, the latter being very important for implementation. Much before he occupied the highest position he would passionately speak and write on the future direction needed to be taken by the Indian power sector, indicating that he had a binocular perspective from the early days. His book *Indian Power Sector: Challenge and Response*, a compilation of papers, prior to his joining as Power Secretary, covers the entire range of issues and challenges and also provides strategy to address them.

Everyone we talked to said the following about Mr Shahi:

He is not only a dreamer, he is a doer. He knows how to ensure that vision is converted into action on the ground. 'I have seen many persons who have big dreams, but few strive to convert their ideas into action. Mr Shahi is an exception in this regard'; 'To him the end goal was clear—bring electricity to the country. He did whatever was required to make this dream a reality'. He has been a great strategist, a true follower of the dictum begin with the end in mind and do the backward integration with action plans and strategies. He not only had big picture thinking but also a grounded practical approach to make things happen. People talked about him as a Midas touch leader because of his success in turning around Unchahar, and Badarpur plants of NTPC as well as success in BSES. While he was Secretary Power, he dovetailed his vision with sound strategy for implementation, and therein lay his success.

He was well aware that the Electricity Act 1910 and Electricity Supply Act of 1948 had tremendous limitations and was fully associated in preparation of successive drafts of new electricity bill, even though he was not in the ministry then. When he joined the ministry, the electricity bill pending in parliament needed to undergo scrutiny of the Parliamentary Standing Committee on Energy. The bill did need a number of changes as the Standing Committee undertook a nationwide consultation with stake holders. Shahi took on the daunting task which involved interactions with state governments, a number of other organizations, industry bodies, the Parliamentary Committee and others and redrafting various provisions. It was daunting because (a) creating consensus among stakeholders with conflicting interests was a challenge, (b) a number of state governments felt that with this central legislation their jurisdictions and authorities were getting diluted, (c) de-licensing of power generation did affect the authority of many agencies and hence the resistance to change and (d) above all the NDA Government did not have majority in the Rajya Sabha, and the Bill to become an Act did need approval of the Rajya Sabha as well.

As a matter of fact, while the Bill was passed in the Lok Sabha, the opposition parties in the Rajya Sabha led by Congress suggested more than 80 amendments to the Bill already passed in Lok Sabha. It was indeed very difficult to convince the various opposition parties on how most of the amendments suggested would be adequately addressed through three important statutory Policy documents envisaged in the Bill—National Electricity Policy, Tariff Policy and

Rural Electrification Policy, which will have equal force to take care of these concerns. Many of the suggested amendments would fall into the category of Rules. Thus, it was possible to bring the opposition parties on Board with the assurance that couple of amendments out of 84 would be brought by the Government in the next session of Parliament—which was subsequently done. Accordingly, the Bill was passed even in the Rajya Sabha and subsequently notified as Electricity Act 2003 in May, 2003.

However, another major challenge was faced when the new UPA Government came to Power in 2004 with the support of Left Parties. One of the suggestions of the Left Parties was to scrap the Electricity Act. The agreed position was a complete review of the Act. The Left Parties were always opposed to a number of provisions, including re-organization of State Electricity Boards into Generation, Transmission and Distribution Companies. Interactions with individual key personalities in the Left Group explaining the rationale behind various provisions and how re-organized Electricity Boards would deliver better results in the larger interests of consumers, did prove helpful. To cut the long story short, such interactions over several months did dilute the position of the Left Group which gratifyingly did recognize the merit of the legislation, and did not pursue their demand for any major review of the legislation. Besides using the power of logic, analysis and purpose, he also used all his networks to influence the thinking of relevant persons. This is discussed in detail under Constituency Management later. Thus, the Electricity Act 2003 was saved.

To get a perspective on the problems of getting an Act passed, compare it with the Coal Bill which was introduced in the year 2000 and was finally scrapped in 2014. The Electricity Bill could have suffered a similar fate, but for the tireless efforts made to ensure that it got passed.

3. Constituency Management

People brought out an exceptional quality which Mr Shahi demonstrated, which was so important for him to successfully implement his vision, that is, his significant capability to influence various stakeholders, and build consensus.

This has been expressed as follows:

- He knew the importance of building consensus to make things happen (10).
- He is very persuasive, takes pains to explain and reason out (6).
- He had a good sense of timing, knew when and how to convey his point of view to different stakeholders (7).
- His biggest strength has been the effort made to build consensus. Among other things he used his good contacts and rapport with senior political leaders to persuade and influence (3).
- As Secretary Power he would reach out to secretaries and others across various ministers without hesitation and discuss relevant issues and plans with them (3).
- He had the knack of making all the stakeholders comfortable and therein lays his success (3).
- When it is said that he changed the power sector landscape it is no small achievement. The success lays in his holistic stakeholder management. For example before reaching out to SEBs, he met the Chief Ministers of the relevant states and influenced their thinking and got them to see the political benefits of allowing power tariff to be distanced from political management. 'By telling them what's in it for them, I could influence their thinking,' he said. Besides this, he also reached out to various state-level Power Secretaries and mobilized their support. He was clearly determined to make things happen, leaving no stone unturned as indicated by the efforts made to get the buy in of various stakeholders.
- Even within his own ministry he introduced ways and means to build consensus in order to get support of the others (3). Weekly meetings were conducted where everyone would present the progress made and also comment on policy issues being undertaken by various sections. As one of the ex-bureaucrats who had worked with him put it, 'Each person got his space to work without feeling controlled'. The sense of team which resulted enormously helped in building greater cooperation.
- When the authors asked the question how did you influence ministers, unions and others, he said, 'It's how you put

it—you cannot be arrogant. You have to listen, be logical and explain and also show them how it would affect them. You have to articulate and communicate'.

- He was also highly experienced in the art of influencing unions and officers' associations right from the time he was General Manager Personnel (5). A glimpse of this is visible if we go to those times. There was a case regarding the proposed suspension of a senior union leader (of the plant) for assaulting the Chief Medical Officer. Before taking this step in the Left-dominated West Bengal, he used the good offices of a senior leftist union leader to meet the Labour Minister, and explained the circumstances in which the suspension needed to be done. It was only after convincing the Labour Minister and also with due preparation that General Secretary of the Union was suspended, without much of a problem after the suspension.
- Much later when he was Secretary Power he had to intervene when the Public Sector Offices Associations of the whole country gave a strike call. He could persuade the power sector associations to desist from striking by bringing to their notice the level of public outcry which would flare up, if the country had to go without power even for a few hours. Secondly, he convinced them that their negotiating power with the Government would go down if they did not appreciate the importance of maintaining this essential service and restored to strike. He could successfully influence their thinking as indicated by the fact that while other Public Sector Officers struck work, Power Sector Companies did not participate.

This type of networking, reaching out to relevant people from different sectors and explaining to them the rationale and need for an approach, or a direction or a decision, has been a signature quality exhibited by Mr Shahi all through his career. On the basis of our interview with him, we could understand that his power of influencing others depends on his ability to empathize with the other person; try to assess what he or she would find relevant and use this logic to convey views to the concerned individual or representative, or organization. He would think through the issues not only from the organizational perspective, but also from all perspectives and therefore he is able to guide, advise and help as mentioned by most of the persons (9). This approach helped him to solve many knotty problems while dealing with Workers Unions, Officers Associations and even bureaucrats and ministers.

He could successfully build consensus by using these approaches. People listened to him because they had faith in his words, knowing that he 'walks the talk'.

4. Entrepreneurial Path Breaker

In this category are competencies which together throw light on the entrepreneurial behaviour of Mr Shahi characterized by risk taking, innovative problem solving and walking the un-trodden path. Interviewees (10) said the following about him, indicating various components which converge into an entrepreneurial and path-breaking approach:

He is courageous; he is bold and daring; a great problem solver; he would put his attention to problem identification followed by problem solving; he had great capability to understand and assess a situation. He used to go the extra mile by trying to understand the likely risks and make plans to mitigate them. He always demonstrates a great combination of the power of analysis and innovation. He combines domain knowledge with commercial aspects, a true business leader. Being so open-minded and issue focused, he had the unique capability to come out with multiple ideas, options and solutions. He is a true professional and is therefore issue focused rather than person focused. Issues are viewed rationally, practically and with an open mind. While discussing matters, his focus is on the issue and he influences using the power of logic and analysis. If we went to him with a problem, he would invite two or three other colleagues for a brainstorming on the issue to produce other perspectives. Being very knowledgeable and logical along with being open minded helps him to frame problems with multiple solutions. He brought out the best in his team by focusing on the argument, rather than on who said what. The combination of open mindedness with problem-solving approach along with sensitivity to people resulted in consensus building. His open-minded approach gives immense opportunity to people to express their views confidently, and develop greater self-esteem and sense of belonging.

He is clearly focused on solving problems and his open-minded listening, without applying any types of filters, helps him focus on the quality of the idea. It is through his power of entrepreneurial orientation—risk taking, creative problem solving, outcome focus—that he could successfully change the architecture of the power sector in India. The passing of the Electricity Act brought an end to the hitherto requirement of licensing to set up power plants. This change threw open opportunities for private players by de-shackling the sector. In the last 10 years, following the Act and Policies being put in place, electricity generation capacity by the private sector has increased by almost 100,000 MW from 10% to 35% and much more are in the pipeline. The earlier plight of running from pillar to post to get permissions and licensing was thus a distant memory from the 'license-quota permit raj' which was prevalent prior to these changes.

Another aspect of his entrepreneurial effort is the Unchahar project, which was then owned by the Uttar Pradesh Government. They wanted to expand the capacity, but had no funds. As Director Operations of NTPC, he was assigned the responsibility of takeover of this project to negotiate various aspects and to develop formulation acceptable to all. In the end, it actually worked out because of the win–win package which was developed by Mr Shahi. The languishing plant load factor (PLF) at 17% in Unchahar was radically increased to more than 60% within 100 days. Subsequently, this plant became one of the best even among NTPC plants and crossed 90% PLF mark. Later, Badarpur plant which had a PLF of 31% could shoot up to 75% thanks to Mr Shahi's path-breaking and innovative solutions.

At the national level, apart from Electricity Act, National Electricity Policy and Tariff Policy, under his leadership as Secretary Power, ultra mega power projects were conceived and awarded transparently within 18 months, according to an ex-bureaucrat who worked with him in that period. Among the many initiatives given prominence was the task of rural electrification, Rajiv Gandhi Vidyutikaran Yogana, which was given fresh impetus in 2005. Within a decade more than a 100,000 villages were electrified. To give a perspective, even after 60 years of Indian independence, in 2001, only

56% of India had access to electricity, and 10 years later, this has risen to 80%. What is unique is the manner in which this was creatively achieved. The strength of all energy companies in the public sector was brought to support the states to complete the task. This was done through turnkey projects with 100% government funding (90% grant and 10% loan by Rural Electrification Corporation).

5. Radar-like Mindset

This category refers to a cluster of attributes of thinking and environment sensing exhibited by Mr Shahi. All the persons we talked to highlighted the following:

He is always updated on the latest developments. He is always in search of new ideas and futuristic solutions to the problems of power in India. He applies his reading to the context in which he is working. He is a voracious reader as well as a writer. As a practical person, he looks for practical solutions to problems. Nothing escapes his radar.

His radar-like mindset also absorbs information and ideas from people around him as indicated by most of the interviewees (8).

He is very open-minded and considers all views. He intently listens to people. He visits and meets people and senses opportunities. By listening to different views, he is able to connect and integrate different ideas. It is this mindset which helps him stay in touch with the latest happenings, keeps him close to futuristic developments, helps him solve problems creatively and tap into emerging opportunities. It is this which helped him bring many new ideas into the country. The idea of developing a power exchange, as well as of developing a SAARC grid for power, has emerged out of his radar-like alert mindset.

6. Global Perspective

This refers to benchmarking with best practices prevalent globally, understanding and learning from the best, with a view to implementing good ideas in the country. The focus is on keeping track of the changes in the global energy sector, identifying new ideas and learning from the best globally.

Most interviewees (8) said the following on this aspect:

He looked at the globe for best practices. He never benchmarked with India. Whatever he did, he had the global perspective in mind.

Having done a diploma in Advanced Industrial Management from Holland, after his MBA, a global perspective was built into him from the beginning of his career. Through his travels he was impressed by the best practices he saw in the power sector abroad. He was particularly impressed by the power exchange which has been prevalent in Europe for many years. He was convinced that it was a useful mechanism for India with its imbalanced power availability in different parts of the country. Through his efforts, this exchange has now been implemented in India and is available to Indian consumers who can now buy power on the exchange in 15 minutes time block. Another aspect of global perspective is the practice of applying global standards to Indian organizations in terms of quality and time and of focusing on continuous improvement.

7. Ethical

Mr Shahi has been viewed as an ethical and fair person in dealing with customers, unions and officers. Almost all the interviewees (9) said the following about him:

'He was always honest and candid while dealing with people'. 'Nothing was secret, and everything was accessible owing to the large transparency in the system. He did not believe in secrecy'. His integrity and honesty are of a very high order. He never took credit for work done by others. All his focus was on performance. If someone did well he was appreciated. 'He was fair and firm, and very ethical'. He was scrupulously honest. He is a man of his words and says what he means, means what he says. 'Once he has committed something people trust that he will do it'. Through experience everyone knows that he is reliable and dependable. He has never let anyone down— whether officer, staff or union leader.

One of the ex NTPC executives who had seen him operating his during his stint as head HR in Badarpur Power Plant shared a story about an IR decision which RVS had taken. There was a hue and cry and workmen were agitated. During the protest against suspension of a prominent union leader, one of the senior union leaders gave a speech criticizing Mr Shahi. However, he also added 'we can blame Mr Shahi for many things but not for his integrity and honesty, although he has been harsh in this case'. That two of his sons are studying in the Central School in Badarpur shows his honesty. Any other 'prosperous' officer would have sent his kids to an elitist school and not to this local school. This is high praise coming from union leaders who would routinely cast aspersions on so many officers as part of their strategy, especially in the era of the 1980s when unionism was at its zenith.

The above indicates that Mr Shahi conducted himself like a thorough professional with all the relevant stakeholders (9). He respected people, listened to them and responded to the issues without ego, status or position interfering in the process (6). It is no wonder, therefore, that he was able to build good teams and attract people's respect, liking and willingness to go with him.

His strong ethical orientation is also visible in his passion to work for the end user, that is customer, public and larger society. It emerged from our conversation with Mr Shahi that his idea of ethics is not only to live up to his role but also to go beyond it. This facet of his leadership profile has built an extremely high level of credibility and deep trust among the people who worked with him.

8. Humble and Unpretentious

All the interviewees unanimously expressed that Mr Shahi was a humble person. They said this in different ways as indicated follows:

He is a simple person, not given to any extravagance. Though he occupied such a high position as power secretary, he did not throw his weight around. He was never arrogant, and always humble and down to earth. He is a good human being and encourages people to express their views which he listens to with rapt attention. As a leader, he believed in an open door policy. He was highly accessible and approachable. We could walk into his office at any time. It is a pleasure and privilege to work with such an unpretentious person. These days we see too many people showing mock humility. He is not like that. He is genuine and authentic, and respects people.

He behaved with the same level of consideration which he showed me before he became my boss.

Being simple, accessible and listening to others seem to be the core of the reason why people respect and value him. These qualities brought him closer to people and everyone including the unions respected and trusted him. This has been the major secret of his capability to mobilize people.

9. Olympian

Interviewees (6) made the following observations about Mr Shahi which convey his determination and continuous efforts to raise the bar of excellence for himself:

He is a self-made man always learning and developing himself. Hard work, dedication and continued learning are his basic qualities. He loves challenges and did many turnarounds in his life. He never said no to challenges. He always rose to take on bigger challenges. He kept shifting the goal post. He never satisfied with status quo.

Like the true Olympic champion, his method was to compete with himself and to keep raising the benchmarks. This is evident from the way he kept expanding his given role, going beyond what was expected of him as well as expanding his horizons, indicating his need to do the best and to strive to be the best.

10. People Developer and Team Builder

All have said in one breath that Shahi, the leader, is known for developing people and building teams. Both are being presented together because they are closely related. The challenges of team building which he experienced as Secretary Power were considerable. As an 'outsider' to the bureaucracy he had to work hard to build his acceptance and then go on to build the team. In the ministry, he brought people closer by getting joint secretaries together for presentations, where each one got a chance to present progress in their domains and then discuss things threadbare.

In fact, he introduced a system of weekly meetings in the power ministry. While in the ministry, he expanded the definition of teams to include the State level Energy Secretaries, Electricity Boards (SEBs). Most people would have restricted the definition to include only their actual team, in this case the ministry. By bringing the State Energy Secretaries SEBs on Board—the key organizations at the state levels, transformation was achieved in Andhra Pradesh, Rajasthan, Gujarat, West Bengal, etc.

According to an ex CMD who had worked with him while in NTPC, his belief in building teams was so high that early in his career as GM-HR, in NTPC, he created National Bipartite committees consisting of members across over 50 unions. He took many initiatives to bring people together. For example to strengthen team feelings, he started inter project cultural and sports meets across NTPC plants (5).

As Secretary Power he created an HR forum in the power sector. He himself would attend the meetings and as a result all CMDs of these companies would join in. Many productive decisions were taken to collaborate and share resources with each other like guest houses, hospitals across the power sector were used in this way.

Most people we talked to (9) expressed the following thoughts about him:

'He was a strong proponent of brainstorming to arrive at better solution. He was very supportive of his team, encouraged and nurtured talent'. 'He believed in supporting talent'. 'He never criticized others'. 'Heard people out'; 'patient listener'; 'come with me' has been his approach rather than 'do as I say'; even when he took a strong stand on an issue he would get things done without reprimanding people. His empathy with people was so high that he never made people feel small. He encouraged his own personal assistant to teach typing skills to his peon, so that the latter could have a better future. This was done wherever he worked. He was a warm-hearted people leader. His style of inclusivity and involvement helped bring people closer to him. He is very positive, smiling and radiating warmth. He enjoyed being with people. He was always very helpful and supportive. He was never angry and was cool and calm while interacting with people. Even if he gets angry, he will not show it. He has been highly involving as well as trusting, empowering and transparent as a leader. 'He had no biases of any kind; he encouraged talent'. If someone makes a first-time mistake, he is forgiven. He strongly valued human dignity and treated people with respect.

'He never threw his weight around, and never believed in hierar-chy'. He had tremendous openness; in fact, he practices open door approach. 'I have seen him feel agitated when site level GMs had to wait to meet him. When he came to know, he would rush to bring them into his office. He empowers and guides; never imposes'. He is very helpful and can go out of his way to help out someone. He has counselled and advised me when I was about to make a major mistake in my career. He is a perfect gentleman. He brought an amazing people perspective to the toughest decision, so that issues could be handled carefully and well sorted out.

The above seems to bring out that although Mr Shahi is deeply analytical, logical and goal focused, he is equally sensitive to people and their feelings. According to him, empathy is one of the great-est qualities needed to build people and teams. He built teams by bringing people together, respecting human dignity, coaching and counseling people, being inclusive, supportive, empowering and decisive when needed. Closely entwined with building teams was the building of the next line of leaders for the organization.

11. Leading by Example

Mr Shahi has been an exemplary leader. He set examples on mul-tiple fronts, be it work, negotiation, networking, influencing, open-ness, decision making, problem solving, dealing with teams or taking on challenges. By displaying honesty, ethical orientation, compas-sion and concern for people, he developed tremendous credibility among all stakeholders. All the persons we spoke to said, he is a true role model; he is the type of leader, young officers should aspire to become. 'It's a huge learning to observe how he manages to balance situations and manages himself regardless of the situation, no mat-ter how difficult it is' (5).

R.V. SHAHI: THE PERSON

After going through long sittings trying to grasp the inner world of Mr Shahi and getting a 360° feedback about him, we have been able to conclude the following about him as a person, his philosophy and value systems:

Mr Shahi is a highly pragmatic, practical person who combines unfettered thinking with logic and brings innovative solutions to problems. He also has a strong work ethic and always believed in going far beyond the stated role in his attempt to deliver the best in the roles he occupied throughout his career. His humanistic values bring tremendous sensitivity and compassion for fellow humans and an inclusive approach to carry everyone along. His value system is characterized by giving back and working for larger cause of uplifting the lives of people. He is a person who set his agenda for his life and work, governed by his strong value system.

He was clear about his career direction from a very young age and shaped himself accordingly. He developed and expanded his capabilities and grew into higher roles because of his high learning capabilities, combined with high alertness to the environmental context. He is courageous and fearless, highly positive and optimistic person. His mythological hero is Rama, who according to him has been a great team builder and leader. He appears to be a spiritual person with deep faith in a higher consciousness. He is a karma yogi in the sense of possessing detached attachment as advocated in the Gita. His great source of inspiration has been his father, a man of profound knowledge with poetic temperament. It was he who shaped his basic life values in the direction of giving and working for a larger cause. It is therefore no wonder that Mr Shahi says, 'Can I make things happen?; can I make a difference?'

APPENDIX II.1: MR SHAHI—POSITIONS HELD, AWARDS, PUBLICATIONS AND QUALIFICATIONS

Positions Held: Chairman or Member on Boards of Directors of various companies also in the Audit Committees of the Boards, during different periods (1991–2002). Member on the Board of NTPC; Member on the Board and Audit Committee of Power Grid Corporation. Chairman of World Energy Council—Indian

Member Committee (WEC-IMC) during April 2002 to January 2007. Member (2003–2006) on the Policy Group of Carbon Sequestration Leadership Forum (CSLF), a US-led global initiative; Member (2005–2006) on the Govt. Steering Committee for the US-led global initiative on Zero Emission Future Generation Project. He has been closely associated with industry bodies such as Confederation of Indian Industries (CII), Federation of Indian Chamber of Commerce & Industries (FICCI), Associated Chamber of Commerce and Industry of India (ASSOCHAM) as Member and Chairman of various Committees. He was also a member on more than 16 Committees and Organizations covering diverse topics related to Energy, Environment, Human Resource Development and Education. Chairman (2006) of the Government constituted Working Group on Power for Eleventh Five-Year Plan (2007–2012). He was on the Board of Xavier Institute of Management, Bhubaneshwar (2000–2006). He was on the Board of Governors of Indian Institute of Management (IIM) Lucknow (2000–2007). He was on the Board of Management Development Institute (MDI) Gurgaon (1997–2010). He was the Chairman, IDFC Energy Advisory Board (2007–2013).

Awards: He was a recipient of Diamond Jubilee Award of CBIP (1993), India International Gold Award-1994 of the NRI Institute and Udyog Ratan Award-1994 of the Institute of Economic Studies, Top Professional Manager Award of the Institute of Marketing and Management (IMM), 1997—Indira Gandhi National Award, 2000, Special Award conferred by Lion's Club International and 2000 'Excellence in Corporate Governance Award' conferred by Rotary International District 3050-Ahmedabad; Power-Telecom Convergence Award 2000 by IPPAI; 'BEST POWER MAN of the Millennium Year 2000' Award by National Foundation of Indian Engineers; Distinguished Fellow Award 2002 conferred by the Institute of Directors. Eminent Engineer Award by Institution of Engineers, International Executive Award by USEA; Powerline Expert Choice 'Award'06 for Biggest Individual Contribution to the Power Sector' on the basis of a survey of power professionals.

Publications: Contributed and presented many papers at various National and International Conferences. Edited a book entitled

100 Years of Thermal Power in India (2000). Has authored a book entitled *Indian Power Sector—Challenge and Response* (2005). Another book *Towards Powering India: Policy Initiatives and Implementation Strategy* (about 500 pages) was released in November 2007. The book *Energy Security and Climate Change* (over 700 pages) was released in December 2009. The fifth book *Light at the End of the Tunnel? Way Forward for Power Sector* (570 pages)was released in 2013.

Academic Qualifications: Graduation (Mechanical Engineering), Post-graduation (Industrial Engineering), Post-graduation (Business Management) and Diploma in Advanced Industrial Management (Delft, Holland). He is a Fellow of the World Academy of Productivity Sciences, a Fellow of Institution of Engineers (India), a Fellow of International Institute of Electrical Engineers, and a Fellow of the Indian National Academy of Engineering.

APPENDIX II.2: LEGISLATIVE AND POLICY INITIATIVES UNDER MR R.V. SHAHI

1. **Accelerated Rural Electrification Program (AREP) Initiated (2002–2003):** The AREP, operational since 2002, provided an interest subsidy of 4% to states for RE programs. The AREP covers electrification of un-electrified villages and household electrification and has an approved outlay of ₹560 crores under the 10th Plan.
2. **Accelerated Power Development and Reforms Program (APDRP) Scheme Initiated (2002–2003):** It aimed at rejuvenating distribution system in towns and cities, and was restructured with two components: (a) Investment Component, and (b) Incentive Component.
3. **Accelerated Generation and Supply Program (AG & SP) Extended to the 10th Plan (2002–2003):** The Accelerated Generation and Supply Programme (AG&SP) was extended to the Tenth Plan to provide funds to critical on-going schemes at subsidized interest rates.
4. **Electricity Act 2003 Enacted (2003–2004):** The objective of the act was to consolidate laws relating to generation,

transmission, distribution and trading of electricity, and the act aimed at promoting competition, protecting customer interests, supply of electricity to all areas, ensuring transparent policies on subsidies and promoting efficient and environmentally benign policies.

5. **CEA Clearance Exempted for Generating Projects Costing Less Than ₹2500 Crores (2003–2004):** This initiative was aimed at reducing the gestation period of power projects and thereby increasing the confidence of investors and lenders.

6. **Three-stage Clearance Adopted for Central Sector Hydro Projects (2003–2004):** A three-stage clearance procedure has been introduced for central sector hydroelectric projects to minimize time and cost overruns.

7. **50,000 MW Hydro Initiative Launched (2003–2004):** The initiative launched by Government of India in May 2003 started with preparation of feasibility and detailed project report, where 162 schemes were identified with aggregated installed capacity of 50,560 MW and were to be taken for execution during 2007–2017.

8. **The National Electricity Policy Notified (2004–2005):** After the new government took charge in 2004, after two more amendments to the previous draft, National Electricity Policy was notified.

9. **Appellate Tribunal for Electricity Established (2004–2005):** As provisioned in the Electricity Act 2003, Appellate Tribunal for Electricity was established in the year 2004–2005, which completely separated the government involvement from Power Sector.

10. **Guidelines Issued for Procurement of Power through Competitive Bidding (2004–2005):** With the taskforce recommending that 'A significant portion (which could be up to 50% of the new capacity) should be committed to trading or other forms of competitive power markets' Central Government came up with initial guidelines for facilitating the same in 2004–2005.

11. **100,000 MW Thermal Initiative Launched (2004–2005):** It involved development of about 70 projects in the categories of pit-head stations, coastal stations and Load Centre

stations, with the objective of identifying projects which would deliver relatively comparatively cheaper power.

12. **Inter Institutional Group (IIG) and 'Green Channel' Constituted to Facilitate IPPs (2004–2005):** Inter Institutional Group (IIG) of financial institutions and a 'Green Channel' in the Ministry of Power were constituted in January 2004 to facilitate the financial closure of private sector projects likely to come up in the Tenth Plan. The IIG and 'Green Channel' were to provide a forum for interaction amongst promoters of power projects, banks and financial institutions and the Ministry of Power.

13. **National Tariff Policy Notified (2005–2006):** The objective of the National Tariff Policy was to ensure availability of electricity to consumers at reasonable and competitive rates, ensuring financial viability of the sector and attract investments, promoting transparency, consistency and predictability in regulatory approaches across jurisdictions and minimize perceptions of regulatory risks and promoting competition, efficiency in operations and improvement in quality of supply.

14. **Rajiv Gandhi Grameen Vidyutikaran Yojana (RGGVY) Launched (2005–2006):** It was aimed at building rural electricity infrastructure and household electrification towards the goal of access to electricity for all. Under the scheme, 90% capital subsidy was to be provided by Government of India for overall cost of projects.

15. **Launch of Ultra-Mega Power Projects (2005–2006):** Ministry of Power launched a unique initiative in 2005–2006 to facilitate the development of Ultra Mega Power Projects (UMPPs) each having a capacity of about 4000 MW, at both the coal pitheads and coastal locations aimed at delivering power at competitive cost to consumers by achieving economies of the scale.

16. **Guidelines Formulated for Merchant Plants/Coal Linkages (2006–2007):** Guidelines were formulated on Merchant Power Plants with an aim of restructuring the electricity industry on 3 November 2006. Under this policy, coal blocks/coal linkages were to be provided to the successful bidders in setting up thermal power stations.

17. **Guidelines Issued for Encouraging Competition in Developing Transmission Projects (2006–2007):** The guidelines were aimed to promote competitive procurement of transmission services, encourage private investment in transmission lines, and facilitate transparency and fairness in procurement processes.
18. **Cabinet Approval of IPO for Power Finance Corporation, Rural Electrification Corporation, National Hydroelectric Power Corporation and Power Grid Corporation of India:** PFC IPO opened on 31 January 2007 (2006–2007).

APPENDIX II.3: ACHIEVEMENTS IN POWER SECTOR DUE TO INITIATIVES UNDER MR R.V. SHAHI

1. In any Five-Year Plan in the past India could add only 15,000–20,000 MW. Now 15,000–20,000 MW is getting added in one year. In 2014–2015, more than 22,000 MW was added.
2. In the last Five-Year Plan (2007–2012), 55,000 MW was added. In this plan (2012–2017), it could be more than 80,000 MW.
3. In April 2002, total installed capacity was 105,000 MW. In April 2015, it is 261,000 MW. More than 155,000 MW has been added.
4. Private sector role in power generation has increased from 10% in 2002 to 40% in 2015, and is increasing. Almost 100,000 MW has been added by private sector in the last 10 years.
5. Rural electricity access has improved as is evident from the following:

	Total households	Electrified	Percent
2001 (Census)	138 Million	60 Million	43
2011 (Census)	167 Million	118 Million	71*

*By March 2015 it is estimated to exceed 80%.

Year	Total villages	Electrified	Percent
2005	594,000	474,000	80
2015	597,000	579,000	97

6. Change in total transmission capacity is outlined as follows:

Parameter	2002	2015
Line (Ckt Km)	152,000	310,000
Sub Station (MVA)	182,000	586,000

Case III: Major General D.N. Khurana, Change Master

ACHIEVEMENTS AND CONTRIBUTIONS

This case purports to sketch the profile of Major General Khurana, who has been a Change Master par excellence, who could revitalize and turn around a decaying organization and successfully moved it to the next horizon.

Major General Khurana joined as Director General (DG) AIMA in 1994 and retired in 2006. Before mapping his virtuous qualities as a leader, we are very briefly highlighting later his career trajectory, which will serve as a backdrop to understand and appreciate this leader (for further details, please refer to Appendix III.1).

He is the man who has been a much honoured and awarded leader for his contributions in the Indian army, with appointments in staff, command and instructional fields. He was closely involved in many strategic army missions where he rose to be a Major General. He was persuaded by Ram S. Tarneja (board member AIMA) and Rajinder Singh (President AIMA council and CMD NTPC) to take charge of the 'sinking ship' AIMA. Subsequently as DG AIMA, he could architect a new landscape for management education in both the business world and academia. He made landmark contributions to take Indian Management beyond borders (see Appendix III.2 for details).

THE PRESENT CASE

The present case sketches the profile, competencies and capabilities of Major General Khurana, the leader, which enabled him to become a change master. He is a highly admired leader for his contributions to transforming AIMA. Before writing the case, we wanted to get a feel of the work culture of AIMA, and hence did a rough sensing by talking informally to five persons from the bank (see Appendix III.3 for the details).

Content analysis was done of the in-depth interviews conducted with various persons (20)—10 who had worked with him at AIMA since he took over as the Director General, and 10 who had joined at different stages under his leadership. Major General Khurana was also interviewed and based on these interviews the following themes of his leadership have emerged:

1. Entrepreneurial Path Breaker
2. Himalayan Vision with Oceanic Depth
3. Connecting Horizon with Ground Realities
4. Consensus Builder
5. People Builder and Shaper
6. Leading by Example
7. Olympian
8. Constituency Management
9. Radar-like Mindset
10. Global Perspective
11. Ethical
12. Humble and Unpretentious

Each of the above leadership themes has been discussed here.

1. Entrepreneurial Path Breaker

Major General Khurana has been a great risk taker and challenge seeker as indicated by the fact that he even agreed to lead a 'sinking ship—AIMA' which did not even have the money to pay salaries for the month when he joined. Interestingly, he joined at a ridiculously low salary. When we asked him, why he took up this assignment, he replied that he took it as a challenge.

The views shared by the interviewees (20) on these aspects are mentioned here. They provide details on Khurana and his ability to take on the challenge and deliver. 'He always spoke about possibilities'. 'He was an innovative thinker'. 'He was highly proactive'. 'His ideas for building AIMA were creative'. 'He revived the dying Advanced Management Program and gave it a new direction with collaboration with London Business School, Harvard, Stanford, Kellogg and others'. 'He was not afraid to get into new territories'. 'He created something new every time as a leader.' 'How to create the next curve was his major concern'.

Interviewees (11) said that in the most difficult situations, he found solutions to the problems of AIMA. He believed in planting new seeds, which then grew into vibrant activities, generating revenues for AIMA. He could spot the opportunities in the education space and then launch products to serve the customer. The following were either introduced or modified initiatives and made into very successful products at the all-India level in this period. They conclusively bring out his orientation to be an innovative path breaker.

AIMA as a think tank: Three important initiatives were taken to establish AIMA as a think tank—B-School ranking survey was initiated. Primary research on growth of MSME sector was initiated and this exploded many myths and enabled the government to understand the ground reality of this sector. AIMA played a major role in drafting India 2020 report, highlighting India's contribution to the world and how India can prepare for the future.

According to the interviewees (11), he introduced the Directors Conclave to bring together industry and academic; MAT was grown into a national test from its earlier avatar as a test run for a handful of universities; testing services like aptitude, individual assessment, recruitment, promotion were developed. He introduced four to five public awards like Best Paper Award, Life Time Achievement Award, Public Service Excellence Award, awards which immensely helped in building the AIMA brand. He also introduced the Young Leaders Award in collaboration with IIML and the JRD Tata, Corporate

Leadership Award with the support of Tata group. Many national competitions like national management games, national management quiz, student management games and student management quiz were introduced. Management simulation games were introduced with both national and global reach. Faculty development initiatives like AMT-accredited management teachers were introduced. AIMA introduced Shaping Young Minds Programme where established leaders spoke to young minds not only about success stories, but also about hurdles, failures and the learning therein. This initiative was taken to prepare leaders for tomorrow.

People (11) also said that specific initiatives were taken in the MSME sector to deliver capacity-building programmes for entrepreneurs, providing avenues for marketing and financial support. This was done with a view to preparing Indian entrepreneurs to compete more effectively. The UNDP concept of cluster building was supported by AIMA; a two-day workshop for MSMEs operating in South East Asian countries was introduced for mutual learning and exchange; and Learning Centres were launched in collaboration with IGNOU via satellite to connect with students across India to deliver the PGDM program via distance-learning made.

His risk taking and challenge seeking, his ability to spot opportunities and create new products and going into new territories make him an entrepreneurial path breaker. The activities of AIMA generated enough revenue to turnaround its financial fortunes within three years. By the time Khurana retired 12 years later (2006) he had ensured a healthy bottom line and a corpus fund of 28 crores for AIMA.

2. Himalayan Vision with Oceanic Depth

Khurana had a grand vision for AIMA. He could see the possibilities for it to become not only a vibrant national body closely involved with the corporate sector as well as academic, but to also create global footprints. He visualized the power and reach of an All India body, well supported by regional chapters which were themselves very strong and robust.

People (15) said the following about this aspect of Khurana's leadership: 'He would think big'. 'He was not satisfied with AIMA's role and size. He felt it could do much more'. 'He was very concerned about capacity building in the education sector and felt that AIMA was the body which could do this'. 'When he addressed us we used to feel thrilled to listen to his dreams which seemed quite impossible to achieve'. 'He made AIMA robust by strengthening the chapters'. 'By introducing testing services and consolidating it, he expanded the AIMA's expertise levels'. 'He made MAT a national level test and after CAT it was most sought after test in India for a while'. 'He took AIMA from a small national player to a respected body on the national and the world stage'.

Thus, the power of a grand vision for AIMA as an overarching body for management education is evident in the above. It is this vision which immensely helped in shaping the direction of AIMA over 12 years from 1994 to 2006.

3. Connecting Horizon with Ground Realities

Major General Khurana could see the possibilities for an organization like AIMA. He married this vision with his passion for capacity building for the country. He had a grand vision to make a difference to society. When the education industry for corporate executives was still nascent (1994), he could perceive a huge opportunity both in training and in management education. Some of the new products which he planned to introduce were, in fact, those which he had seen abroad and felt that there was a good market for these products in India. In that sense, he was aiming at offering niche products to the customer and was extremely successful at it.

Many of his dreams for AIMA would have stayed unrealized had he not made efforts at building the organization on multiple fronts. His first step was to manage resistance to change and increase his acceptance among the employees. Right in the beginning he addressed the employees, sought their cooperation and said 'if you don't work we will sink' (10); he gave the call for hard work (6). He reorganized the internal structure (how?) and redistributed responsibilities. In fact, it was his style of management to modify the structure to align with emerging market realities. He focused on developing internal talent and networking. He helped restructure the Local Management Associations and introduce the concept of Regional Presidents.

Khurana created AIMA's future through his power of passionate visioning and determined actions. People (10) who had worked with him since inception said the following about Major General Khurana:

'He had a very high vision and dream for AIMA'. 'He was very proactive'. 'He had both a great strategic mindset as well as excellent implementation skills'. 'When he talked about so many new products one after the other, we were excited'. 'There was plenty of enthusiasm to work with a leader who could think big'. 'I was thrilled'. 'He did a root cause analysis to understand the problem and then solved it'. 'The best part about Khurana Sir's vision was his thrust on implementation'. 'His strength lay in execution'. 'He had great execution skills'. 'He had a great eye for detail'. 'He was extremely detail focused'. 'He could pinpoint mistakes'. 'He was a meticulous planner'. 'Nothing was left to chance'. 'He would drill down to the details'. 'Strict monitoring was done along with delegation. He would sometimes make surprise visits on the night before an event'. 'He believed in follow-up'. Everyday there was an SOP checklist and a thorough follow-up; 'there was close monitoring'. 'He put the right people on the right job'. 'He knew everything that took place at AIMA'. 'He had the pulse of AIMA in his hands'.

The above quotes bring out clearly that along with dreaming big dreams, he was an excellent implementer. He picked the right people for the job. He believed in close monitoring and follow-up and left nothing to chance. In fact, the collective morale went up significantly when the Annual Day Celebrations of AIMA (1994–1995) went off perfectly well and they got kudos from the council members and guests. This was a turning point in people accepting him as a leader.

4. Consensus Builder

Khurana was a consensus builder and spent considerable time building consensus among the members of the AIMA board as well as the AIMA steering committee, which consisted of distinguished leaders and captains of industry. He made efforts to give relevant inputs regarding what was needed and how AIMA could be revived. It is only after he earned their trust and cooperation, that he could go ahead with speed, expand and grow the business of AIMA. In fact, he could develop such a fantastic rapport with these industry honchos that they were there to support him whenever he needed any help from the industry to support the cause of AIMA. Thus, it was a collective effort which got launched to not only keep AIMA from sinking but to stabilize it and move with speed.

5. People Builder and Shaper

According to all the interviewees when Khurana joined as DG, 'People were highly individualistic', 'they were working in silos', 'there were trust issues', 'people did not cooperate across departments'. 'There were lots of conflicts', some of them were downright rude and nasty. 'It was not at all a congenial situation', Khurana said, 'When I joined, I sensed that people had to be brought together so that they can work as a team'. They also needed to be groomed and mentored. According to people (10), as a first step, Khurana started bringing people together. 'He used to address us and ask for suggestions on how to bring improvement'; 'he used to ask for ideas'; 'only ideas were asked for and not criticism'. 'He was open to ideas, and if something was good, he would make sure that it was implemented'. 'A suggestion box was placed so that anyone could give their ideas and suggestions'. 'He believed in the young and was keen to hear their thoughts and ideas'. 'He had great ability at E-3—energize the team, engage with them and empower and support the team members'. One of the early steps taken by the DG, according to a senior officer of AIMA, was to introduce the buddy system—that is allotting two persons to a job, so that learning got enhanced, people got closer and work did not suffer.

All said that initially he was tough. This was because he wanted to establish discipline and standards (5). He spent time mentoring people on some of the minute details of how things should be done: brochures, conference arrangements, program organization, etc. Once he found people meeting high performance standards through the mentoring process, he began to empower them. He would say, 'give your best; your decision is my decision' (4). He is known to have sat through conferences and workshops just to get a feel of quality and when needed step in to support the staff and then give developmental feedback.

'He was very concerned about capacity building within AIMA and focused on holistic development of all employees' (4). He has made statements such as, 'it is my responsibility to develop my people in a holistic way' (7). To this end, he encouraged employees to go for programmes on management skills, on yoga, meditation and spirituality. One of his important contributions besides building a team and sense of harmony was to mentor, groom and develop people. The interviewees said, 'He initially guided everyone and then empowered them. If, someone got stuck he helped them' (6). 'As a leader he built relationships and established creditability through execution' (7). 'He told us we could contact him at anytime' (9). In fact he requested for honest feedback about mistakes saying that, if 'I come to know in advance then I will do something about it' (3). He was extremely unbiased. Never encouraged chamchas (6). He instilled the art of contingency planning in people; plan for the best prepare for the worst was the approach (2). 'He believed that all human beings have great potential which stays latent till it is used'. Thus, people were given roles and responsibilities and given the right empowerment (6); 'Highly approachable, although he did not tolerate fools' (7); I am a better professional … because of him I got to learn a lot. 'I feel sincere gratitude to him. It was a pleasure to learn from him and work with him. I have implemented many things I learnt; from him' (1). He believed in strong human touch as indicated by the views shared in the following paragraphs.

People shared the following about their experiences with him: 'I had once achieved a fantastic job and shortly after he was there to appreciate'. 'When he scolded me badly for some mistakes I would be so demoralized that I would take leave the next day. Next morning, he would call, try to placate me, send a car to pick me up, bring me to the office'; 'as a leader he first focused on building relationships and then established credibility by execution'.

People (14) said that he was so people centric that at time he even went beyond rules to address their genuine concerns. 'He went beyond rules—had a style of human touch and recognition'. 'He was very helpful, supportive'. 'He gave people freedom to people to do their jobs'. 'If a person did well he was praised if he did badly he was questioned'. 'Achievers were recognized and poor performers were given feedback and if required they were reprimanded'.

All said that they were taken care of once AIMA began to taste success and do well. Compensatory off was introduced, lunch allowance was provided for those who had to work on a Saturday; cars were made available to drop lady staff if they were working beyond 7 PM. 'Families were brought together once or twice a year for celebrations and DG would appreciate the employees before them'. This boosted their self-esteem and positivity and perhaps helped them to view his reprimands and scolding in a more benign and tolerant fashion.

The above clearly reveals that Khurana valued people, built teams, focused on developing their morale, developing their capability, motivating them, grooming and developing them and giving recognition for work done. In the process, people started working together, cooperated with each other and together contributed to improving AIMA's performance. A congenial work culture got created. In fact when a fire broke out in the office building people came from long distances to help salvage things although this was on a holiday, indicating the extent to which people had developed a feeling for the organization.

6. Leading by Example

One of the outstanding qualities of Khurana as DG-AIMA has been to lead by example. When it came to apologizing to students for an error made by an employee, he was the first one to go ahead and do this. When a fire broke out in the office premises he was there. When he insisted on quality work by the staff, he himself was the acme of perfection in delivery. On matters of discipline and punctuality no one could beat him. 'In fact he was always ahead of us'. Even the initial low salary, at which he joined AIMA, indicated his intention to build the place rather than use it as a parking slot. Accepting such a challenging job post retirement for such a pittance itself heightened his credibility. People said about him, 'He never expected from others what he himself did not do' (8). 'He never said I. It was always we' (7).

7. Olympian

Like the typical Olympians, Major General Khurana was never satisfied by the quality of work done and always sought to improve it to the best possible levels of excellence. People described the high focus on excellence which the Major General brought to the table.

One of the employees gave the example of a well-known political figure, Najma Heptullah, who had been invited as the Chief Guest at one of their annual events. She reached 20 minutes in advance. She told the organizers, 'I thought it best to reach early because I know that Major General Khurana will start the programme without me if I am a little late'. His reputation for discipline and punctuality was thus well known and established. He inculcated discipline and gave a strong message on punctuality. People (20) said the following about him:

He was always punctual. 'Quite early in his term he undertook the task of benchmarking AIMA with other management associations in order to reach and exceed those levels'. 'There was a high focus on quality. Even a single mistake was not tolerated'. He tolerated only first-time mistakes. He would say, 'if you repeat your mistakes, it means you haven't learnt from them'. He set clear goals at the DG level, and at other positions down the line, so people knew what was expected of them. Work manuals were developed for every employee. 'His excellence focus was so high that two years before the Asian Association of Management Organizations (AAMO) president ship was scheduled to come to India, he began to meticulously plan initiatives'. The lead time of two years is what impressed his team. While guiding his team members he encouraged them to perform saying, that, only if you perform, you will make mistakes. 'He was a lion within AIMA'. No one had the guts to face him, if they made a mistake. I once found a mistake in my brochure only after it was printed—a night before the event. I was so upset, that I got it reprinted overnight so that it was perfect. 'I learnt from him how to do a perfect job'. 'I learnt from him how to bring detail focus to the job at hand'.

One of the interviewees described an event which brings out Khurana's excellence focus. A national level conference had been organized in Hyderabad where the conference hall could fit around 900 guests. Khurana decided to turn away 150 cheques because he felt that more than 900 guests would cramp the seating in the hall and reduce the comfort level of the participants. The local organizers just could not fathom the reasoning. In the Major General's view, 'we should give the participants a great experience'.

8. Constituency Management

A tremendous focus was laid on connecting with different stakeholders of AIMA. According to one of the executives who witnessed the event, it started on the very first day when he walked into the AIMA building and found many people loitering around. He realized that they were students and parents. He asked why proper arrangements were not made if so many people were expected. He quickly got to the bottom of things and realized that although the PGDM programme was a distance learning programme, it was not made clear to the parents and students owing to some miscommunication. He gathered everyone in the auditorium and 'with folded hands apologized to them'. He said, 'sorry we have not made proper arrangements her'. He honestly shared that it was a distance learning programme, not a fulltime programme. He was upfront and honestly apologized on behalf of team AIMA. That impressed the students, parents and the AIMA community a whole lot. It is obvious that he gave a clear message about handling the stakeholders fairly and maintained the name and image of AIMA, rather than annoy the constituency which was so important to them—students and parents.

From connecting with students (and parents), he moved to the Governing Council level. He developed a good rapport with the Council; he shared his plans and gave detailed inputs. When they approved, he then moved ahead to execute the ideas with full enthusiasm and drive. He moved on to networking with the large number of AIMA Local Management Associations (around 48). Local chapters were strengthened and AIMA's national level brand value steadily got enhanced. When he retired in 2006 there were 56 active chapters with a good connect with the parent body. DG himself further did intense networking with various corporate heads and thereby developed a large group of willing supporters for AIMA, whom they could reach out to whenever help was needed. 'I could reach out to any of them when I needed support of any kind— whether nominations, participants in competitions or sponsorships, etc'. He also focused on networking with various industry bodies such as FICCI, ASSOCHAM, CII and others such as bureaucrats and political elite. Then, he networked with associations globally across over 30 countries and made a respectable place for the AIMA brand on the world stage.

From the above, it is clear that Major General Khurana was highly proactive and savvy in connecting with his constituency and building positive relationship with them.

9. Radar-like Mindset

Major General Khurana displayed a highly alert and perceptive mindset about happenings, events and developments in the education space. By visiting different associations at the national level he could identify the gaps in the offerings of these peer organizations. This helped him, in turn, to develop new products which AIMA could launch (mentioned on pages 195–196). Thus, he could sense opportunities and take advantage of them for the benefit of the organization. When he visited international events by different associations, he realized the absence of a South Asian Association of Management and founded the same. Further, he could identify new products and offering during his international visits like the business simulation games from Singapore. For many years AIMA enjoyed the advantage of being one of the select few organizations, running such games in India and thereby introducing a (then) cutting edge pedagogy to the Indian Corporate Sector. He partnered with international bodies such as American Management Association, Chartered Institute of Management, UK, European Association of Management Organizations, Asian Institute of Management Manila, RMIT Australia, Carnegie Melon University USA, HENKEY management College, UK, etc. Management development activities increased dramatically as they began to offer new products.

People (16) said the following about him:

'He was a very good listener. This helped him understand ground realities at AIMA'. 'His alertness and sharp observation skills helped him in assessing his team's strengths and non-strengths which he later used to place the right person on the right job'. The biggest indicator of his opportunity-sensing mindset is his perception of AIMA before he joined as the DG. Although what was visible was a loss-making doomed organization, he could see the possibilities and opportunities which AIMA had should it choose to take advantage of them. In fact, his attitude was that every problem also throws up opportunities.

10. Global Perspective

Khurana did not compare his organization to peers in India. He thought about global benchmarks for AIMA. After the initial consolidation, he got the best global minds to talk to his team and inspire them at a 2-day retreat. His notion of quality was anchored on global standards set by the best management associations in the USA, the UK, Asia and Australia.

This global perspective meant that he tried to drive the organization to become competitive at both the national and the international levels. Regional level influence was also increased by setting up the Asian Association of Management with Pakistan, Nepal, Sri Lanka and Mauritius as members. By developing a large number of MOUs across the globe, he ensured an inflow of global ideas and practices. Above all, he also brought in a focus on technology, for example, technology was used for training of accredited management teachers and PGDM Programme.

It was the urge to reach global standards that made him bring in business simulations to India and to also facilitate competitions which would take the top Indian teams abroad to compete internationally.

This also helped him initiate closer collaboration with international bodies, as mentioned above.

11. Ethical

People have mentioned that he was a highly ethical person in every possible way—ethical to the organization and ethical to his role as

DG-AIMA. All have spoken about Khurana's high ethical standards and expressed this in the following manner:

'He is a man of high integrity. He never compromised despite losses incurred and unpleasant outcomes'. When he apologized to students and parents about the miscommunication regarding the PGDM programme (mentioned earlier), it indicated his integrity. As the face of the organization, he said sorry on behalf of his team, on day 1 of joining the place. 'This matters … this made us feel excited to work with such a man'. 'He was transparent and shared all information'. 'He never expected us to do what he did not'. 'He took the lead, he showed the way'. 'By setting expectations, he made it clear what we were expected to do'. 'If our performance was up the standards, we were instantly recognized. If someone did a bad job he got scolded'. 'Man of great honesty and integrity'. 'His focus was on organization building and making contributions'. 'Worked tirelessly to build AIMA'. 'I was thrilled and excited to work with such a great leader, a man of such integrity, who spoke the truth to the customers'.

'It was an uplifting experience to work with him'. 'He challenged us with his high standards but never made us feel insecure or small'. 'He was a man of his word and we trusted him'. 'It is remarkable that he gave due credit to people, unlike many heads who take credit for the work of others'. 'I have worked with many DGs but he was one who gave me tremendous learning opportunity'.

The above quotes beautifully bring out that Major General Khurana upheld high values, treated people fairly, did not manipulate them, took care of them and above all developed them. It is a testimony to his being absolutely ethical, grounded and realistic when he decided to quit in 2006, although he could have stayed in longer. He was thus a great role model for AIMA employees.

12. Humble and Unpretentious

Many interviewees (12) talked of the way he conducted himself—humble, unpretentious and accessible. They shared their views as follows:

'He used to respect people'. 'He was not at all status conscious'. 'He was as comfortable with a President of the country as with a cab driver'. If a person had a good idea he valued it, without bothering who gave the idea. 'I have not seen him throw his weight around'. 'Although he was initially tough, as things stabilized he showed us his softer side'. 'He would walk into anyone's office to discuss with them'. He would ask 'what are you doing? Do you need my help'? 'He used to listen carefully when people spoke'. He was an open-minded person and not rigid. He was unassuming. He was not at all status conscious. If a person had merit even if he was young, he would address as 'Sir' or 'Maam'. 'One of the interviewees shared a heart-warming example of Khurana and his driver. Khurana encouraged the driver to give his graduation examinations. During the examinations, he would personally drive him to the centre, wish him luck and then drive down to work'.

The above quotes indicate a level of humility and unpretentious-ness which is rare at the top level. It is no wonder that he was able to influence people and mobilize them to achieve a turnaround and script a path-breaking growth trajectory for AIMA.

MAJOR GENERAL KHURANA: AN ANALYSIS

The following quotes from Major General Khurana's interview sum up his core value system:

> *A wise old bird sat on a tree*
> *The more he saw the less he spoke*
> *The less he spoke the more he heard*
> *On why can't you be like the wise old Bird?*
> (Inscription in the Defense Services Staff College, Wellington)

This quote brings out very sharply the belief in acquiring wis-dom through listening, absorbing and learning from everyone.

> *Safety, Honor and Welfare of your country, comes first. Always and every time*
> *Honor, Welfare and Comfort of your Men comes next*
> *Your ease, comfort and safety comes last always and every time*
> (Inscription in the Indian Military Academy, Dehradun)

The above brings out the primacy attached to the well-being of one's country, one's people highlighting Major General Khurana's core value of patriotism and nationalistic pride.

He believes that a self-actualizing and fully functioning person is highly action centric, and he sees meaning in life in terms of work and action. He believes in relentlessly and doggedly pursuing, striving and making things happen. He believes that thought without action does not have any value and that action without thought is a futile exercise. Another core belief held by Khurana is time-bound and meticulous action. Further, he believes more in the power of the man behind the gun than the gun itself, alluding to the criticality of grooming, building and taking care of people. He admires leaders such as Subhash Chandra Bose for the sheer courage to stand up and give an alternative to the country, and Atal Bihari Vajpayee for his statesmanship. Among mythological heroes, he admires Arjuna for his relentless quest and endeavour at consummate mastery over weapons in a manner that he could shoot at the speed of sound.

APPENDIX III.1: CAREER TRAJECTORY, AWARDS AND CONTRIBUTIONS

All India Management Association (AIMA)

He assumed the assignment of Director General of All India Management Association (AIMA) in 1995. AIMA is the national apex body of professional management in the country. During this period of nearly 12 years, he has steered the National Management Movement in the country and knitted together 63 Local Management Associations spread across India and abroad. He has built AIMA as a strong institution which is truly acknowledged as a leader in Management Development Movement not only in India but also whole of Asia. During this period he has established very close rapport with industry, business, government, professional bodies and NGOs across the country through close networking. This has been achieved through setting appropriate HR strategies for a diverse work force, designing and implementing controls and procedures and strict financial discipline. Many new and innovative products and services of high quality for enhancing professional competence of Indian managers were introduced during this period.

Institute of Directors

He was the founding Director General of Institute of Directors India for two years. Institute of Directors (IOD) is an apex association of company directors committed to improving the competitiveness of Indian business through development of its leadership.

Army Background

After distinguished service of over four decades, General Khurana retired from the Indian Army in 1991. Although he was commissioned in the Corps of Signals (Electronics and Telecommunications) in the army, he had the rare distinction of being specially selected and inducted in the General Cadre of the Army on being promoted to the rank of brigadier. As a general cadre officer, he had the honour of Commanding an Infantry Brigade and Infantry Division. He had a major role in planning and conducting military operations in Sri Lanka and Maldives. During his army career, he has held some of the most prestigious command, general staff and instructional appointments at the Army College of Combat, Mhow and Defence Services Staff College, Wellington. Being a highly decorated soldier, he was commended by the Army Chief for exceptional service and awarded Ati Vishist Seva Medal by the President of India for distinguished services of exceptional order.

APPENDIX III.2: ACHIEVEMENTS AT AIMA

Major General Khurana, during his 12-year-long association with AIMA (1995–2006), undertook many structural changes as well as path-breaking initiatives, and the major initiatives are documented as follows:

1. **Initiatives for Working Managers:** Following initiatives were taken by AIMA under the leadership of Major General Khurana for working managers.

   - Nation-wide network of nodal centres opened for reaching out to practicing managers (1995)
   - 1st National Management Convention (NMC) conducted by CMD-AIMA becomes a landmark event (1997)
   - Asian Management Games conducted by AIMA at Kolkata (1998)
   - Simulation Games launched as in-company training tools by AIMA (1998)
   - Launched Global Senior Management Program in association with INSEAD, France to help benchmarking with European standards (2004)

2. **Collaborative Ventures with B-Schools:** It was under the leadership of Major General Khurana that AIMA increased its association with B-Schools manifold and some of the landmark initiatives are as shared below:

   - Management Aptitude Test (MAT) started for admission into AICTE approved B-Schools (1997)
   - Director's Conclave aimed at increasing industry-academia interface started (1997)
   - 'Chanakya', an indigenous developed Business Simulation Game software launched for B-Schools (1997)
   - 10 scholarships of ₹60,000/- each instituted for students from Economically Weaker Sections (EWS) at B-Schools (2003)
   - MAT scholarship for bright students announced (2003)
   - 1st ever National Management Student Quiz launched with stupendous success (2003)
   - Approval of MAT by Ministry of HRD and its ISO-9001-2000 certification (2003)
   - National Case-Study Writing Workshops conducted in Delhi and Bangalore (2004) to increase pedagogical effectiveness and also to attract more and more people to write India-specific cases

- AIMA launched first-ever National Paperwriting Contest on Management for B-Schools (2004)
- 'Young Managers Confidence Index' launched to find out the views of Indian companies about B-School graduates (2004)

3. **Going Global:** Major General Khurana was one of the early pioneers in Indian Management Education to understand the importance of internationalization, and under his leadership several initiatives were undertaken to make AIMA go global, as outlined in the following:

- Successful collaboration with Carnegie-Mellon University to deliver AP-SCORE (AMP) in Pittsburg (1995)
- AIMA plays a key role in setting up of South Asian Association of Management Organizations (SAAMO) and Major General D.N. Khurana takes over as its Secretary General
- As part of India–Africa Partnership Initiative, AIMA conducted two-day workshop on 'Awareness for Entrepreneurship Development' for students of Uganda, Tanzania and Kenya (2000)
- Signing of MoU with ISC Switzerland for joint management education projects, Research, Faculty Exchange and facilitating their participation in AIMA's major programs (2001)
- Formation of Qatar and Mauritius Management Association (2001)
- AIMA conducts its first-ever program overseas (Mauritius-2002)
- Setting up of Center for Public Governance in association with George Mason University (2003)
- Provided instrumental support in organizing first-ever Middle-East National Management Convention in Qatar (2003)
- AIMA obtained grant from EU to promote EU India research with specific objective of producing, collecting, organizing, sharing and disseminating among major stakeholders in India (2005)

4. **Internal Architecture of AIMA—Strategies, Structure, Systems and Processes:** One of the prime concerns that Major General Khurana faced upon his joining was related to architecture of AIMA, be it the infrastructure condition at AIMA, or the relationship with LMAs. To bring around desired change, this was one of his first priorities and the following achievements highlight the sincere efforts and visible changes that happened during his tenure.

- Setting up of Centre for Management Development CMD (1997)
- Starting of LMA CEOs workshop fostered closer interaction between LMA and AIMA (2000)
- Conducting 1st Management Convention on e-Business in association with Hyderabad LMA, once again aimed at fostering closer ties (2001)
- ERP and MIS implementation in AIMA (2002)
- AIMA newsletter 'COMMUNIQUE' goes online, ensuring wider reach and closer connect (2002)
- Financial support scheme to LMAs to help them build their infra was well appreciated by all stake-holders (2002)
- Advisory Panel of Past Presidents formed to ensure smooth transactions (2002)
- AAMO constitution was edited to incorporate and adopt the new additions in activity portfolio (2003)
- A.C. Nielson and ORG-MARG conducted Brand Audit survey for AIMA to outline brand strengthening strategies (2003–2004)
- Signing of Charter with 46 LMAs to ensure mutual cooperation between AIMA and LMAs. LMA Support committee formed to re-enforce the AIMA-LMA relationships (2004)
- AIMA constitution amended to give permanent seats to eight LMAs and eight other LMAs given rotating memberships
- Upgrading of infrastructure and designing a charter for each member in Secretariat

5. **Positioning of AIMA among Corporate and Stakeholders:** It was therefore no surprise that under able leadership of Major General Khurana, AIMA not only received several awards but also undertook many path-breaking initiatives, as mentioned in the following:

- AIMA selected to totally administer J.R.D. Tata Corporate Leadership Award annually (1995)
- AIMA starts with Public Service Excellence Award (1998), marking a great addition to its national stature
- AIMA conducts recruitment tests for Delhi High Court, Indian Airlines and Kashmir University, a testimony to increasing popularity of its testing services (2000)
- Creating High Level Strategy Group (HLSG) under the chairmanship of N.K. Singh, Member Planning Commission, to come up with report 'India's Opportunity 2020' and presenting the same to Prime Minister, President to serve as a ready reckoner for ways to tap the lurking opportunities (2001)
- AIMA conducted the 1st National Conference on Public Governance aimed at bringing Public Governance into focus (2002)
- To help liaison effectively with Small Enterprises, Dr J.S. Juneja award for Creativity and Innovation launched (2003)
- Commissioning of survey to understand 'IMPACT OF GLOBALIZATION ON SMALL ENTERPRISES' (2003)
- To involve youth in National Management Movement, 'Shaping Young Minds Programme' taken up (2004)
- Release of book 'PASSION TO WIN' outlining the salient contours of Research Commissioned by AIMA on 'How Winning Companies Develop & Sustain Competitive Edge'
- 1st Service Marketing Summit held by AIMA (2003)
- AAMO journal 'ASIAN MANAGEMENT REVIEW' launched (2005)

6. **Financial Performance of AIMA:** Under the leadership of Major General Khurana, the surplus at AIMA increased the

surplus from ₹969,907 to ₹74,072,215 (increase of 75 times in 12 years).

7. **Awards and Accolades:** The illustrious career and contribution of Major General D.N. Khurana is also reflected in the awards and accolades he received. Some of the major awards and accolades are as shared here:

- AtiVishistSeva Medal for Services of Exceptional Order by the President of India
- Life Time Achievement Award in Management-Global Excellence Awards by World HRD Congress
- Competition Success Review Gold Medal Award as Super Brains Super Personality
- Indian Brand Summit Award for Outstanding Contribution to Industry
- ITM Business School Award as India's Greatest HR professional
- NIMT Commendation Award 1999 for Promotion of Management Education in India

APPENDIX III.3: AIMA WORK-CULTURE ATTRIBUTES

Culture attributes	Before	After
Teamwork	Low	Very high
Commitment to organization	Low	Very high
Motivation	Low	Very high
Conflicts	High	Low
Inter-department collaboration	Low	Very high
Top-down comm.	Moderate	Very high
Bottom up comm.	Low	Very high
Excellence	Low	High
Target and performance orientation	Low	Very high
Global benchmarking	Low	High

Case IV: M.D. Mallya, Towards the Next Curve

ACHIEVEMENTS AND CONTRIBUTIONS

Mr M.D. Mallya has been Chairman and Managing Director of Bank of Baroda, from May 2008 to November 2012. In the ex-officio capacity, he headed the bank's several domestic/overseas subsidiaries and joint ventures. During the tenure as Chairman and Managing Director, Bank of Baroda recorded a high growth rate, beyond the industry level at over 30% doubling its business in 3 years. The net profit touched a new peak of over ₹5000 crores. Prior to this, he was Chairman and Managing Director, Bank of Maharashtra (March 2006 to May 2008); Executive Director, Oriental Bank of Commerce, New Delhi (July 2005 to March 2006), and held various positions in Corporation Bank where he worked until he reached the position of General Manager.

The story of Bank of Baroda (BoB) under the leadership of Mr Mallya (CMD) is a rare example of a public sector bank which achieved excellence despite the internal and external constraints. Under Mr Mallya, BoB moved into a phase of consolidation and moved into the next orbit of growth and performance. The bank has received many accolades and awards in the year 2008–2012. The share value of the bank zoomed up from ₹360 in March 2008 to a high of ₹860 in March 2012. International operations grew from ₹51,874 in March 2008 to ₹209,444 crores in September 2012. (For Award, Accolades and Financial Performance, see Appendix IV.1, a, b, c and d.) It is remarkable that these milestones were reached without unrest and by retaining the positive image of the bank in the volatile business environment post the global financial meltdown.

Besides this, in terms of total business, BoB raced ahead of its peers. BoB grew at around 26–27% in the 2011–2012, while the industry grew at 18–19%. Their international operations multiplied four times. BoB doubled its performance every three years right from 2008. In the words of the chief economist of the bank, 'Our major achievement is not growth but rather growth with quality'.

In the year 2011–2012, the bank attained the number one spot in terms of percentage of total business growth year on year, which is a distinctive achievement dreamt of by every public sector bank.

Mr Mallya's exemplary performance record, the legacy he has left behind in Bank of Baroda, the magnitude of change that he could achieve, his relentless endeavour to take the bank to the next curve, made us curious to understand, who is this man as a leader; how does his mind work, and what kind of a persona does he possess? It is in this context that we decided to write this case. Before writing the case, we wanted to get a feel of the work culture of Bank of Baroda, and hence did a rough sensing by talking informally to five persons from the bank (see Appendix IV.2 for the details).

THE PRESENT CASE

To get a broader view of Mr Mallya's profile, we had extensive interviews with 20 members of the top and senior management team who had worked closely with Mallya. The present case sketches the profile, competencies and capabilities of Mr Mallya, the leader, which enabled him to work towards the next curve of excellence. On the basis of content analysis of the in-depth interviews with top, senior and middle level officers as well as Mr Mallya, we have identified the following leadership features:

1. Visionary Strategist
2. Binocular Vision with Microscopic Details
3. Constituency Management
4. People Developer and Team Builder
5. Open, Empowering and Participative
6. Humble
7. Balanced Person
8. Ethical
9. Radar-like Mindset
10. Olympian
11. Close Monitoring and Review
12. Leading by Example

1. Vision Strategist

Everyone we interviewed highlighted that Mallya as a man with Himalayan vision. Mr Mallya joined BoB in May 2008, from Bank of Maharashtra where he was the CMD. According to the GM HR who accompanied him from Pune to Mumbai soon after he took over he said, 'My dream is to see that the bank's annual profit grows fourfold in four years and this was achieved by the bank in 2011–2012'.

All the interviewees said that he would clearly talk about the emerging business context, paint the big picture and highlight the vision and goals. He exhorted them to work passionately towards achieving the vision. Some of the GMs (8) shared that 'In the first six months when he said we should make ₹5000 crores profit for the full year, people were sceptical but finally we have achieved the goal!'. According to many of the senior-level officers (12), he had a crystal clear vision of where he wanted to take the bank right from the beginning'. 'His initial vision—to grow four times in size—was an audacious goal, one which no one believed at that time' (8). In every speech and address to employees on various occasions, he gave them the vision that 'we have to be the most admired bank'. 'He gave everyone a clear path, a very clear vision' (15).

What he visualized for the bank is what was achieved in 2011–2012. This took the bank to the number one position among Indian public sector banks (after SBI). This vision provided clear direction to the bank. What is most interesting, however, is that barring specific occasions when numbers were discussed, Mr Mallya always talked about values, contribution and so on, raising the level of consciousness of the people.

People (15) also indicated that he is highly strategic. The strategy of conducting business by focusing on building a diversified portfolio—spreading the risk across various products—was the foremost observation made by everyone about him. People said that while in many cases it was not obvious at the time that they applied for large loans, later we realized that Mr Mallya's assessment of the credit worthiness of this company was accurate as subsequent events have shown. The second important aspect mentioned by most of the persons interviewed was the focus on leveraging technology. Clearly, the direction for public sector banks lies in moving in the direction of new age banking and he took the bank on this established path.

The third important point mentioned by the group of GMs has been the focus on international expansion since this contributes to the balance sheet in terms of high value. Today, it contributes to 25% of the bank's profits.

The most important indicator of Mr Mallya's strategic thinking is his focus on achieving growth through people. As a public sector banker he knows the issues and challenges faced in the scenario of scarce leadership talent and decided to handle it himself. He became the role model and educated and tirelessly coached his senior team to become better leaders.

From the above, it can be concluded that Mallya is a man not only with big dreams, but also is strategic in his approach to realizing the same.

2. Binocular Vision with Microscopic Details

This leadership attribute can be defined as capability to dream big and have clear understanding of ground-level issues, which is very important in achieving a grand vision. Most people (18) spoke about his masterly business acumen; his awareness of both big picture and the ground realities of the business and the market movements. In fact, one of the GMs brought out that when Mr Mallya took charge that was the year when the global financial meltdown took place and he did not have an easy time in growing the bank. Yet BoB established confidence in the minds of the public as well as the investors and continued on its growth path through strategic moves. It is his power to see the macro picture and integrate it with ground realities which makes him such a great banker. The proof lies in the quality of the business, especially where so many public sector banks have badly suffered by making decisions which proved unsound in hindsight.

People expressed their views as follows:

'His knowledge and mastery in the domain of banking is unparalleled'. 'He has a great command of the economic scenario and also has a firm grip on the pulse of the market'. 'His assessment of different sectors of the economy is on the dot'. 'There is no doubt that he is a great great banker'.

Benchmarking vis-à-vis peer banks was done on various parameters like business levels, growth, profitability, return on assets and return on equity. This was shared with people at every opportunity so as to build the collective momentum.

Enormous efforts were made to prepare people for change. For example, BPR implementation for example was handled through communication, clarification and help from the corporate BPR team. In fact, the team visited many zones and regions and addressed the relevant people and showed them how the new process would reduce their burden and help them. Soon the word spread and various regions and zones began to invite the team to their own locations.

The above illustrates that Mr Mallya can not only fly at 60,000 feet but also walk effortlessly on the ground. In other words, Mr Mallya demonstrated capability of connecting horizon with ground reality.

3. Constituency Management

Being a seasoned public sector banker and having moved across three other banks, he was familiar with what lays in store for him as he took charge. He thus deliberately started his innings in BoB in a measured and slow way. Many interviewees (16) said, 'He made himself acceptable to the people by his approach. People were relieved, and, to be frank, the fear psychosis vanished'. GMs (10) said, 'CMD created the growth momentum by involving people at the grass root level'. A good environment was created, no stress in the work place and people began to work. Everybody worked and brick by brick the organization grew with the collective efforts of all; according to most of the GMs and DGMS (18) whom we interviewed, Mr Mallya acted decisively and quietly without much fanfare. As one of the GMs put it, 'Mr Mallya leveraged the practices initiated by his predecessor; Mr Mallya capitalized on the strengths of the bank and took forward most of the initiatives which were taken in the regime of the previous CMD (12). By not seeking to deride or destroy the initiatives of the previous incumbent, he also got the cooperation of many of the old timers who had worked hard during the previous years. Mallya built a congenial relationship with union leaders and the officers' association. Early efforts were made to create a homogenous and unified top team moving in the same direction. A top management conclave (top 100) was held where 'we discussed the bank's growth agenda and also got to understand each other better'. People came together, stayed together, ate together and talked to each other. 'The conclave helped in building bonds with the top management' (GM HR).

Customer service was emphasized along with the need for positive attitude towards the customer. A strong message was given to the ZMs at various meetings (to give quick responses on loan applications). The message of quick response to the customer spread throughout the organization. People said, 'CMD himself is very responsive to the customer and believes in quick decision making and we do the same'. Two of the GMs said that one of Mr Mallya's greatest contributions to this bank is to make it a marketing bank … 'we have not reached there as yet but we are on the way'.

He worked to gain acceptance not only of the internal stakeholders, but he also focused on creating strong bonds at the board level. As a result, he got their support for many of the key issues. Further, according to the chief economist of the bank, Mallya consciously cultivated investors by transparent sharing of information.

The above brings out that Mr Mallya has been an excellent constituency manager. This enabled him to start a collective march towards his goal, which was whole heartedly supported by all the stakeholders.

4. People Developer and Team Builder

GMs and ZMs (20) whom we met expressed that in the first year, wherever CMD visited, he met people across levels in small, large and very large groups. They said the following about his style:

'He involved people at the grass roots level in his communication'. 'He is passionate about connecting with people'. 'Everyone spoke admiringly about his speeches'. In the initial phase his speeches were peppered with statements such as, 'This bank has great potential; this bank has lots of capability; we have good people here; you are capable of doing many things here especially when there is so much opportunity'. He used the communication opportunity to boost up the morale of people and their self-esteem and pride. He did not miss any opportunity to appreciate and boost the morale of people, for example, when the contract with the brand ambassador was ending, he said, 'we don't need another brand ambassador, you 40,000 persons are my ambassadors...'.

According to most (18) of the people we talked to, Mr Mallya is a man who believes in personal touch. 'He believes in personal touch', 'when there is any invitation for a social event, he makes it a point to visit'. 'When we meet socially he will make it a point to remember to ask about the progress of the family'; 'he is a great human being, when there are personal problems he goes out of his way to help'. His orientation to meet people, answer calls, be available and approachable all indicate his human touch. Many people mentioned that due consideration is given to human factors and constraints when transferring people. 'He is friendly and smiling', 'has a great smile'. 'Even if there are a 100 people in a gathering, he never fails to shake hands with each and every one of them and exchange pleasantries'.

Another aspect has been his high level of accessibility. According to many interviewees (15), people could call him or message him and he would either take the call or, if he was busy, he would call back; senior-level officers of the bank found that they could walk into his office without any appointment if the matter was important.

Mr Mallya has shown how people can work together and achieve business results. He actually lived up to the slogan—trust, transparency and togetherness—as reflected in the statements (20) given as follows:

'He has always emphasized working together'. 'He made efforts to bring various teams together and build tremendous bonds and this has been an important part of his leadership style right from the day he took charge'. Whether it is his top team, the board, the unions and federations, the top 100 (ZMs and RMs), he paid attention to bring them together; 'people came together, stayed together, ate together and discussed about the bank together' he said and this built the bonds.

An important aspect of his people management has been his focus on the positives as mentioned by many people (11). 'He did not focus on the negatives according to the GMs; he always focused on the positives'. One person narrated, 'even if I went to him complaining about another colleague's behaviour, he would look calmly and say, ok now let us do what needs to be done'. 'He completely discouraged all negative discussions'. In fact, he has been described by many (15) as a very highly positive person with a positive agenda for the bank.

Teamwork was demonstrated right from the top level. This was well summed up by one of the GMs, 'When people saw CMD and the Executive Director on the same wavelength, others down the line followed this example'. CMD himself made all efforts to bring people together by involving larger numbers in meetings and bringing together people across the hierarchy. People came together for new product launches; foundation day and conclave for DROs. People (10) said that, most importantly corporate office became highly responsive and supportive. They became more friendly and professional. Since Chairman himself was so helpful and responsive when ZMs and RMs and customers approached him, the corporate office followed this behaviour. His supportive attitude further helped in enhancing the team spirit and culture of collaboration. Information sharing with all further cemented the 'esprit de corps' and sense of team. One of the RMs said, 'Earlier there were groups and so we were cautious in communication. Now we are all Barodians'. Chairman's habit of giving credit of all achievements to the 'Barodians' rather than taking credit himself at the annual meets, further reinforced the message of team spirit.

Above all, the hallmark of Mr Mallya is his high level of trust in the team (19). This was conveyed to people by the following actions. The fact that he did not change the top team when he took charge; the fact that he delegated and empowered people indicated to all that he trusted them and in turn they felt the need to rise up to his expectations. 'He trusts people to deliver and does not micro manage. People feel so empowered that they actually feel like rising up to his expectations'. He gave the slogan, 'Employee First'. Each opportunity was used to convey the direction in which the bank should grow the available opportunities and constraints; his vision of how BoB should do business and so on. The change in process mentioned above, as well as the slogan, 'Employee First' gave people the self-belief to act. This slogan gave a positive result—people believed CMD's statement because of the way he treated people right from day one.

Another aspect of Mallya's style has been his connect with the senior team. According to the interviewees (18), Mr Mallya maintained connect with the top 400 (up to chief manager level) and through them with the next 400–500 managers who are their direct reportees. People (18) said the following about his team connect:

Team connect has been done through various channels including planning and review meetings; large group communications such as town hall addresses; and through grooming, guidance and accessibility over phone. Regular communication took place with all 42,000 employees—wherever possible through face-to-face meetings, video conferencing, newsletters sharing the latest happenings and plans through the in-house magazine. Likewise, connect was established with the unions and federations. In fact, a constant connect was maintained with them on a quarterly basis all through, keeping the focus on business growth expectations and growth of the bank. He showed the same consistency in his dealing of people and proved to the staff of BoB through his actions that he really did put the employee first—all his subsequent efforts showed that whether it was empowerment, meetings, delegation of powers or project sparsh, or recognition schemes, it has all shown how much he values and puts the employees first.

Tremendous focus has been placed on leadership development within the bank. Apart from efforts made through the 'Sparsh' initiative to educate, train, groom and develop people, CMD has been deeply concerned about the talent crunch at senior levels and in fact he has been using various meetings to first speak on how to be a good leader; what are people's expectations from a leader; how to be a better leader.

The above description brings out that Mr Mallya lived up to his slogan of trust, transparency and togetherness and brought people together through this powerful mode.

5. Open, Empowering and Participative

Openness, empowering and participative style have been the hallmarks of Mr Mallya's stint as CMD of Bank of Baroda. All people said that there is tremendous openness to express views. They said, 'the manner in which meetings are conducted encourages people to freely express their thoughts and ideas'. 'People speak out and good ides do come out of these meetings'; 'there is free interaction and exchange of ideas'. 'There is confidence that these ideas will be heard and if accepted they will be appropriately implemented'; 'this is one of the reasons why change has taken place'.

Target setting process was made both bottom up and top down according to all the Barodians we interviewed. One of the GMs said, 'Before the meeting, CMD circulated a mail giving the SWOT analysis of the bank. He commenced the annual budget exercise by giving the macro perspective of the emerging business situation. Then to the utter surprise of the zonal heads and regional heads, he said, now it is up to you what target you want to set; you know your regions and zones the best. That was a great message and gave the feeling that field and corporate office are one. And everybody tried to see that the target was achieved'. In all subsequent meetings, the ZMs and RMs were given the freedom to set their targets. He stuck by his initial statement in the first exercise, 'I am not going to impose any targets, whatever are the targets you have to self-impose. You tell me what you are ready to achieve, I can only give you a broad vision of what I want us to achieve'.

According to some of the ZMs, 'The concerned ZM was given the freedom to make his own assessment of the potential of the zone and plan accordingly, no doubt with the guidance of the CMD when needed'. Some of the reactions to this approach to target setting are given as follows:

'We were very surprised because we had never experienced anything like this before'; 'we were used to being told that this is the target you have to achieve...'; 'he sat through the entire target setting meeting and listened with rapt attention to everyone'; 'in the last four years he has never forced us to do something even if he disagreed with us'.

The process of target setting continued on this pattern and over the years the heightened transparency led to even the first-level officer being aware of the targets. In fact, the move to put up the targets of various zones on the intranet along with the details of targets achieved by each zone and region by the year end, available for all to see, has been appreciated by one and all. According to many of the interviewees (12), 'the best part is that whatever has been achieved has been done with the consent of all concerned and with their whole hearted participation'.

The high empowerment culture and collective vision building and target setting created high involvement and ownership. Apart from target setting, empowerment also took the form of encouraging decision making at different levels. Lending powers as well as administrative powers have been revised upward according to people across various levels. According to the interviewed ZMs (8), 'We get a free hand to canvas business, to sustain growth and take care of all operational issues. We don't need to ask anybody, whatever is good or bad is our decision'. 'There is freedom and autonomy to work here'.

Transparency and involvement in meetings and discussions has been another important route through which ownership has been created. According to all the interviews, 'meetings are conducted here in a very calm and composed way and a culture of analysis pervades the meetings'. 'He sits through each meeting and listens very carefully and this helps up people tremendously'. Empowerment and participation unleashed the collective passion and self-drive of the bank to perform and prove themselves.

This created a generally positive attitude to work among the people expressed in the following ways, 'we are happy and we work'; we are happy because of the positive attitude and approach'. 'We don't mind sitting late to complete the work'. 'Today openness has increased and therefore everyone knows what's happening in this organization'. 'Tremendous culture of teamwork, cooperation and coordination has developed in BoB', 'good relationships in this bank'. Leaders are highly supportive and helpful. 'There is a supportive and encouraging culture in this bank'. 'It's a human environment. I feel connected to the organization and to the people, although the money is lower than private sector....' In fact some people (DZM level) actually said, 'if we look back what we got in the last four years? No extra money, no extra benefits; what we have got is prestige, honor name and fame in the industry. Feel so proud to be Barodians'.

Above all, there is a culture of trust, transparency and positivity in this bank. People have become receptive and open-minded and volunteer new ideas in meetings because they have seen things change and because they have seen the results.

6. Humble

Everyone we met highlighted that Mr Mallya treated everyone politely and with dignity. No one was shouted at or humiliated in various meetings. This is the one of the most important qualities of Mr Mallya as a person which all have highly appreciated. Most persons we talked to described him as humble. Most persons (18) we talked to described him as humble. 'He does not act like a CMD'. 'He behaves like he is one of us'. 'He queues up with us to pick up lunch when he comes to inaugurate a training program'. 'He is very practical and down to earth; 'interacts so freely with us when there are meetings, you don't feel that you are talking to the CMD of an organization'. On annual day celebrations he stands at the gate to welcome guests, said some of the interviewees.

Everyone we talked to highlighted this personal quality which they admired. 'He listens'; 'very patient listener', 'when we go to him we know that we will get a patient listening', 'if he is busy he will complete what is before him and then he will give you complete attention. He never pays only half attention', 'in meetings we speak out because we know that we will be heard and our ideas can also be taken up'. This is a valued quality because the typical style of CMDs in banks has been more to address and advice others, rather than to listen and take inputs from people around them. His listening helped him not only to absorb information but created immense impact on Barodians.

7. Balanced Person

Everyone expressed that Mallya is a very calm, smiling and friendly person and described this as follows:

'He is so calm'. 'He is a gentleman very polite and very calm'; 'he never gets irritated or angry', 'he has never lost his temper or shouted at people', 'never insults people', 'treats people with dignity'. As one of the DGMs said, 'See basically the moment you are not shouted at and you are treated properly there is comfort'. One person mentioned, 'I am very highly strung and get agitated easily. When I go to him and say sir, this is the problem', his response is very normal and he says, let's find the solution; I feel calmed down when I meet him', another GM said, 'I have never seen him moody or erratic. His consistency level has been remarkable'. 'His approach is gentle and assertive'. 'He is friendly and smiling', 'has a great smile'. As a result of this behaviour combined with listening, people experience his style as soothing. 'Even if there are a 100 people in a gathering, he never fails to shake hands with each and every one of them and exchange pleasantries'.

8. Ethical

Everyone mentioned that BoB operates in an ethical and honest manner thanks to the CMD's own approach. All the interviewees highlighted that he was completely focused on the growth of the bank through the right route and not by taking short cuts. He cautioned people to focus on business growth with quality, rather than recklessly focusing on short-term growth. All business decisions were taken in the interest of the well-being of the bank. This was visible when promotions were given and transfers were done. 'It was clear that his focus is on putting the right person on the right job'. This is no small achievement considering that from 2008 to 2012 he had effected 15,000 promotions. He clearly took his role very seriously and tried his best to do justice to it. Another aspect was the manner of doing business. By emphasizing goal focus, transparency, increasing participation, information sharing and empowering people for business decisions and by not interfering in their decisions, Mallya conveyed his high level of ethical orientation.

9. Radar-like Mindset

All the respondents (20) said he was very alert and observant and expressed this as follows:

'Nothing misses his eye', 'every move made in the market is known to him'. 'He knows what is happening in the market, has tremendous market intelligence with him', 'keeps track of all large corporate clients and their movements'. 'He is very very alert and his antennas are very very sharp'. 'He understands things at the macro level and gives guidance to the regions and zones. It is thanks to this that the quality of advances by the bank has been of good quality'. He is very quick and sharp along with being highly meticulous, well prepared and organized.

'When he comes for meetings he does thorough homework and is well prepared'. 'He knows where to focus, knows exactly what questions to ask'; 'he is extremely quick and intelligent and he runs faster than all of us'. Field-level officers (ZMs and RMs/DRMs) (11) said that while lending large amounts he comes out with information about a client history from 5 years or ten years ago. This helps in taking a clear decision which otherwise would have gone wrong because of the apparently clean profile on paper. Along with alert antenna, everyone spoke about his elephantine memory. 'He has a tremendous memory for numbers', 'he remembers what was promised by whom in the target setting and review meetings—you can't fool him'. He has his little notebook on which he puts down important/relevant information and otherwise he is entirely dependent on himself for information.

The above shows that he had his ear to the ground and knew what was happening in the relevant circles. Along with this grip on ground-level information relevant to the bank's business, he also had a powerful memory and both together aided him immensely in follow-up and in making good business decisions.

10. Olympian

Mallya has been an Olympian, driving himself and mobilizing people for high-quality goal achievement. His large vision to grow the bank resulted in having to operate like a true Olympian, relentlessly pursuing the goal, never satisfied, continuously moving ahead. People (10) said that, 'When he comes for meetings he does thorough homework and is well prepared'. 'He knows where to focus, knows exactly what questions to ask'; 'he is extremely quick and intelligent', 'very very sharp', 'he runs faster than all of us'.

All interviewed officers were unanimous in saying that Mr Mallya is a highly focused person. 'He never loses sight of the goal', 'is crystal clear about the goals and direction', 'all energy focused on achieving the goal', 'nothing distracts him'. 'He means business and he calls a spade a spade'. His high focus is supported by superb time management. All the interviewees have observed this quality in Mr Mallya. One person described it very well—'I have been to so many meetings. At every meeting he looks at his watch and commences his speech—it's a flawless delivery—and completes it well in time'.

A strong business focus was developed and conveyed to everyone relentlessly. The message given was of growth with quality. Mr Mallya clearly told people that they should follow procedures and that there was no need to take any shortcuts and that it was up to them to decide whether the proposal was bankable or not. They were told that there was no pressure either way. People were advised that sector-wise exposure was to be balanced and skews were to be avoided. He himself gave focus on asset quality and better NPA management. Review systems were robust and feedback was given in a logical and assertive style which clearly conveyed the expectations.

According to an AGM, the focus was on issues not on exercising authority and power ... this is the best thing which has happened here. In fact, the focus on results was so high that CMD was known to call up on his own and talk to ZMs sometimes even RM. In due course, the same focus percolated down the line as the next levels began to ask the same set of questions to their deputies and the culture was reinforced.

His Olympian goals combined with a focused approach undoubtedly immensely help him in keeping things on track, monitor and follow up.

11. Close Monitoring and Review

The empowerment and involvement is dovetailed with close monitoring, review and analysis. The bank continued the existing performance review systems; however, to everyone's relief those who did not meet the targets 'were not humiliated', 'there were no brickbats'. The approach utilized was more developmental, in terms of asking questions and giving suggestions on handling specific problems faced by the people. While there was freedom in target setting, once we have committed then we have to achieve it. CMD has his own diary where he would note down relevant figures and unless some major calamity happens targets are not revised.

The credit-monitoring department keeps track of early warning signals and sensitizes the operating units about the need for monitoring. Another initiative mentioned by the interviewees is the fortnightly reporting of pending issues with corporate office (if unattended for more than a month). Thanks to the introduction of this process, people made efforts to ensure that no issues were left pending. In due course, all these initiatives have led to close coordination across the hierarchy according to many of the field level interviewees leading to quick response to the customer.

Healthy internal competition was generated across the regions by displaying all target and performance-related information on the intranet. Besides this zone-wise performance, performances of the verticals are ranked based on selected parameters and displayed on the website.

Mallya insisted that all meetings must be regularly held. In fact, unlike CMDs over the years who participated briefly in these meetings, he sat through each meeting and presentation and listened very seriously. Meetings therefore became very important events in the organization and taken seriously by all. Everyone clearly understood the focus of the CMD on performance.

12. Lead by Example

As a public sector banker, he knew the issues and challenges faced in the scenario of scarce leadership talent and decided to handle it himself. One of the outstanding aspects of Mr Mallya's leadership style is the phenomenal way in which he became a coach and mentor for the top 100–400 (from GM to DRM level). This aspect is now discussed as follows. All the interviewees expressed their view about his leadership as follows:

He became the role model and educated and tirelessly coached his senior team to become better leaders. The descriptions of his style very clearly bring out that he played this role to perfection—'always available', 'every time you meet him you learn something new', 'you can approach him anytime and discuss with him'. 'He does not micro manage but if you approach he will clarify things'. 'He gives us very good guidance and ideas at the quarterly meetings'. 'He gives guidance on where to focus in the business based on the latest trends in the economy'. 'He gave us a good module and excellent technique for providing branch level leadership' indicating the extent to which Mr Mallya has gone to groom leaders. One of the managers brought out that while they have been working day in and day out for the last few decades, 'Mr Mallya helped us to rediscover what we are capable of doing with motivation. He probably rediscovered the talent in us....' He has never had to use his position/power to get things done. He has focused on his personal power of persuasion and inspiration. When things go wrong he still does not lose control, rather he focuses on giving assertive and clear feedback for improvement without getting aggressive or abusive. Many people have learnt by observing him how to do marketing.

In fact, it is through this style of educating, handholding and his highly motivational speeches that he built the self-confidence of people and gave them the courage to act.

As a result of this developmental approach and firm feedback, he has been able to develop many leaders down the line according to many of the GMs. People down the line including officers have expressed in unison that they 'feel proud of the bank', 'it's great to get recognition in the market', 'when we go out people recognize and treat us differently'. They used adjectives like feel 'proud', 'prestige', 'honor', 'name and fame' to belong to BoB. This is because, 'we get recognition in society', 'feel so happy and proud'. One of the managers described the feelings very eloquently, 'our hearts swell with pride. Ten years ago we were shy to introduce ourselves as Barodians'.

APPENDIX IV.1A: CAREER TRAJECTORY, AWARDS AND CONTRIBUTIONS

Current Assignments: Nominated as a Member of Governing Council of Centre for Advanced Financial- Research and Learning (CAFRAL), Member on the Board of India Infradebt Limited (Infradebt), Emami Limited, Nitesh-Estates Limited, Indigo Airlines, Coffee Day. Nominated as Permanent Invitee to the Board for Payment & Settlement Systems (BPSS) of Reserve Bank of India.

Advisor to Tata Capital Ltd and its subsidiaries (NBFCs), Member of the committee constituted by Finance Ministry to develop a road map for operationalizing the Bharatiya Mahila Bank; Member on Central Board of the State Bank of India.

Other Assignments: On the Board of Advisory Council of Centre for Advanced Financial Research and Learning (CAFRAL), the apex intellectual knowledge dissemination institute for Financial Sector. Chairman of Indian Banks Association from April 2011 to July 2012. He headed Government/RBI-appointed various expert Committees and contributed to shaping up better prudential policies benefiting the financial sector. He is a Member NIBM Governing Council. He has been Director on the Board of The New India Assurance Company Limited, Exim Bank, and IndiaFirst Life Insurance Company Limited—fastest emerging life insurance company. He is the President, Indian Institute of Banking and Finance (IIBF), the apex professional and educational institute in banking in India. He is the Chairman of the Governing Council of Institute of Banking Personnel Selection (IBPS).

Accolades Awards and Qualifications: Individual accomplishments: 'Business Standard' conferred upon the 'Banker of the year award' in 2010 and again in 2012, also recognized as the 'Banker of the year—2011' by *Business World*, considering the exemplary leadership role and personal excellence demonstrated as the Chairman and Managing Director, Bank of Baroda. 'Outstanding Finance Professional in 2010' by MCX-CNBC–TV 18; awarded 'Best CEO-Public Sector—2012' by *Forbes India.*

During his tenure, Bank of Baroda has consistently won several awards. It was adjudged as the 'Best Bank 2010' by *Business India*, Best Bank by CNBC, Fastest growing Bank among PSBs by *Business World*; and Bank of the Year 2010 (for India) by *Banker* Magazine UK-London. The Bank also won the 'Best Bank 2012' award of *Business India* for the second time, which is a unique distinction to receive such recognition. Thus, the inspiring leadership and innovative strategic thinking has not only taken Bank of Baroda to new heights of glory, but also enabled the Bank to receive wider recognition from the media in the form of awards and accolades.

Educational Qualification: Mr Mallya has a B.E. with distinction, from Regional Engineering College, Suratkal, Karnataka; a Post Graduate Diploma in Management from Indian Institute of Science (IISc), Bangalore and a Certificate in Industrial Finance, Indian Institute of Banking and Finance.

APPENDIX IV.1B: TOTAL BUSINESS OF BOB AND OTHER PUBLIC SECTOR BANKS (₹ IN CRORES)

Public sector banks in India	2008	2009	2010	2011	2012
Bank of Baroda	258,735	335,648	416,297	534,115	672,248
% Growth	24.07	29.73	24.03	28.30	25.86
Punjab National Bank	285,959	364,463	435,931	555,006	673,363
% Growth	20.92	27.45	19.61	27.32	21.33
Bank of India	263,487	332,617	398,253	515,040	567,049
% Growth	28.64	26.24	19.73	29.32	10.10
Canara Bank	261,310	325,112	403,986	506,440	559,544
% Growth	8.48	24.42	24.26	25.36	10.49
United Bank of India	178,125	235,236	289,355	353,447	400,751
% Growth	20.71	32.06	23.01	22.15	13.38
Oriental Bank of Commerce	132,423	166,869	203,747	234,962	267,943
% Growth	22.46	26.01	22.10	15.32	14.04
Corporation Bank	94,610	122,496	155,937	203,597	236,611
% Growth	30.85	29.47	27.30	30.56	16.22

SOURCE: Data received from BoB, 2013.

APPENDIX IV.1C: COMPARATIVE RANK (TOTAL BUSINESS) OF BOB AND OTHER PUBLIC SECTOR BANKS

Public sector banks	2008	2009	2010	2011	2012
Bank of Baroda	4	2	2	2	2
Punjab National Bank	1	1	1	1	1
Bank of India	2	3	4	4	3
Canara Bank	3	4	3	3	4
Union Bank of India	5	5	5	5	5
Oriental Bank of Commerce	6	6	6	6	6
Corporation Bank	7	7	7	7	7

SOURCE: Data received from BoB, 2013.

APPENDIX IV.1D: COMPARATIVE RANK (IN TERMS OF % GROWTH) OF BOB AND OTHER PUBLIC SECTOR BANKS

Public sector banks	2008	2009	2010	2011	2012
Bank of Baroda	3	2	3	3	1
Punjab National Bank	5	4	7	4	2
Bank of India	2	5	6	2	7
Canara Bank	7	7	2	5	6
Union Bank of India	6	1	4	6	5
Oriental Bank of Commerce	4	6	5	7	4
Corporation Bank	1	3	1	1	3

SOURCE: Data received from BoB, 2013.

APPENDIX IV.2: CULTURE ATTRIBUTES AT BANK OF BARODA

Culture attributes	Before	After
Teamwork	High	Very High
Commitment to Organization	High	Very High
Motivation	High	Very High
Conflicts	Moderate	Low
Inter-department Collaboration	Moderate	Very High
Top-down Comm.	Very High	Very High
Bottom up Comm.	Moderate	High
Excellence	High	Very High
Target and Performance Orientation	Very High	Very High
Global Benchmarking	High	High

Case V: R.K. Dubey, Connecting Horizon with Ground Realities

ACHIEVEMENTS AND CONTRIBUTIONS

The leadership journey of Shri R.K. Dubey is studded with many landmark achievements in the positions he occupied, whether PNB where he rose to become General Manager; or in Central Bank of India where he was Executive Director for two and half years (September 2010 to January 2013); or in Canara Bank where he was Chairman and Managing Director for 21 months (details of his career trajectory and awards and accolades are given in Appendices V.1 and V.2). He has an impeccable track record of not only doing things differently but also doing different things. He effortlessly enfolded both the approaches to achieve the goals. He demonstrated tremendous passion and commitment for contributing beyond the prescribed role boundary. As a leader, he seamlessly integrated thought, emotion and action, indicating a rare capability to be a holistic leader (for details of his contributions as CMD Canara Bank, see Appendix V.3).

THE PRESENT CASE

He is a man who is known, admired and respected for his unique and significant contributions in every position that he occupied as a leader and therefore considered a role model by anyone who came in contact with him. The present case sketches the profile, competencies and capabilities of R.K. Dubey the Leader, which enabled him to strive throughout his life, to move relentlessly from one orbit to the next. Before writing the case, we wanted to get a feel of the work culture of Canara Bank, and hence did a rough sensing by talking informally to five persons from the bank (see Appendix V.4 for the details).

We had extensive interviews with 10 individuals who worked closely with Mr Dubey, while he was in the Canara Bank. On the basis of content analysis of the 20 hours of in-depth interviews with various individuals, we have identified the following themes of his leadership as perceived by the interviewees.

The following case highlights the ways and means by which Mr Dubey could make tremendous contributions to the transformation of Canara Bank from its state of slumber. The content analysis-based information has been organized under the following leadership capabilities:

1. Connecting Horizon with Ground Realities
2. Entrepreneurial Path Breaker
3. People Power
4. Constituency Management
5. Olympian Zeal
6. Strategic Vision and Long-term Perspective
7. Leading by Example
8. Humane
9. Radar-like Mindset
10. Ethical

1. Connecting Horizon with Ground Realities

One of the most powerful and visible leadership capabilities of Mr R.K. Dubey has been connecting horizon with ground realities, by not only carrying big vision but also executing the same. Right from the time he joined the bank, it was clear to people that he was clear about the direction for the bank. People who heard his initial speech after taking charge said, 'it was apparent that he had ambitious plans for the bank' (5).

He had to prove his mettle within a short tenure of 21 months; however, the ground realities were completely unsupportive. In fact, at the very first Top Management Committee (TMC) meeting, he could see the low morale of the people in the bank. The whole bank had been struggling to make a total business of 5 lakh crores and was trying hard to cross a level of 6 lakh crores for more than a year but was not able to do so. At that point of time, the total business stood at 5.31 lakh crores. He knew this meeting was a make or break meeting and hence retorted, 'then this bank does not need a Chairman'. People were taken aback and then the discussions started. Through a lot of back and forth discussions and encouragement, the team came forward voluntarily to cross a level of 600,000 crores, which was far higher than the moderate one of ₹560,000 crores they mentioned earlier.

His first focus was on understanding the people because, 'I knew that only through people will execution be possible'. He was acutely aware that imposing a target would not get the results and hence he said, 'It is up to you, you decide how much you want the bank to achieve'. According to the interviewees (8), he took the opportunity to remind them about the bank's 100-year-old history and its most illustrious icon, Mr B. Ratnakar, chairman of the bank in the 1980s. He tried to activate their pride and the need to live up to the bank's earlier achievements and stature.

Describing the scenario when he took over as CMD, all the persons whom we interviewed said the following:

'The bank was directionless'. 'It was a divide and rule culture'. 'There was a fear culture because around 14,000 charge sheets had been issued during the previous regime'. 'There was a fear psychosis'. 'We felt frustrated, there was so much uncertainty'. 'There was no growth and there was too much disconnect and negativity'.

'A culture of excuses had sprung up'. Describing the situation most people said (7), 'We felt suffocated'. 'We were in low spirits'. 'We were in our cocoons'. People had to be shaken out of their deep slumber, which he did through a multitude of approaches discussed in detail in the section on people management. He gave clear goals to the entire bank—CASA, thrust in retail, cross selling—fee income and recovery—NPA management. According to the eight GMs we interviewed, he was very supportive and said, 'Tell me what hurdles you are facing and I will remove them'. 'He set priorities and gave clear directions'. 'You do the work and I will facilitate you'; 'tell me what business growth you want to achieve and I will do it'. People (10) said, he made an effort to understand us and our requirements. He committed to support us and when he kept his word we felt compelled to work hard.

Mr Dubey therefore began confidence-building exercise by visiting each of the 34 circles. In fact, he was the only CMD to have visited all the circle offices. According to all the interviewees, he visited most of the circles within a short span of three months and the remaining few were also visited in the next three to four months. At every circle, he met all the branch managers and executives, listened to their grievances and suggestions and also met the prominent customers invited over breakfast/lunch/dinner/high tea. He also addressed the entire staff of the circle. Press and media were also addressed during every such visit to boost the brand image. The general feeling in the bank was that, if he is working so hard for the bank, why not we? The General Managers we talked to (6) said that the targets became binding because, 'we had set the targets ourselves'.

Once the targets were agreed upon, systems were put in place to monitor performance of the senior team. This was shared by most of the interviewees (6) as follows: 'He drove the targets positively through follow-up'. 'His execution skills are of a very high order'. 'He was not only ambitious, he knew how to make things happen'.

The third major step taken was to restructure the bank to bring sharp focus. According to all the persons we talked to, new verticals were added. For example, two General Managers were designated for NPA handling—one to focus on large-value NPAs and one to handle small-value NPAs, since each needed a different approach. Two GMs were appointed for advance monitoring of accounts likely to turn NPAs. Lok Adalat schemes were used extensively for reduction of small-to-medium value NPA/suit-filed accounts. Results were far beyond expectations at some places. A transaction wing was created to implement installation of more than 3000 onsite ATMs before March 2014. He closely monitored progress on a weekly basis. When feedback was given about their lending rates being uncompetitive on MSME, agriculture, retail, etc., some sensing and verification was done and policy modifications were made to facilitate ease of lending.

He used the power of communication to great effect. Key information was shared with each and every employee. Thus, mobile numbers of more than 45,000 employees were gathered and regular SMSs and important information about new initiatives and products were shared with all. On the above matters, mailers were also sent to all the branch managers and above. Every month a bilingual communication was sent from CMD's desk to the entire staff, reviewing the previous month and setting the direction for the current and next month. This kept everyone updated and focused on clear priorities.

Above all, there was plenty of freedom and empowerment. Almost everyone (8) said, 'He trusted us so much that we used to be scared of making mistakes'. 'Once a decision was made, he focused on getting the result. He did not micromanage'.

By galvanizing people, setting focused targets along with restructuring and close monitoring, Mr Dubey successfully connected, horizon with ground reality. In addition, tremendous thrust was given to come up with new and innovative ways of attracting customers and mobilizing business. This is discussed at length in the next leadership capability given as follows.

2. Entrepreneurial Path Breaker

Mr Dubey showed tremendous entrepreneurial capability to find solutions to many problems of trying to teach the elephantine bank to dance. As one of the GMs said, he had promised in the first TMC, 'I will make the elephant dance and he did it in such a short span of time'.

According to one of the GMs who had met him just as he took charge of the bank, 'He was very clear from the very beginning what he wanted to do. We realized this when at the time of the formal joining day at the bank, he gave a one and half hours speech on strengths and weaknesses of the bank, and his agenda for the bank'.

All the persons we talked to said in different ways that the bank was a monolith, saddled with many problems including downward trends in the business, in the credit portfolio, in the ranking as well as in the general sentiment. Galvanizing people and restructuring as well giving clear direction was only a good start. How to actually mobilize the customer and ensure greater credit disbursement, better business and above all create a better brand image? This was one of the core challenges facing him.

All the interviewees described his approach as follows: He was courageous and bold in decision making. He did not hesitate to take risks in pursuit of the goal. 'He came up with many innovative products and solutions and he encouraged us to come up with new products and solutions'.

All the interviewees said that:

- 'There were campaigns every week'. 'Road shows were done for CASA and retail. Wherever a road show was held, he would visit'. 'Whenever he visited in connection with a road show, he would address customers as well as the employees. There would be huge publicity and media would be present at these events'. 'At such road shows CMD would address press meets and customer meets, there would be media and TV channels and a branch inaugural would also take place'.
- Media presence at these road shows attracted more people to participate. For example, car loans, home loans and CGTMSE cases without collateral, without personal guarantee under MSME were widely publicized. The public was promised clearances on the spot. This attracted people in large numbers.
- Tie-up was made with all the major auto dealers. For Maruti, they had the highest credit financing for two consecutive years, that too during the auto slowdown, among all the PSBs and even got ahead of some of the major private peers.

Explaining how innovatively business was done people said the following:

- 'We brought together the bank, customers as well as auto companies and builders at a common venue'. Prospective customers could explore, decide on a product, book it with a seller and apply for a loan with the bank. Instant clearance was given subject to legal scrutiny (7).
- Tie ups were done with channel partners—builders, dealers, etc. (10).
- Approvals for housing loans were done within a day on the website to widen the reach to Gen. Y customers (6).
- Advertisements were placed on social media platforms (6).

Another new idea which was introduced to the bank was to focus on earning through volumes rather than through high cost. 'In fact Canara Bank lowered its interest rates on almost all the type of loans to below that of SBI as base rate of the bank was brought down by 5 basis point compared to all other banks'. Earlier, we were higher than them. People laughed at us but within a year our business volume grew tremendously—retail growth of more than 50% y-o-y and more than 25% on all other loans.

- We could beat Axis Bank and ICICI that year on retail business (8).
- As a result of these initiatives, customers who had fled us came back (5).

Many new schemes targeting customer-specific needs were developed. In an unprecedented move for a public sector bank, these were shared with zonal managers/circle heads and customers to get feedback. Suggestions were taken, schemes were modified and quickly launched (5).

The power of video conferencing technology was used to get all the 34 circle heads at the TMC on a fortnightly basis. This is being highlighted because although the technology existed in the market, the IT department had not added this feature and as a result not all circle heads could participate at the TMC meetings. It is the introduction of this technology which helped him to conduct bi-monthly meetings in the presence of the entire top team, hence deepening the relationship.

Decision making from the Head Office (required for certain value of loans) also happened quite smoothly. Further at the policy level, things were simplified and greater transparency was introduced.

In an unprecedented move, at a Branch head meeting Mr Dubey asked a non-performing manager, 'Tell me if you are uncomfortable in your job ... if so I will transfer you to a portfolio where you can do better'. This was initially viewed with scepticism by all. When the person concerned was given a good portfolio, people were convinced that CMDs focus was on performance and not any vendetta.

The spirit he tried to instil in the bank was to above all, 'never miss an opportunity'. The result of the focused thrust was soon visible. Retail loans shot up from 10% to 40% in less than a year; retail growth increased to about 60–65%. Gross NPAs were down to 2.5% and the bank received four awards for technology. By any standards this has been a creditable performance by the bank.

3. People Power

One of the most important routes through which Mr Dubey achieved many of the targets was through people power. This is noteworthy because when he joined the bank people were withdrawn, frustrated and fearful. Yet within a couple of months he was able to revive their competitive spirits.

All the persons that we interviewed said the following about how this was achieved:

'He always focused on the positives'. 'He took the pains to reach out to all of us through the circle visits'. He travelled relentlessly for three months, reaching out to the whole bank. 'He was like a cool gentle breeze on a hot summer day'. 'He introduced a more participative style. Nothing was imposed'. 'He reminded us about our glorious past'. 'He asked us to work and said I will support you'. 'He said don't be afraid of punishment, I will protect you if you make a genuine mistake'.

'He attacked the major impediment which was creating fear and inaction among employees—1000 charge sheets which were issued in the previous dispensation'. People (10) said he gave assurances that if mistakes were unintentional people would not be harassed; 'he was very protective of the people'. The number of pending charge sheets was brought down to 67 within a short span of 6 months. These 67 were the cases where fraud/court cases were involved.

He not only said this, he also worked to deal with them—he worked closely with all concerned agencies and ensured that within a few months, the number of pending complaints was brought down from 400 to below 100.

In the process of reducing the fear levels in the organization many initiatives were taken. People shared about the many steps which were taken to become highly accessible to all:

'A hotline was created by which anybody could reach out to him'. 'This was the first time ever, that people down the line could, approach the CMD and talk to him'. 'This accessibility gave a real boost to all of us'. 'He brought in the rule that all charge sheets should be closed six months before a person retires'. 'In this way people could retire with dignity without the shadow hanging over them towards the fag end of their careers'; 'once the target was fixed and agreed upon, he did not interfere'.

All the interviewees said that as a result of his accessibility, people found that 'he was a very helpful person—if anyone went to him with a genuine problem, he would go ahead to support the person'. 'He had a humane approach'; 'he was a very trusting person'. 'Fear of taking decisions and lending was gone'.

'Most significantly, when people responded to his call and brought results, Mr Dubey did something unheard of in Canara Bank—he distributed about 35 crores (of government-approved scheme for payment to employees) as cash incentives. Decision to give the incentives was not taken in the previous three years despite this facility being available'.

He not only made himself accessible, but also reached out to people on his visits both formally and informally. The following observations were made by all the interviewees we talked to.

'Wherever he visited, he called for Town Hall meetings where he addressed all employees, including the staff levels'. 'When people spoke or complained, he listened to them very carefully regardless of level. He tried to help wherever possible'. 'He believed in personal touch'. He motivated performers at General Manager level through early promotion interviews. As a result, 10 Canara Bank GMs became eligible to attend Executive Director interviews (conducted by the government) in 2014. 'He succeeded because he had a very inclusive approach' (10). 'He had no favourites—everyone felt equally close to him' (6). 'There were many opportunities to celebrate. Families were also invited' (7). 'We became one big family' (10).

The results of these initiatives have been tremendous, as indicated by the following statements by all the interviewees:

'We felt highly motivated and surcharged'. 'We felt proud to be a part of this bank'. 'We felt lots of respect'. His various actions made us feel that he was genuinely concerned about us. 'We experienced his care and love'. 'Our confidence increased'. 'All of us were his fans'—everyone down the line. 'We felt important'. 'We felt that he is a part of us, therefore always felt that he was with us. It was fantastic'.

As the above section brings out, Mr Dubey mobilized, enthused and motivated people by walking with them, leading them as well as following them.

4. Constituency Management

Mr Dubey was keenly aware about the various constituencies that he had to manage in order to attain his vision for the bank. He made efforts to develop a good relationship with the employees, customers, board, media and analysts, i.e., all the stakeholders.

He strived to reach out to them all in different ways. All interviewees said the following about his efforts at managing various constituencies and analysts:

He listened to all employees at all levels and helped solve their problems. He paid attention to complaints from employees, listened carefully to them. Anyone down the line could send sms or give him a call. He always took calls. If he was busy he would call back. He took care of people and they became his biggest ambassadors. Even with unions and officers associations credibility was built about his intent for the bank. For example, laptops and mobile phones were given to Branch Managers before they became a union issue.

Employee grievances (registered on the website under the Samadhan scheme) were handled and resolved within two days. 'Over a period of a few months he knew his team members by name'. 'He uplifted the mood of the people'. 'He enhanced their competitive spirit'. 'He could inspire the team to bring the name of the bank on top'. Tremendous efforts were made at brand building. 'We got plenty of publicity thanks to the many campaigns and activities, where CMD himself addressed and media followed him'. He built one-to-one relationships with board members. In his words, 'When I needed help of any kind, I explain rationally and then requested them personally and they would respond'.

He brought customer delight by sanctioning loans, in principle, on the same day at credit camps. We made customers further happy by bringing the builder, the auto company together on the same platform as the banker; similarly, we delighted the customer by sanctioning loans online. He paid keen attention to listen to customers. His door was always open for them. Time to resolve customer complaints was reduced from 60 days to maximum 7 days.

By connecting with different stakeholders, by making them feel recognized and valued and by taking care of their genuine problems, Mr Dubey managed to get the goodwill of all stakeholders. They in turn supported him through various situations.

5. Olympian Zeal

Mr Dubey has an Olympian mindset. He said, 'I am an impatient person, I have no tolerance for delays ... over the years I have become more patient and perseverant because of my need to win and continuously excel'.

Before joining Canara Bank he had already done his homework on the bank and made his plans. He was keenly aware that he had a short stint of 21 months and yet was determined to produce outstanding results. He was successful at this (see Appendix for details).

He reached his seemingly impossible goals by setting four clear thrust areas as mentioned earlier. At the same time, he worked on the people side and activated the collective body as he realized that without their collective efforts, his ambition would not have taken the bank too far. Thus by inspiring people, by getting their participation in the target-setting process and by empowering them, he galvanized people. All the persons we met highlighted the following aspects of Dubey's style, which enabled the bank to reach the tough goals:

He closely monitored performance on a weekly basis. 'He drove performance positively. There was positive pressure; there was no negativity at all'. He enabled speed of functioning through active use of technology for communication with the entire top team. 'He achieved the impossible through these efforts, where he himself was actively involved in the entire process'.

There was high quest for excellence. He was never satisfied. 'He was a tough task master'. He was highly competitive. In fact, discussions in the weekly TMC meetings were focused on market share and how to beat other banks.

Whenever there was some achievement of a private sector bank in the news, he would call up the Executive Directors and say, 'why can't we do this?' (according to the Executive Director whom we interviewed).

In an unusual move, Canara Bank looked to the private sector for benchmarking purposes. The speed of the bank enhanced significantly because of the speed of decision making and empowerment down the line. For example, the clearance time for retail, MSME and agriculture proposals went down from 1.5 months to 1–2 days. Canara Bank raced ahead of different competitors in different segments—on retail we beat Axis and ICICI.

Dubey was in such a hurry that to cope with what he had unleashed, he would sometimes have to clear a mind-boggling 500 files every day according to an executive director who worked closely with him.

From the start he was clear about performance focus. He did not tolerate non-performance. One of the General Managers gave the example of the target for completion of their new office in Mumbai. Mr Dubey visited the premises and said 'let's plan the inaugural for May (6 months before the scheduled date in November) … I am inviting the Finance Minister for the inauguration'. He gave the target and left it to us. He gave a pep talk to the engineers. There was no micromanagement subsequently and the building was completed as per the new date and the FM, indeed, inaugurated the new premises of circle office Mumbai at BKC on 25 May 2013.

Similarly, he gave a challenge to the top team to open 1000 odd branches during 2013–2014. They achieved 800 in that period with onsite ATMs. Normal lead time to open a branch is 2–3 months. On the matter of creating onsite ATMs, he gave hourly clearances to achieve the target. The board of the bank decided that more branches are required in North, Central, East, West, not ignoring South so that CASA of the bank could be improved in 2–3 years, hence the efforts to expand.

The above finding brings out that Mr Dubey is a man with tremendous Olympian zest, continuously raising the bar. He is a truly excellence-seeking leader.

6. Strategic Vision and Long-term Perspective

Mr Dubey had a futuristic approach to create the next growth trajectory for the bank. Many of his decisions and actions were designed to sustain the life of the organization into the future.

People (7) said, 'he had clear plans for the bank'. He knew where he wanted to take the bank; he communicated this plan to people in a simple way so that it reached one and all; he decided profit figures in advance and then worked towards it.

'He asked us to prioritize and work only on four clear domains, which would benefit the bank in the long term'. He pushed for long-term sustainability by changing the product portfolio mix. Greater thrust was given to retail transactions which in his judgement would be stable. In contrast, bulk deposits were not given a push, since they could vanish at any time and were high cost to the bank. Parallel thrust was given to NPA recoveries so that bad debt was reduced for improving the financial health of the bank.

Tie-ups were done with housing, vehicle and education loans for the convenience of the customer. Massive recruitment—about 15,000 in 2013–2014 was done keeping in view the large-scale retirements—3000 every year in the coming three years so that the bank's growth is not hindered for lack of manpower as also to have adequate manpower at all the levels, including rural and semi-urban branches for faster delivery and smooth functioning. Another aim was to bring down the average age of employees from above 50 to below 40, which was subsequently achieved. This, in turn, brought a wave of tech-savviness and enthusiasm in the cadre.

Thrust was given to technology-based products which Gen-Y would be happy to use since they form a significant percentage of total users. The focus was on top line growth. All round thrust was given to growth and speed of decision making (for sanctioning loans) was drastically reduced from 75 days to 1–2 days as mentioned earlier.

Even the incentive money was strategically given. Those who excelled in the thrust areas of the bank were given a larger percentage. Those who excelled in fee-based income were rewarded the most. Credit limits were increased and strategies were developed for CASA.

He did everything in large volumes, added more than 1800 branches taking total to over 5600 branches, added more than 4000 ATMs taking total to over 8000 ATMs, next only to SBI among PSBs. He added over 15,000 new recruits taking total to more than 45,000 employees. Number of e-transactions increased from below 40 to above 60 per day in just one year. Although he did not articulate a large dream or vision to the employees, the above actions clearly indicate a large vision and concern for the future of the bank. Thus, his entire efforts were focused on creating tomorrow today.

7. Leading by Example

Mr Dubey led team Canara Bank in a very efficient manner. He practiced what he preached and did what he promised. Through this approach, he successfully created and mobilized a large team. Most people (8) said the following about him:

'When he committed something, he delivered as per his promise'. 'Through empowerment and by observing Mr Dubey, we learnt how to make decisions'. 'We actually learnt a lot about how to run a bank'. 'It was the first time somebody explained to us the reasons for making a business decision, alternatives and their implications'. 'We learnt how to handle a large enterprise'. 'In the case of large value NPA companies, he would himself do video conference with them and resolve the matter then and there'. When we had doubts, he would say, 'Let's make it happen'. 'We learnt the power of empowerment through him'.

Since in every way Mr Dubey showed exemplary behaviour and tasted success, and therefore people rightfully looked up to him a role model.

8. Humane

Mr Dubey was well known for reaching out to people, regardless of level, down to the class for staff and freely relating with them.

People (10) said the following about him:

'Chairman took pains to talk to everyone including class four employees'. 'When Town Hall meetings were arranged, he wanted every employee of the circle to be present; he would listen carefully when people spoke; he did not ignore feedback and complaints'. 'He was always positive and never criticized any actions taken in the past'.

Some persons (4) said, 'He even helped those who were not positively inclined towards him'. All the interviewees talked about his humane and positive attitude as follows:

He treated people extremely well. He had so much love, care and concern for us. He genuinely cared for us, was kind hearted, sensitive and concerned about people. He would appreciate with a full heart, was a good listener, he meant what he said, was very reasonable. If we give logic and explain, he could be convinced and change his stance; he never said no to genuine cases. At the same time, he could see through people if they tried to mislead him.

While people mentioned the above, all of them also said the he was upfront; he was kind yet tough and he expected people to keep their commitment. In fact, one of his favourite phrases was 'Tough Love'.

The above quotes tell a tale of a man who was socially sensitive, humane, caring, a person who focused on the task and drove it through a human contract and a gentleman's agreement based on trust rather than using position power; or create, fear and threat to make people work. It reflects the profile of a balanced person who did not succumb to the irresistible and heady lure of power and the seductive comfort of sycophancy.

9. Radar-like Mindset

Mr Dubey's radar-like mindset is evident from his close touch with happenings around him. One of the major benefits he got by listening to complaints was an understanding of ground reality of the bank. By listening to different viewpoints, he could tap into new ideas.

He kept track of what the competitors were doing and this information he shared with his team members sometimes to challenge them, at other times to motivate them.

People (7) said the following about his information orientation, 'He exhorted branch managers to go out in the field and observe what the competitors were doing'. He used to encourage us (GM level) to go to the market, check competitors' products and design something similar or better with innovation for the bank. He told us (GM level) to watch other banks. He was so alert that nothing missed his attention. Many new products were introduced through such sensing and smelling of the environment. In this way, he could ensure that the bank kept up with others; that new ideas were brought in. There was no arrogance, throwing his weight around, showing off or being status conscious.

10. Ethical

Mr Dubey has a strong reputation as an ethical banker. Although he was highly competitive it was not at the cost of ethical norms of functioning. One powerful indicator of this orientation is his approach to those who were denied promotion. In an unprecedented move he allowed the system of appeals. The complaints were examined seriously and up to 10.00 (genuine cases) were promoted.

Another indicator is his habit of not putting down his predecessors or criticizing them for their actions. In fact, he dipped into the past only to bring out motivating stories (7).

While he was a positive person, for the organizational cause he was tough on nonperformers and defaulters (8). People (7) said the following about Dubey's ethical orientation. 'He did not use any dubious means'. 'He meant what he said'. He was upfront'. 'He was a man of integrity', 'we felt that we were in safe hands', 'he was very fair and just leader'. The most powerful indicator of his ethics and concern for employees was the way in which he fought the injustice meted out to more than 1000 employees who were charge sheeted mostly on minor matters some of which were even undeserved. By giving focus on solving these cases by actively representing with the agencies such as CVC, etc., he showed his ethical orientation.

The above brings out that Mr Dubey is inner directed. He powerfully integrates thought with action by focusing both on ideas and execution. He walks the talk, demonstrates courage of conviction and in a true sense emerges as a leader of men, having immense faith in people power. It demonstrates high capability of managing constituencies of different stakeholders—both internal and external.

MR DUBEY—INNER ARCHITECTURE

Mr Dubey's spiritual quotient is of a very high order. He has deep faith in a higher power, bordering to a belief in destiny. He is fundamentally a peace lover and harmony seeker who likes to create such a positive environment wherever he goes. His tolerance of diversity is very high and he believes in bringing people together and harmonizing diverse and contradictory forces. He is basically a consensus builder with immense faith in teamwork. He is a man of ambition who has constantly sought to leave a legacy.

Mr Dubey's work ethic has been of a very high order. He is known to have relentlessly worked 16–17 hours a day for weeks on end. He is always receptive and open to new ideas, regardless of the source. His life goal is highly contribution centric with a relentless focus of shifting the goal post. Being a hard-core optimist, he is never disheartened by setbacks and failures. In fact, he believes in learning from his failures and mistakes and converting them into future successes.

His role models are Abraham Lincoln, A.B. Vajpayee and A.P.J. Abdul Kalam. He mentioned Jawaharlal Nehru's words 'I don't believe in excuses for delay, I believe in getting things done' reflecting a temperament of task execution. He has a deep connection to the lines of the poem by Emerson:

The woods are lovely, dark and deep,
But I have promises to keep
And miles to go before I sleep

These lines indicate his deep commitment and hard work. He also mentioned that Jonathan Livingstone Seagull is his favourite book, perhaps reflecting his endeavour to fly higher and higher, never satisfied and complacent, charged up with a ceaseless zest to fly higher and higher.

APPENDIX V.1: R.K. DUBEY—ACHIEVEMENTS

Chairman and Managing Director, Canara Bank (January 2013– September 2014): During his tenure as CMD Canara Bank, the total business increased by over ₹240,000 crores as on 30 September 2014 registering a growth of 45%. The bank opened over 1800 branches, added more than 3800 ATMs and recruited over 14,000 young staff to expand and manage the business. In this period, Canara Bank achieved one of the lowest NPAs (GNPA of 2.49%) in the banking industry registering a record cash recovery of ₹5494 crores during financial year 2013–2014—a creditable achievement where most of the banks are paralyzed by rising NPA levels.

In this period, innovative products and services were developed to deepen financial inclusion. A centre for 'Entrepreneurship Development of Women' was established to train rural women in micro finance.

Projects 'Udaan' and 'Project Shikhar' were introduced in this period to transform the work ethics and culture of the bank, enhancing levels of motivation and commitment of employees.

Canara Bank effectively meets the targets on financial inclusion in 1624 villages with more than 2000 population, and 3860 villages with less than 2000 population. Canara Bank garnered a total business of 5588 crores through 536 newly opened branches. Through the use of business correspondents, ₹280 crores were made and innovative processes, systems and technology were used in the achievement of these objectives. Many initiatives were taken to spread financial literacy; 1.19 lakh persons from the general public as well as 30,000 school children in Uttar Pradesh along with their teachers underwent sessions.

A number of large-scale initiatives were taken under CSR—64 self-employment training initiatives were supported in 17 states and 51,790 members of the public were trained through this initiative. Mr Dubey's performance track record was equally outstanding in Central Bank where he was ED from September 2010 to January 2013. He revamped HR policies of the bank and introduced a robust marketing thrust, and retail banking and cross selling received special emphasis. Above all, Mr Dubey was able to awaken the sleeping giant and made its presence felt across the nation.

Recruitment of badly needed staff was relaunched with vigour to support the bank's growth plans. Through dialogue with unions, officers associations, the concept of co-partnership was evolved. He introduced many welfare schemes to look after the employees of the bank. All such strategies significantly boosted the sagging morale of the staff which had become weak due to frequent confrontation between management and unions. Rationalization of RRBs, financial literacy, credit-counselling centres and rural self-employment centres as per the Government of India's mandate were implemented in all the 56 lead districts of the bank.

He has been the Chairman of Canbank Venture Capital Fund Limited, Canara Bank Securities Limited, Canbank Factors Limited, Canbank Computer Services Limited, Canara Robeco Asset Management Company Limited and Canara HSBC Oriental Bank of Commerce Life Insurance Company Limited for the period January 2013 to September 2014; Director of Cent Bank Home Finance and Cent Financial Services Ltd., while being the Executive Director of Central Bank of India; Member of Managing Committee of Indian Banks' Association (2010–2014); Honorary Fellow of Indian Institute of Banking and Finance (IIBF) and Member of the Governing Council; Chairman—IBA Committee on Agro Business and MSME for the year 2013–2014 (most of the recommendations of the committee were accepted by RBI and are under implementation); Member—CII National Council on Financial Sector Development 2013–2014.

Mr Dubey has 37 years of work experience in three large public sector banks in India. He assumed the office of Chairman and Managing Director of Canara Bank from January 2013 and superannuated in September 2014. Previously, he held the office of

Executive Director of Central Bank of India from September 2010 to January 2013. He has a total experience of working as a whole-time director on the board of both the nationalized banks for more than 4 years on policy making, strategy crafting and administration. He commenced his banking career with Punjab National Bank as a management trainee in November 1977 and rose to the level of General Manager in 2008 and covered all operational areas of banking including administration at rural, semi-urban, urban and metro all over the country before moving to Central Bank of India as an Executive Director.

APPENDIX V.2: AWARDS, ACCOLADES AND QUALIFICATIONS

Awards and Accolades

Best Banker Award 2012 conferred by RBI Deputy Governor; Best Banker of the Year 2013 conferred by Bangalore Management Association; 'Best Banker Award' for nurturing the RSETI movement in the country for the year 2012–2013 awarded by Ministry of Rural Development; Golden Peacock Award for Corporate Governance by Institute of Directors at London; 'Mahatma Gandhi Pravasi Samman' and a gold medal by NRI Welfare Society of India at the Global Achievers' Conclave held in the House of Lords, London; 'Outstanding Banker of the Decade 2013 award' by Unity International Foundation, New Delhi; Corporate Social Responsibility (CSR) by Institute of Directors and HR Excellence—2012 for excellence in HR Policies and Procedures; Greentech HR Award 2013; Conferred with Platinum Award under 'Best Strategy' and 'Training Excellence'. Conferred with 'HR ORIENTED CEO' (Platinum) for the valuable contribution to the HR arena and the Award for Best HR Strategies and Innovation in Employee Retention in the year 2011.

Life Time Achievement Award by Greentech International Foundation and ABP-BFSI, Mumbai; Inspirational Leader of the Year conferred by CMO Asia at Singapore; CEO with HR Orientation conferred by Institute of Public Enterprise (IPE) during Asia Pacific HRM Congress; Distinguished Fellow of Institute of Directors for the year 2013; Skoch Award 2013 for Corporate Social Responsibility; Global Visionary Award instituted by VISION Foundation, Ahmadabad; Top Rankers Excellence for CEO of the Year by Top Rankers Management Consultants, New Delhi; Outstanding Entrepreneurship conferred by Enterprise Asia and the Organizing Committee of the Asia Pacific Entrepreneurship Awards 2014 India, New Delhi; Legends of Bangalore by the Chamber of Commerce for India and International Business and Industries, Bangalore; Platinum Award for Innovation by Skoch Group.

Academic and Professional Qualification

He graduated as Bachelor of Science and M.A. in English Literature and followed it with the Certificated Associate of Indian Institute of Bankers (CAIIB) conducted by Indian Institute of Banking and Finance. He completed graduation in law (LLB) and post-graduation (MBA-HR) and also did a Post Graduate Level Program on Development Banking (Victoria University, Manchester, United Kingdom). He also did a specialized course in strategic management of financial institutions from Christ College, Cambridge, UK. He was also part of the Advanced Management Program on Leading Change by MDI Gurgaon in Europe and London, UK.

APPENDIX V.3: COMPARATIVE PERFORMANCE ANALYSIS OF CANARA BANK VIS-À-VIS PEERS FOR FY 2014

Performance of Canara Bank as of March 2014

The following are the major strengths for Canara Bank compared to its peers:

- **Strong Business Growth:** CB registered strong business growth in FY14 at 21% compared to BoB (20%), PNB (14%) and UBI (12%). BoI registered 26% growth in business.

- **Better Asset Quality:** CB's gross NPA ratio at 2.49% was the lowest compared to PNB (5.25%), UBI (4.08%), BoI (3.15%) and BoB (2.94%). Net NPA ratio for CB was at 1.98% compared to PNB (2.85%), UBI (2.33%), BoI (2%) and BoB (1.52%).
- **Growth in Non-interest Income:** CB registered the highest growth in non-interest income at 25% compared to 23% (BoB) and remaining peers were in the range of 8–14% growth.
- **Capital Adequacy:** CB's capital adequacy ratio is at 10.63% compared to UBI (10.12%) and BoI (9.97%). BoB's capital adequacy ratio was the highest at 12.28%, followed by PNB (11.52%).
- **Higher Productivity:** CB's productivity, measured in terms of domestic business per branch, was at ₹143 crores, highest among the peers. The domestic business per branch of PNB was at ₹117 crores, BoI (₹134 crores), BoB (₹134 crores) and UBI (₹130 crores) and CB was the highest in both domestic deposits per branch and advances per branch compared to peers.
- **Delivery Channels (Domestic):** CB opened 1027 branches and 2786 ATMs during the year, taking the total tally under the domestic branch network to 4750 and ATMs to 6312 as of March 2014 compared to PNB (6200 branches and 6940 ATMs), BoB (4874 branches and 6254 ATMs), BoI (4646 branches and 4225 ATMs) and UBI (3869 branches and 6429 ATMs). CB's ATM-to-Branch ratio was 133% compared to 166% (UBI), 128% (BoB), 112% (PNB) and 91% (BoI).

Weaknesses

CASA Deposits

- Due to concerted efforts, CASA ratio of CB improved to 25.90% from 25.12% in the previous year (2012–2013). However, it is lower compared to PNB (41.31%), BoB (31.76%), BoI (29.01%) and UBI (29.50%).

- During the year, the Bank added ₹17,219 crores CASA deposits (y-o-y growth of 20%) compared to ₹26,506 crores, 22% (BoB), ₹19,528 crores, 13% (PNB), ₹11,667 crores, 12% (BoI) and ₹6166 crores, 8% (UBI).

APPENDIX V.4: CANARA BANK WORK-CULTURE ATTRIBUTES

Cultural attributes	Before	After
Teamwork	Low	Very High
Commitment to Organization	High	Very High
Motivation	Low	Very High
Conflicts	High	Low
Inter-department Collaboration	Low	Very High
Top-down Comm.	Moderate	Very High
Bottom-up Comm.	Low	Very High
Excellence	Low	High
Target and Performance Orientation	Moderate	Very High
Global Benchmarking	Low	Moderate

PART IV: COMPARISON OF QUALITATIVE AND QUANTITATIVE FINDINGS

Perusal of the findings from both the questionnaire and interview data clearly brings out the high degree of similarity between findings using both the methods. The cases have brought to life the meaning of the virtuous leader attributes featured in the questionnaire. Virtuous leaders demonstrate humanistic approach, sensitivity to people, humility, ethical behaviour and performance focus. They also groom and build people, led by example, along with being visionary and courageous.

Key Conclusions from Qualitative Data

Weaving together the common strands emerging from the profiles of the five virtuous leaders brings out the following salient features which are conceptually grouped into 14 broad categories:

1. Looking Beyond—Creating Tomorrow Today
2. Looking Around—Alert Antenna
3. Looking Within—Evolving Self
4. Self-directed and Inner Directed
5. Heightened Ambiguity Tolerance
6. Unconventional
7. Nonegoistic Problem Solver
8. Heightened Social Sensitivity
9. Detached Contribution Focused
10. Ethical
11. Consensus Builder and People Shaper
12. Humanistic—Philosopher—King
13. Gestalt Holisticity—Integrating Thought, Emotion and Action
14. Philosophy and Purpose of Life

1. *Looking Beyond—Creating Tomorrow Today*

From times immemorial, kings used to call upon astrologers, palmists and oracles, like the oracles of Delphi, to predict the unfolding future, so they could prepare today for tomorrow. Such an urge is equally prevalent among common human beings. Those leaders who are unable to intuit the emerging future will be like the blind leading the blind into a tomorrow without being prepared for it. Mighty kingdoms and organizations, which revealed in the past and present but ignored the future, decayed and died down.

It is heartening to note in this context that the five virtuous leaders demonstrated tremendous desire, inclination and capability to envision the emerging future. They used their visioning power to prepare the organization for tomorrow. They did not stop at visioning; they also architected strategies, evolved appropriate structure and carved out suitable processes to build organizational readiness. This was done by them in order to cope with and effectively manage future eventualities.

2. *Looking Around—Alert Antenna*

One of the fundamental prerequisites for one's survival is sensitivity to the environment, so that one can adapt, accommodate and cope with the emerging challenges. This is not only true for human beings for their survival and growth, but also equally critical for the survival, growth and sustainability of organizations. In fact, today's business world is complex, full of ambiguities, uncertainties and volatility. Figuratively speaking, it is a battleground which not only spans the immediate physical surroundings of the city, the state or the region, but also encompasses global environment. In the last two decades, global competitive forces have intensified making survival a tough task for organizations because no one can predict who the competitor is and who will gain an edge in the market overthrowing the current market leaders. In such a scenario, economic size and scale is no longer a guarantee for survival, growth and sustainability since many Goliaths are being struck down by young Davids. In this upside-down world, small fish are swallowing the big fish.

It is in this perspective that organizations need to look around—develop radar-like mindset, evolve robust market intelligence, benchmark with best and learn on the feet. Only such organizations will, needless to say, have a competitive edge. All the virtuous leaders in our study amply engaged with the environment, made efforts to understand and prepare the organization for the same.

3. *Looking Within—Evolving Self*

In our long experience of working closely with the corporate sector as consultants and counsellors, we have seen that many companies do make efforts to look around and beyond; however, few are the companies which make the effort to look within in a constructive fashion and align themselves accordingly to the environment. This peculiar organizational behaviour is equally prevalent among leaders. As long as they get positive feedback and reinforcement about their styles and actions, they feel comfortable and look for more such reassuring and even flattering inputs. However when they find some feedback which does not confirm their thinking, the normal reaction is to immediately deny and reject the same. They use defence mechanisms to rationalize and justify their actions.

Such behaviour is more visible among arrogant and ego-centric CEOs who overrate themselves. Because of this attitude, rather than taking the organization on a growth trajectory, their attitude results in organizational complacency, stagnation and decay. We have seen many such leaders and organizations paying a heavy price for carrying such a disposition.

It may be worthwhile mentioning that individuals, who look within, who to take up self-responsibility and who own up to who they are, are able to continuously reinvent themselves and take a rebirth in their consciousness. Such people are highly evolving, growing and able to lead their lives functionally, creatively and productively—the essential aspects of virtuous leaders. In fact, self-introspection and self-acceptance constitute the basic fulcrum for growth, development and change. They relentlessly move towards higher consciousness and greater integration of their multiple selves—physical, emotional, intellectual and spiritual. These virtuous leaders continuously strive to move from id to superego, ignorance to enlightenment, *tamoguna* to *satoguna* and from instinctive and conditioned self to the intellectual and spiritual self. They have courage to face themselves and accept who they are including their follies and foibles. They make constant effort to change and transform. They are open to share their problems and get feedback from others. In leadership positions, they follow the 360° feedback approach. They are highly idealistic and truly self-actualizing in a Maslovian sense. They therefore lead their life creatively, productively and functionally.

Such evolved leaders have a sense of equanimity and equipoise enabling them to see multiple facets of reality, rather than being bogged down by their opinions and views. They do not get hijacked by their unconscious conspiracies, personal biases and prejudices and the dark shadow of the self. Therefore, their decisions and actions are more rational, realistic and practical, in the interest of both the organization and themselves.

Leaders with a capability to see the multiple facets of reality are more open-minded and demonstrate heightened capacity for ambiguity tolerance, diversity and dissent. All the virtuous leaders who feature in this research are characterized by being self-reflective, close to ground realities, combined with a sense of unpretentiousness and therefore are able to lead themselves and their organizations most productively.

4. *Self-directed and Inner Directed*

Being inner directed refers to the psychological disposition of virtuous leaders to carve out their own path, not influenced by fads, fashions, whims and fancies. Their direction is governed by their inner compass of purpose, beliefs and values. Such people are very clear about their goals, priorities and action plans to move ahead. They have the courage of conviction to take self-responsibility for their lives. They are strong realists who own up their failures and learn from them and move ahead. They are autonomous and do not necessarily conform to norms and mores. They operate more out of meaning, purpose and beliefs rather than being governed by social expectations, pressures and demands. Thus, such virtuous leaders are bold and courageous and not afraid of swimming against the tide. They believe in the lines from Invictus—'I am the master of my fate and captain of my soul'.[1] These people focus more on the larger issues and if needed compromise on trivial matters. They are highly futuristic, believe in looking ahead and preparing for tomorrow today.

Contrary to this, other directed individuals tend to be governed by societal forces pushing for conformity. They are not masters of the self unlike inner directed people who have truly mastered themselves. Globally, most of the iconic leaders have been found to be inner directed, not treading the beaten path, having the courage of conviction to overcome hurdles, rather succumbing to them. Virtuous leaders in this study abundantly revealed the qualities described above.

5. *Heightened Ambiguity Tolerance*

A healthy person is open minded, receptive and willing to explore divergence without being afraid of either change or differences. This person is highly inclusive in approach and is comfortable with contrarian and divergent views. Thus, such a person is able to perceive multiple facets of reality and thus has a comprehensive and holistic understanding of the same. Consequently, such a person has the ability to make objective decisions.

6. *Unconventional*

The unconventional person does not follow the beaten track; has the knack of seeing things differently, perceiving beyond the obvious, connecting the dots and finding new meanings in situations and events. Unconventional people focus more on the goals and outcomes rather than following conventions. Thus, they have the capability of devils advocacy, not accepting things at face value and even the courage to walk alone if needed. Such people even become crusaders for the right cause. People like Mandela, Lincoln, Einstein, Martin Luther King and Gandhi embodied the spirit of being unconventional.

7. *Non-egoistic Problem Solver*

These persons are the epitome of humility. They are emotionally stable and self-confident enough not to be destabilized by criticism from others. They respect fellow human being and treat them with dignity. They are positive, trusting and empowering and are open to learn from anyone. They are non-hierarchical and believe in an egalitarian value system. Above all, they are result focused and to this end, they solve problems which come up on the way. They integrate both rationale—emotive thought processes and are therefore able to make objective and implementable decisions.

8. *Heightened Social Sensitivity*

Humanistic orientation is at the core of the person with high social sensitivity. Such people are compassionate, loving, caring and full of empathy, while dealing with people around them. They understand the pains and pleasure of fellow human beings and are able to empathize with them and when needed they go all out to help others. They are basically people oriented and take care of their constituency and followers when they are in leadership positions.

9. *Detached Contribution Focus (Karma Yogi)*

The healthy person is a karma yogi believing in actions as duty without focus on rewards. They are excellence seekers, relentlessly raising the bar of performance and shifting the goal post. Completing the work excellently, they consider, is the greatest reward. Such people are self-motivated, resilient and rarely get demoralized. They believe in the saying, *blessed is he who has found his work.* They believe that they must do the best they can with what they have. They are strong followers of the saying by Mary Pickford[2] there is always another chance … this thing that we call 'failure' is not falling down but staying down. In a nutshell, they believe in moving towards the next orbit and creating the new curve without bothering about rewards.

10. *Ethical*

The ethical person is morally and financially above board. Such a person is not only personally ethical but also ensures ethical behaviour among the constituency members and followers. Decisions, actions and styles of these persons are geared towards the larger purpose and well-being of the nation, organization and various stakeholders. It is such ethical persons who follow the Gandhian principle of trusteeship. They are not greedy and therefore truly selfless and detached. They, in fact, alternate between attachment and detachment. They are the people of strong character and self-discipline. They believe in the dictum expounded by Cyrus[3]— 'A man's own is the arbitrator of his fortune'. Ethical persons are thus highly courageous and bold.

It is worthwhile mentioning at this stage that all the characteristics of the healthy person discussed above have been found in our case studies of virtuous leaders. There is generally agreement and awareness on the importance of the above characteristic to become a virtuous leader. The key, however, is regarding the ways and means by which one can become a virtuous leader. It would be worthwhile mentioning again that only a psychologically healthy and evolved human being can become a virtuous leader. This section now attempts to chart out the way and means to become a virtuous leader.

11. *Consensus Builder and People Shaper*

Organizations are able to successfully take on the competition only when they build people power and channel the same for goal achievement. Most of the research into the area of building competitive edge in organizations has come to the realization that competitive pillars such as cost leadership, customer leadership, innovation can provide only short-term competitive edge. They have concluded that it is only people power and culture of the organization which cannot be easily imitated and can therefore provide sustainable competitive edge. This was beautifully articulated by Henry Ford who said,

> *You can take my factories, burn up my buildings, but give me my people and I will build the business right back again.*

Great leaders are able to excite and motivate people through the power of their vision, involving people, adopting a participative and brain-storming approach, personal chemistry and engaging in grooming and developing people. The impact of such a participative and consensus building approach is remarkable, resulting in people feeling empowered, owning the decisions and actions and pursuing implementation with a sense of ownership.

As the great quote from Tao Te Ching[5] aptly emphasizes:

> *The greatest type of ruler is one of whose existence people are hardly aware*
> *Next best is a leader who is loved and praised*
> *Next comes the one who is feared*
> *The worst is the one who is despised*
> *When a leader doesn't trust the people, they will become untrustworthy.*
> *The best leader speaks little.*
> *He never speaks carelessly. He works without self interest and leaves no trace.*
> *When the work is accomplished, the people say: 'Amazing: we did it all by ourselves'.*
> (verse 17, The Art of Leadership, Lao Tzu, Tao Te Ching)

Such leaders are always with their teams, sometimes leading from the front, sometimes walking with the team and sometimes guiding from behind. In fact, the films *Chak De* and *Lagaan* illustrate the spirit of working together and winning together. Such builders invest in mentoring, counselling, coaching their team members and in this way they harness the collective potential of the team.

The narratives of all the five leaders bring out this phenomenon very powerfully. All have been great team builders, consensus seekers and people builders.

12. *Humanistic—Philosopher—King*

The ancient saying, 'No King can be a great king without being a greater philosopher' from the times of King Janaka, made clear prescriptions on characteristics of a virtuous king. Likewise, Plato eulogized that no philosopher can be a great philosopher without having a king's mind. In other words, both Janaka and Plato powerfully advocate that greatness lies in the integration of the minds of king and philosopher.

In China, a similar paradigm existed in ancient times for selecting kings and superiors. They used to ask questions designed to assess the presence of a holistic mind, integrating qualities of both philosopher and kings. For example, has he got a poetic temperament, does he have interest in music, drama, theatre?; does he have an artistic temperament, does he have evolved sensitivity about people's pains and pleasures?; is he a great warrior demonstrating mastery over weapons used in the battle field? This ancient wisdom is universally applicable and equally valid today. A study of the lives of leaders such as Gandhi, Mandela, Einstein, J.R.D. Tata, Martin Luther King, Jamsetji Tata, G.D. Birla, Lincoln, Jefferson, Roosevelt, Charles de, Nehru and Vajpayee amply demonstrates the presence of both kinds of qualities—that of philosophers as well as of kings. All virtuous leaders in the study have been strategists, worldly wise, practical with deep sensitivity and compassion for fellow human beings, an ability to relate with anyone and everyone, going beyond the barriers of positional hierarchy.

13. *Gestalt Holisticity—Integrating Thought, Emotion and Action*

Pedestrian leaders, who are trapped by the pulls and pressures of multiple forces around them, are not in a position to transcend and effectively manage conflicting and contradictory forces. They often get hijacked either by excess cognitive power (if they are the logical type) or get carried away by emotive power. They either became too thought centric or get overly action centric, obsessing over mundane and minute details, and micromanaging and missing the wood for the trees. In contrast, virtuous leaders integrate cognition, conative, affective and spiritual powers within themselves. They see their lives and roles holistically and are rarely trapped by their unconscious conspiracies. Since they have a highly evolved conscious self, they are able to manage their shadow—the dark side of their psyche. Analysis of their persona and styles, mindsets and value systems brings out their unique quality synthesizing and integrating their own inner diverse forces. This emanates from their emotional stability and inner balance.

14. *Philosophy and Purpose of Life*

The history and geography of a human life ultimately rests on one's life purpose. In fact, people do not follow leaders; they follow the purpose which the leader stands for and pursues. Leaders such as Gandhi, Mandela, Lincoln, Roosevelt, Martin Luther King, Lenin, Nelson Mandela, Charles de Gaulle, Jamsetji Tata, G.D. Birla and J.R.D. Tata had a large following because of the larger cause that they stood for. Purpose is like the engine which drives one's life and therefore once the purpose of one's life is achieved, one's life is over, unless one creates a new purpose. The life of great leaders demonstrates that they were continuously creating a new purpose, thereby inspiring and mobilizing people.

It is interesting that bulk of Indians who pray to Lord Krishna do not know where and how he died. In trying to understand the reason for the same, we stumbled upon the realization that Krishna died—in the minds of people—the day the war of Mahabharata was over. This is because people remember him dominantly for the role he played in this epic war.

Without purpose, human beings are directionless and fritter away their time and energy. Therefore, to become virtuous leaders, clarity of life purpose is essential. The five virtuous leaders in this study demonstrated tremendous clarity of purpose and aligned their roles and goals with the same.

Appendix

TABLE A3.1

Virtuous Leadership Attributes by Age: Frequency, Percentage and Ranks

Item no.	Virtuous leadership behaviours	Group 1			Group 2			Group 3		
		Age <30 years (268)			Age 31–45 years (233)			Age >46 years (233)		
		frequency	%	Rank	frequency	%	Rank	frequency	%	Rank
3	Humble and empowering	212	79.1	2	188	80.7	2	195	83.7	1
2	Respectful about the dignity of others	224	83.5	1	194	83.3	1	172	73.8	3
4	Good listener	200	74.6	3	174	74.7	3	163	70	5
5	Provide clear sense of direction for performance	166	61.9	5	152	65.2	6	165	70.8	4
13	Approachable	190	70.9	4	146	62.7	10	135	57.9	8
6	Ethical and honest	137	51.1	10	149	63.9	8	177	76	2
7	Dynamic and radiates positive energy	149	55.6	7	132	56.7	12	150	64.4	6
18	Make people feel that they are valuable	146	54.4	8	168	72.1	4	110	47.2	15

17	Mentor and coach	156	58.2	6	150	64.4	7	111	47.6	14
1	Demanding and performance centric	95	35.4	15	159	68.2	5	147	63.1	7
9	Lead by example	137	51.1	11	141	60.5	11	122	52.4	11
8	Impartial	126	47	12	130	55.8	13	132	56.7	9
11	Visionary	95	35.4	16	147	63.1	9	115	49.4	13
14	Courageous to take bold decisions	87	32.4	18	129	55.4	14	127	54.5	10
10	Fast in making critical decisions	91	33.9	17	124	53.2	15	120	51.5	12
15	Respect people regardless of levels (non-hierarchical)	109	40.6	14	122	52.4	16	93	39.9	16
12	Kind hearted and supportive	143	53.3	9	100	42.9	17	77	33	17
16	Cool and composed	115	42.9	13	81	34.8	18	74	31.8	18
19	Man of words	81	30.2	19	79	33.9	19	67	28.8	19
20	Always remember person's name	56	20.9	20	72	30.9	20	58	24.9	20

Rho: Group 1 vs. 2 = .74**; Group 1 vs. 3 = .64**; Group 2 vs. 3 = .75**.
** indicates significant at .01 level.

TABLE A3.2

Virtuous Leadership Attributes by Work Experience: Frequency, Percentage and Ranks

Item no.	Virtuous leadership behaviours	Group 1			Group 2			Group 3		
		Work experience <5 years (250) frequency	%	Rank	Work experience 6–15 years (154) frequency	%	Rank	Work experience >16 years (330) frequency	%	Rank
3	Humble and empowering	193	77.2	2	119	77.27	2	283	85.76	1
2	Respectful about the dignity of others	212	84.8	1	124	80.52	1	254	76.97	2
4	Good listener	187	74.8	3	117	75.97	3	233	70.61	5
5	Provide clear sense of direction for performance	155	62	5	88	57.14	8	240	72.73	4
13	Approachable	184	73.6	4	88	57.14	7	199	60.30	8
6	Ethical and honest	127	50.8	11	86	55.84	11	250	75.76	3
7	Dynamic and radiates positive energy	140	56	7	82	53.25	12	209	63.33	7

18	Make people feel that they are valuable	140	56	8	103	66.88	4	181	54.85	14
17	Mentor and coach	153	61.2	6	91	59.09	5	173	52.42	15
1	Demonstrate fairness in working	91	36.4	15	91	59.09	6	219	66.36	6
9	Lead by example	130	52	10	87	56.49	9	183	55.45	12
8	Impartial	118	47.2	12	75	48.7	14	195	59.09	9
11	Visionary	86	34.4	16	87	56.49	10	184	55.76	11
14	Courageous to take bold decisions	78	31.2	18	82	53.25	13	183	55.45	13
10	Fast in making critical decisions	84	33.6	17	63	40.91	17	188	56.97	10
15	Respect people regardless of levels (non-hierarchical)	99	39.6	14	68	44.16	15	157	47.58	16
12	Kind hearted and supportive	135	54	9	65	42.21	16	120	36.36	17
16	Cool and composed	110	44	13	42	27.27	18	118	35.76	18
19	Man of words	71	28.4	19	42	27.27	19	114	34.55	19
20	Always remember person's name	52	20.8	20	41	26.62	20	93	28.18	20

Rho: Group 1 vs. 2 = .78**; Group 1 vs. 3 = .63**; Group 2 vs. 3 = .71** .

** indicates significant at .01 level.

TABLE A3.3

Virtuous Leadership Attributes by Educational Qualification: Frequency, Percentage and Ranks

Item no.	Virtuous leadership behaviours	Group 1 Graduate (342) frequency	%	Rank	Group 2 Post-graduate (392) frequency	%	Rank
3	Humble and empowering	273	79.8	2	322	82.1	1
2	Respectful about the dignity of others	275	80.4	1	315	80.3	2
4	Good listener	258	75.4	3	279	71.1	3
5	Provide clear sense of direction for performance	217	63.4	5	266	67.8	4
13	Approachable	216	63.1	6	255	65	5
6	Ethical and honest	226	66	4	237	60.4	6
7	Dynamic and radiates positive energy	205	59.9	8	226	57.6	8
18	Make people feel that they are valuable	196	57.3	9	228	58.1	7
17	Mentor and coach	209	61.1	7	208	53	12

1	Demonstrate fairness in working	186	54.3	11	215	54.8	10
9	Lead by example	181	52.9	12	219	55.8	9
8	Impartial	175	51.1	13	213	54.3	11
11	Visionary	187	54.6	10	170	43.3	15
14	Courageous to take bold decisions	167	48.8	14	176	44.9	14
10	Fast in making critical decisions	154	45	16	181	46.1	13
15	Respect people regardless of levels (non-hierarchical)	155	45.3	15	169	43.1	16
12	Kind hearted and supportive	153	44.7	17	167	42.	17
16	Cool and composed	128	37.4	18	142	36.2	18
19	Man of words	117	34.2	19	110	28	19
20	Always remember person's name	93	27.1	20	93	23.7	20

Rho: Group 1 vs. 2 = .93**.
** indicates significant at .01 level.

TABLE A3.4

Virtuous Leadership Attributes by Gender: Frequency, Percentage and Ranks

Item no.	Virtuous leadership behaviours	Group 1			Group 2		
		Male (516) frequency	%	Rank	Female (218) frequency	%	Rank
3	Humble and empowering	420	81.4	2	175	80.2	1
2	Respectful about the dignity of others	421	81.6	1	169	77.5	2
4	Good listener	381	73.8	3	156	71.5	3
5	Provide clear sense of direction for performance	334	64.7	5	149	68.3	4
13	Approachable	323	62.6	6	148	67.8	5
6	Ethical and honest	352	68.2	4	111	50.9	9
7	Dynamic and radiates positive energy	317	61.4	7	114	52.2	8
18	Make people feel that they are valuable	292	56.6	11	132	60.5	6
17	Mentor and coach	298	57.8	9	119	54.5	7
1	Demonstrate fairness in working	308	59.7	8	93	42.6	13

9	Lead by example	292	56.6	10	108	49.5	10
8	Impartial	283	54.8	12	105	48.1	11
11	Visionary	260	50.4	13	97	44.5	12
14	Courageous to take bold decisions	254	49.2	14	89	40.8	16
10	Fast in making critical decisions	245	47.5	15	90	41.2	15
15	Respect people regardless of levels (non-hierarchical)	233	45.2	17	91	41.7	14
12	Kind hearted and supportive	238	46.1	16	82	37.6	17
16	Cool and composed	204	39.5	18	66	30.2	18
19	Man of words	172	33.3	19	55	25.2	19
20	Always remember person's name	132	25.6	20	54	24.7	20

Rho: Group 1 vs. 2 = .92**.
** indicates significant at .01 level.

TABLE A3.5

Virtuous Leadership Attributes by Family Type: Frequency, Percentage and Ranks

Item no.	Virtuous leadership behaviours	Group 1			Group 2		
		Nuclear family (433) frequency	%	Rank	Joint family (301) frequency	%	Rank
3	Humble and empowering	347	80.1	2	248	82.3	1
2	Respectful about the dignity of others	358	82.6	1	232	77	2
4	Good listener	324	74.8	3	213	70.7	3
5	Provide clear sense of direction for performance	280	64.6	5	203	67.4	5
13	Approachable	294	67.8	4	177	58.8	8
6	Ethical and honest	254	58.6	7	209	69.4	4
7	Dynamic and radiates positive energy	268	61.8	6	163	54.1	11
18	Make people feel that they are valuable	238	54.9	9	186	61.7	7
17	Mentor and coach	230	53.1	11	187	62.1	6
1	Demonstrate fairness in working	227	52.4	12	174	57.8	9

9	Lead by example	238	54.9	8	162	53.8	12
8	Impartial	230	53.1	10	158	52.4	13
11	Visionary	190	43.8	15	167	55.4	10
14	Courageous to take bold decisions	211	48.7	13	132	43.8	16
10	Fast in making critical decisions	189	43.6	16	146	48.5	15
15	Respect people regardless of levels (non-hierarchical)	175	40.4	17	149	49.5	14
12	Kind hearted and supportive	200	46.1	14	120	39.8	17
16	Cool and composed	173	39.9	18	97	32.2	19
19	Man of words	127	29.3	19	100	33.2	18
20	Always remember person's name	122	28.1	20	64	21.2	20

Rho: Group 1 vs. 2 = .87**.
** indicates significant at .01 level.

TABLE A3.6

Virtuous Leadership Attributes by Resilience: Frequency, Percentage and Ranks

Item no.	Virtuous leadership behaviours	Group 1 Low resilience (400) frequency	%	Rank	Group 2 High resilience (334) frequency	%	Rank
3	Humble and empowering	332	83	1	258	77.2	2
2	Respectful about the dignity of others	306	76.5	2	289	86.5	1
4	Good listener	291	72.7	3	246	73.6	3
5	Provide clear sense of direction for performance	250	62.5	4	233	69.7	4
13	Approachable	250	62.5	5	221	66.1	5
6	Ethical and honest	244	61	6	219	65.5	6
7	Dynamic and radiates positive energy	235	58.7	7	196	58.6	8
18	Make people feel that they are valuable	229	57.2	8	195	58.3	9
17	Mentor and coach	227	56.7	9	190	56.8	10

1	Demonstrate fairness in working	214	53.5	10	187	55.9	11
9	Lead by example	209	52.2	11	179	53.5	12
8	Impartial	196	49	12	204	61	7
11	Visionary	188	47	13	169	50.5	14
14	Courageous to take bold decisions	182	45.5	14	142	42.5	17
10	Fast in making critical decisions	177	44.2	15	166	49.7	15
15	Respect people regardless of levels (non-hierarchical)	170	42.5	16	150	44.9	16
12	Kind hearted and supportive	165	41.2	17	170	50.8	13
16	Cool and composed	146	36.5	18	124	50.8	13
19	Man of words	129	32.2	19	98	29.3	19
20	Always remember person's name	109	27.2	20	77	23	20

Rho: Group 1 vs. 2 = .95**
** indicates significant at .01 level.

TABLE A3.7

Virtuous Leadership Attributes by Work Locus of Control: Frequency, Percentage and Ranks

Item no.	Virtuous leadership behaviours	Group 1 Internal LOC (376) frequency	%	Rank	Group 2 External LOC (358) frequency	%	Rank
3	Humble and empowering	316	84.0	1	279	77.9	2
2	Respectful about the dignity of others	298	79.3	2	292	81.6	1
4	Good listener	277	73.7	3	260	72.6	3
5	Provide clear sense of direction for performance	249	66.2	5	234	65.4	4
13	Approachable	237	63.0	6	234	65.4	5
6	Ethical and honest	251	66.8	4	212	59.2	6
7	Dynamic and radiates positive energy	233	62.0	7	198	55.3	8
18	Make people feel that they are valuable	223	59.3	9	201	56.1	7
17	Mentor and coach	223	59.3	8	194	54.2	11
1	Demonstrate fairness in working	204	54.3	12	197	55.0	9

9	Lead by example	216	57.4	10	184	51.4	12
8	Impartial	192	51.1	13	196	54.7	10
11	Visionary	210	55.9	11	147	41.1	17
14	Courageous to take bold decisions	182	48.4	15	161	45.0	14
10	Fast in making critical decisions	182	48.4	14	153	42.7	16
15	Respect people regardless of levels (non-hierarchical)	168	44.7	16	156	43.6	15
12	Kind hearted and supportive	145	38.6	17	175	48.9	13
16	Cool and composed	128	34.0	18	142	39.7	18
19	Man of words	120	31.9	19	107	29.9	19
20	Always remember person's name	86	22.9	20	100	27.9	20

Rho: Group 1 vs. 2 = .92**.
** indicates significant at .01 level.

TABLE A3.8(a)

Virtuous Leadership Attributes by Values (Egalitarian and Humanistic): Frequency, Percentage and Ranks

Item no.	Virtuous leadership behaviours	Group 1 Low egalitarian (421)			Group 2 High egalitarian (313)			Group 3 Low humanistic (398)			Group 4 High fumanistic (336)		
		frequency	%	Rank	frequency	%	Rank	frequency	%	Rank	frequency	%	Rank
3	Humble and empowering	328	77.9	2	262	83.7	1	319	80.1	2	271	80.6	1
2	Respectful about the dignity of others	339	80.5	1	256	81.7	2	332	83.4	1	263	78.2	2
4	Good listener	307	72.9	3	230	73.4	3	293	73.6	3	244	72.6	3
5	Provide clear sense of direction for performance	273	64.8	4	198	63.2	5	245	61.5	6	226	67.2	4
13	Approachable	270	64.1	5	213	68	4	259	65	4	224	66.6	5
6	Ethical and honest	242	57.4	7	182	58.1	9	220	55.2	9	204	60.7	7
7	Dynamic and radiates positive energy	267	63.4	6	196	62.6	6	252	63.3	5	211	62.8	6
18	Make people feel that they are valuable	224	53.2	10	193	61.6	8	219	55	10	198	58.9	9
17	Mentor and coach	218	51.7	12	170	54.3	13	217	54.5	11	171	50.8	12

No	Attribute	N	%	Rank	N	%	Rank	N	%	Rank	N	%	Rank
1	Demonstrate fairness in working	237	56.2	8	194	61.9	7	229	57.5	7	202	60.1	8
9	Lead by example	178	42.2	16	142	45.3	17	150	37.6	17	170	50.6	14
8	Impartial	223	52.9	11	177	56.5	10	221	55.5	8	179	53.2	11
11	Visionary	229	54.3	9	172	54.9	11	215	54	12	186	55.3	10
14	Courageous to take bold decisions	185	43.9	15	172	54.9	12	190	47.7	13	167	49.7	15
10	Fast in making critical decisions	171	40.6	17	153	48.8	14	154	38.6	16	170	50.6	13
15	Respect people regardless of levels (non-hierarchical)	195	46.3	13	148	47.2	16	187	46.9	14	156	46.4	16
12	Kind hearted and supportive	185	43.9	14	150	47.9	15	179	44.9	15	156	46.4	17
16	Cool and composed	151	35.8	18	119	38	18	142	35.6	18	128	38.1	18
19	Man of words	127	30.1	19	100	31.9	19	111	27.8	19	116	34.5	19
20	Always remember person's name	104	24.7	20	82	26.2	20	97	24.3	20	89	26.4	20

Rho: Group 1 vs. 2 = .96**; Group 3 vs. 4 = .95**.
** indicates significant at .01 level.

TABLE A3.8(b)

Virtuous Leadership Attributes by Values (Hedonistic and Personal Development): Frequency, Percentage and Ranks

Item no.	Virtuous leadership behaviours	Group 5 Low hedonistic (356)			Group 6 High hedonistic (378)			Group 7 Low personal development (332)			Group 8 High personal development (402)		
		frequency	%	Rank	frequency	%	Rank	frequency	%	Rank	frequency	%	Rank
3	Humble and empowering	288	80.9	2	302	79.8	2	229	68.9	2	269	66.9	2
2	Respectful about the dignity of others	291	81.7	1	304	80.4	1	200	60.2	3	251	62.4	4
4	Good listener	248	69.6	3	289	76.6	3	172	51.8	12	193	48	14
5	Provide clear sense of direction for performance	225	63.2	5	246	65	4	190	57.2	6	234	58.2	7
13	Approachable	245	68.8	4	238	62.9	6	182	54.8	8	235	58.4	6
6	Ethical and honest	194	54.4	9	230	60.8	9	108	32.5	18	129	32	18
7	Dynamic and radiates positive energy	224	62.9	6	239	63.2	5	246	74.1	1	279	69.4	1
18	Make people feel that they are valuable	183	51.4	12	234	61.9	7	178	53.6	9	225	55.9	8
17	Mentor and coach	188	52.8	10	200	52.9	12	156	46.9	14	219	54.4	9

#		Group 5			Group 6			Group 7			Group 8		
1	Demonstrate fairness in working	201	56.4	7	230	60.8	8	156	46.9	15	198	49.2	13
9	Lead by example	131	36.8	17	189	50	13	175	52.7	10	189	47	15
8	Impartial	186	52.2	11	214	56.6	10	199	59.9	4	257	63.9	3
11	Visionary	197	55.3	8	204	53.9	11	195	58.7	5	209	51.9	11
14	Courageous to take bold decisions	180	50.5	13	177	46.8	16	103	31.0	19	121	30.1	19
10	Fast in making critical decisions	141	39.6	16	183	48.4	14	174	52.4	11	211	52.4	10
15	Respect people regardless of levels (non-hierarchical)	176	49.4	14	167	44.1	17	186	56.0	7	235	58.4	5
12	Kind hearted and supportive	154	43.2	15	181	47.8	15	86	25.9	20	119	29.6	20
16	Cool and composed	117	32.8	18	153	40.4	18	146	43.9	16	177	44	16
19	Man of words	95	26.6	19	132	34.9	19	159	47.8	13	205	51	12
20	Always remember person's name	79	22.1	20	107	28.3	20	136	40.9	17	175	43.5	17

Rho: Group 5 vs. 6 = .93**; Group 7 vs. 8 = .94**.
** indicates significant at .01 level.

TABLE A3.8(c)

Virtuous Leadership Attributes by Values (Pride and Materialistic): Frequency, Percentage and Ranks

Item no.	Virtuous leadership behaviours	Group 9 Low pride (310)			Group 10 High pride (424)			Group 11 Low materialistic (367)			Group 12 High materialistic (367)		
		frequency	%	Rank	frequency	%	Rank	frequency	%	Rank	frequency	%	Rank
3	Humble and empowering	241	77.7	2	349	82.3	2	288	78.4	2	302	82.2	1
2	Respectful about the dignity of others	242	78.0	1	353	83.2	1	301	82	1	294	80.1	2
4	Good listener	220	70.9	3	317	74.7	3	258	70.3	3	279	76	3
5	Provide clear sense of direction for performance	184	59.3	6	287	67.6	5	228	62.1	7	243	66.2	4
13	Approachable	191	61.6	5	292	68.8	4	256	69.7	4	227	61.8	5
6	Ethical and honest	174	56.1	9	250	58.9	8	201	54.7	11	223	60.7	6
7	Dynamic and radiates positive energy	206	66.4	4	257	60.6	6	241	65.6	5	222	60.4	7
18	Make people feel that they are valuable	170	54.8	11	247	58.2	9	205	55.8	10	212	57.7	8
17	Mentor and coach	153	49.3	12	235	55.4	10	183	49.8	14	205	55.8	9

#	Attribute	n	%	Rank	n	%	Rank	n	%	Rank	n	%	Rank
1	Demonstrate fairness in working	178	57.4	7	253	59.7	7	232	63.2	6	199	54.2	10
9	Lead by example	126	40.6	17	194	45.7	16	130	35.4	18	190	51.7	11
8	Impartial	171	55.1	10	229	54	11	212	57.7	9	188	51.2	12
11	Visionary	178	57.4	8	223	52.5	12	225	61.3	8	176	47.9	13
14	Courageous to take bold decisions	152	49	13	205	48.3	13	186	50.6	13	171	46.5	14
10	Fast in making critical decisions	134	43.2	16	190	44.8	17	153	41.6	16	171	46.5	15
15	Respect people regardless of levels (non-hierarchical)	148	47.7	14	195	45.9	14	191	52	12	152	41.4	16
12	Kind hearted and supportive	141	45.4	15	194	45.7	15	183	49.8	15	152	41.4	17
16	Cool and composed	98	31.6	19	172	40.5	18	136	37	17	134	36.5	18
19	Man of words	99	31.9	18	128	30.1	19	123	33.5	19	104	28.3	19
20	Always remember person's name	76	24.5	20	110	25.9	20	99	26.9	20	87	23.7	20

Rho: Group 9 vs. 10 = .97**; Group 11 vs. 12 = .85**.
** indicates significant at .01 level.

TABLE A3.9

Virtuous Leadership Attributes by Organizational Sector: Frequency, Percentage and Ranks

Item no.	Virtuous leadership behaviours	Group 1			Group 2		
		Indian public sector executives (263) frequency	%	Rank	Indian private sector executives (307) frequency	%	Rank
3	Humble and empowering	218	82.8	1	255	83	2
2	Respectful about the dignity of others	195	74.1	2	263	85.6	1
4	Good listener	176	66.9	4	243	79.1	3
5	Provide clear sense of direction for performance	169	64.2	5	214	69.7	5
13	Approachable	148	56.2	8	235	76.5	4
6	Ethical and honest	183	69.5	3	178	57.9	9
7	Dynamic and radiates positive energy	166	63.1	6	193	62.8	7
18	Make people feel that they are valuable	121	46	14	187	60.9	8

17	Mentor and coach	119	45.2	15	206	67.1	6
1	Demonstrate fairness in working	156	59.3	7	155	50.4	14
9	Lead by example	126	47.9	12	174	56.6	11
8	Impartial	139	52.8	9	169	55	12
11	Visionary	126	47.9	13	135	43.9	18
14	Courageous to take bold decisions	133	50.5	10	138	44.9	17
10	Fast in making critical decisions	132	50.1	11	145	47.2	16
15	Respect people regardless of levels (non-hierarchical)	89	33.8	16	149	48.5	15
12	Kind hearted and supportive	85	32.3	17	175	57	10
16	Cool and composed	64	24.3	19	160	52.1	13
19	Man of words	67	25.4	18	124	40.3	19
20	Always remember person's name	53	20.1	20	99	32.2	20

Rho: Group 1 vs. 2 = .78**.
** indicates significant at .01 level.

TABLE A3.10

Virtuous Leadership Attributes by Industry Type: Frequency, Percentage and Ranks

Item no.	Virtuous leadership behaviours	Group 1			Group 2		
		Service (423) frequency	%	Rank	Manufac- turing (311) frequency	%	Rank
3	Humble and empowering	330	78	2	265	85.2	1
2	Respectful about the dignity of others	346	81.7	1	244	78.4	2
4	Good listener	315	74.4	3	222	71.3	4
5	Provide clear sense of direction for performance	272	64.3	4	211	67.8	6
13	Approachable	269	63.5	5	202	64.9	8
6	Ethical and honest	237	56	8	226	72.6	3
7	Dynamic and radiates positive energy	222	52.4	10	209	67.2	7
18	Make people feel that they are valuable	248	58.6	6	176	56.5	12
17	Mentor and coach	239	56.5	7	178	57.2	11
1	Demonstrate fairness in working	187	44.2	12	214	68.8	5

9	Lead by example	224	52.9	9	176	56.5	13
8	Impartial	222	52.4	11	166	53.3	14
11	Visionary	159	37.5	16	198	63.6	9
14	Courageous to take bold decisions	155	36.6	17	188	60.4	10
10	Fast in making critical decisions	174	41.1	15	161	51.7	15
15	Respect people regardless of levels (non-hierarchical)	184	43.4	14	140	45	16
12	Kind hearted and supportive	186	43.9	13	134	43	18
16	Cool and composed	135	31.9	18	135	43.4	17
19	Man of words	112	26.4	19	115	36.9	19
20	Always remember person's name	90	21.2	20	96	30.8	20

Rho: Group 1 vs. 2 = .77**.
** indicates significant at .01 level.

TABLE A3.11

Virtuous Leadership Attributes by Nationality: Frequency, Percentage and Ranks

Item no.	Virtuous leadership behaviours	Group 1 International executives (164) frequency	%	Rank	Group 2 Indian executives (570) frequency	%	Rank
3	Humble and empowering	122	74.3	2	473	82.9	1
2	Respectful about the dignity of others	132	80.4	1	458	80.3	2
4	Good listener	118	71.9	3	419	73.5	3
5	Provide clear sense of direction for performance	100	60.9	6	383	67.1	4
13	Approachable	88	53.6	11	383	67.1	5
6	Ethical and honest	102	62.2	5	361	63.3	6
7	Dynamic and radiates positive energy	72	43.9	14	359	62.9	7
18	Make people feel that they are valuable	116	70.7	4	308	54	10
17	Mentor and coach	92	56.1	9	325	57	8

1	Demonstrate fairness in working	90	54.8	10	311	54.5	9
9	Lead by example	100	60.9	7	300	52.6	12
8	Impartial	80	48.7	13	308	54	11
11	Visionary	96	58.5	8	261	45.7	15
14	Courageous to take bold decisions	72	43.9	15	271	47.5	14
10	Fast in making critical decisions	58	35.3	17	277	48.6	13
15	Respect people regardless of levels (non-hierarchical)	86	52.4	12	238	41.7	17
12	Kind hearted and supportive	60	36.5	16	260	45.6	16
16	Cool and composed	46	28	18	224	39.3	18
19	Man of words	36	21.9	19	191	33.5	19
20	Always remember person's name	34	20.7	20	152	26.6	20

Rho: Group 1 vs. 2 = .81**.
** indicates significant at .01 level.

REFERENCES

1. poetryfoundation.org. (2015). *Invictus.* Retrieved from http://www.poetryfoundation.org/poem/182194 (accessed on 20 July 2015).
2. Watson, L.E. (1951). *Light from many lamps: A treasury of inspiration* (p. 156). New York, NY: Simon & Schuster.
3. Ibid., p. 161.
4. Leadershipnow.com (2015). Quotes on relationships. Retrieved from http://www.leadershipnow.com/relationshipsquotes.html (accessed on 20 July 2015).
5. beyondthedream.co.uk (2015). Tao Te Ching 17: The Art of Leadership. Retrieved from http://beyondthedream.co.uk/tag/verse-17/ (accessed on 20 July 2015).

4

Leading Consciously: A Road Map for Moving from Toxic to Virtuous Leadership

Human beings are not glorified animals they are repressed angels.
—Viktor Frankl[1]

This chapter is organized in four parts:

- Part I briefly highlights the raison d'être for writing this book—*The Odyssey to Leadership: From Darkness to Light*.
- Part II focuses on (a) the salient findings regarding the behavioural and attitudinal dispositions of toxic leaders and their impact on the psycho profile of their followers; and (b) the mechanisms which followers adopt to cope with the toxic behaviour of their superiors.
- Part III presents on the salient behavioural and value dispositions of virtuous leaders. The findings are further used for higher level of conceptualization and paradigm building.
- Part IV is primarily devoted to the journey which leaders need to take to move from their toxicity (darkness) to their virtuousness (light).

This chapter also attempts to carve out the road map that positional leaders need to follow in order to move from darkness to light, that is, from Id to superego, and from instinctual to conscious behaviour, from *Tamas* to *Rajas* and *Satoguna* so that they can integrate the power of *Rajas* and *Sato* to become philosopher–kings–the crescendo of virtuous leadership. They must also strive to move from the trapping of unconscious living and leading to becoming fully conscious and thereby to become functional, creative and productive leaders.

It may be worthwhile mentioning what the iconic guru Warren G. Bennis[2] once said that if leaders are prisoners of their unconscious conspiracies, they lose their power to become fully functional and self-actualizing leaders. A similar concept has been articulated by leading thinkers such as Maslow, Chris Argyris, McGregor, Eric Fromm, Viktor Frankl, Brandon, Assagioli and others from the humanistic school of thought. In sum, it may be emphasized that leaders must undertake this personal pilgrimage to move from darkness to light to become virtuous leaders.

PART I: WHY THIS BOOK?

The overarching purpose of this work is not to bring out yet another treatise on leadership phenomenon and burden the reader with more of the same. Needless to say, the leadership domain has produced a plethora of theories and paradigms hinging primarily on the behaviouristic framework. As a result, most of the research is centred around measurable leader behaviours, in due deference to one of the core tenets of the 'scientific' method—what cannot be measured and scientifically observed is not worthy of exploration. Many important factors which influence leader behaviour—philosophy and purpose of life, values, beliefs and attitudes—are unfortunately not given due importance by majority of the researchers while studying the leadership paradigm. It is no wonder therefore that bulk of the work dabbles only at the fringes of leadership and overlooks the core factors which govern the leadership phenomenon. Although there is no doubt that the above approach has yielded intellectual understanding of what makes a good leader, yet behaviourally speaking, it does not help a toxic leader to become a truly virtuous leader. We firmly believe that virtuous and holistic leadership is, therefore, needed and can only emerge when the phenomenon is studied comprehensively taking into account various levels of a human being—that is physical self, emotive self, intellectual self and spiritual self.

Another uniqueness of our work has been the study of both toxic and virtuous leaders together. This has been done in order to bring out the contrast between the two phenomena which are located at two opposite poles of the leadership continuum. Both toxic leadership and virtuous leadership phenomena have been studied to extract the learning from both perspectives. In other words, what to do and what not to do, or what to absorb and what to discard, can be learnt through a study of both toxic and virtuous leadership together, the premise being that people learn equally from both positive and negative experiences.

This work therefore lays due emphasis through an eclectic approach on holistic understanding of the leader at the physical, intellectual, emotive and spiritual levels. In our view, this research model makes the work very unique and distinctive. It may be worthwhile mentioning that adapting an eclectic approach to this research has also given us deep and meaningful insights into the phenomenon which typically would not emerge by using either only survey or only case study approaches.

It may be worthwhile mentioning that the foundation of this work is embedded in the core belief that every person is a builder, sculptor, painter and shaper of his leadership destiny. As the Gita powerfully explicates:

> *Man's own self is his friend;*
> *Man's own self is his foe;*
> —Gita (Verse 6)[3]

A second core conviction based on wisdom from the great epic, 'Gita' is that every human being is a *shudra* (ignorant) by birth; it is one's upbringing and socialization which makes a person 'twice born', that is taking 'rebirth' or reinventing oneself; study of the scriptures makes one wise, and understanding the purpose of life makes one a truly enlightened human being, which is the prerequisite to become a virtuous leader. Therefore, in order to become a virtuous leader, it is essential that one has deep understanding of the purpose of one's life and one's existence. The third basic belief underlying this work is that being a good human being is a necessary condition to become a virtuous leader.

The journey of self-actualizing and being fully functional leaders begins once a person embarks on the odyssey of self-discovery and conscious living. Socrates aptly said that, 'an unexamined life is not worth living',[4] indicating the need for constant reflection and meditation about self as a leader, self as a human being and the direction in which one should move to become a fully productive and functional person enabling him or her to become a virtuous leader. This will be the main focus of the present chapter.

PART II: TOXIC LEADERSHIP

This presents (a) toxic leader landscape and (b) key findings from the research study.

Toxic Leader Landscape

Chapter 1 gives a bird's eye view of both the toxic leadership and virtuous leadership. It powerfully highlights the damage which toxic leaders have inflicted on humanity and the potential which they carry to wreak havoc and destruction. This has been brought out through a mix of historical realities as well as contemporary experiences.

Research studies on toxic leadership have brought out that toxic leaders are preponderantly despotic, narcissistic, machiavellian, sadists, tyrants or bullies or any combination of these syndromes. Through their actions and behavioural excesses, they destroy nations, institutions and organizations; they create enormous discomfort, anxiety, fear, demotivation and low morale among the affected followers. In the extreme situations it can lead to revolt. Employees, therefore, become disengaged, uninspired and look for the first opportunity to desert the organization.

Toxic Leaders: Key Findings from the Study

Our study of toxic leaders (see Chapter 2) brought out the following profile:

1. Toxic leaders have been found to be primarily arrogant; they put the blame on others for poor performance, they are close minded; they create insecurity; they indulge in favouritism and are unreliable as well as abusive and ill tempered. In other words, they display characteristics of being narcissistic, machiavellian and sadist.

2. This primary cluster of toxic leadership is observed across all subcategories formed by age, education, work experience, industry sector, ownership pattern and nationality.

3. This pattern is also seen across personality variables—resilience, locus of control as well as their value profile.

4. We can conclude from these findings that there is tremendous homogeneity regarding toxic leaders disposition regardless of the selected independent variables in this study.

5. Examination of the effect of such toxic behaviours on subordinates revealed that it has a deleterious impact leading to emotional distress ranging from feeling upset, giving up, anxiety and worthlessness.

6. Study of the coping mechanisms utilized by the followers while dealing with toxic leaders brings out that they use adaptive, assertive, avoidance and approach in that order. It is possible to deduce that since adaptation is the primary mode of coping used by followers, they neither confront nor discuss problems in depth. Such a mode makes them more compliance centric to ensure their own survival and as a result, the real problems are swept under the carpet and remain unresolved.

7. Variables such as age, work experience, educational qualification hedonistic value system, type of industry (manufacturing or service) and nationality significantly impact levels of emotional distress.

8. Findings on coping strategies bring out than gender, locus of control, ownership pattern, industry sector and nationality

do significantly influence either one or two or three of the previously cited coping mechanisms.

9. Case study findings across the 11 case studies of toxic leaders bring out that they are primarily arrogant, followed by being ego centric and close minded. They publicly run down others; they indulge in 'me' centre agenda, play favourites, become abusive, are untrustworthy, machiavellian and dishonest, as well as are corrupt and lacking in integrity.

10. It is noteworthy to mention that tremendous similarity is evident between the previously mentioned toxic leader characteristics derived from both questionnaire-based research and case study-based research.

11. Findings of the study bring out clearly that toxic leaders are disliked, despised and hated unequivocally regardless of categories and groups that people belong to.

12. Followers working with them feel extremely humiliated, lose their self-confidence, suffer from the feeling of powerlessness, helplessness and disengagement, perhaps even alienation from the workplace. They do not muster courage to confront and resolve issues; they adopt the line of least resistance by using coping strategies such as avoidance and adaptation in order to survive. Therefore, given a chance nobody would like to work with such toxic leaders.

PART III: VIRTUOUS LEADERSHIP

Virtuous Leader Landscape

Our decades-old experience in the corporate sector, as consultants, coach and mentors, brings out that while there is widespread prevalence of toxic leaders, virtuous leaders are in a miniscule minority in all walks of life—politics, business, bureaucracy and academia. There is a dire need for more virtuous leaders since they are the leaders who can make the difference in human life, institutions and society.

Scanning the literature on virtuous leaders has powerfully shown that they have a significant and positive impact on people and organizations. They generate high degree of commitment and high morale. They create enthusiasm, teamwork and pursuit of excellence by triggering the positive energy among followers. They create a performance-centric work culture, encourage expression of ideas and promote creativity and innovation, thereby building a winning organization.

Virtuous Leaders: Key Findings from the Study

1. Salient findings from the present research study highlight that virtuous leaders are seen to be primarily empowering and supporting. They are humble and empowering, are respectful of others' dignity, are good listeners, provide clear direction and are approachable, the ranks being from 1 to 5. In other words, they are humanistic, along with being performance centric, and demonstrate tremendous sensitivity while dealing with people.

2. The second cluster of virtuous leaders' disposition indicates that they are ethical and honest; they are dynamic and radiate positive energy; they make people feel valued and they are great mentors and coaches.

3. Combining the two clusters cited above brings out that virtuous leaders are humanistic, they focus on performance excellence and they are ethical. This means, in other words, virtuous leaders combine beautifully contribution centricity, moralistic approach and humanistic value system.

4. There is significant similarity across the behaviour of virtuous leaders by various categories—age, education, work experience, industry sector, ownership pattern and nationality.

5. This pattern is also seen by personality variables—resilience and locus of control and as their value profile.

6. This indicates that the preference for virtuous leaders' characteristics does not vary by categories and that there is significant homogeneity in the findings regarding virtuous leaders.

7. Deeper study through case methodology indicated that these virtuous leaders are very similar in their value framework and approach while dealing with their followers. They are humanistic and moralistic and at the same time contribution-centric like a karma yogi. In addition to the above characteristics, virtuous leaders in our study are found to be spiritually evolved. Their life is governed by a larger purpose; they are courageous, bold and risk-takers; they are also objective realistic, pragmatic and above all they are ethical. They have a high degree of political acumen as well as immense networking capability while dealing with stakeholders. A study of the lifestyle of the five leaders who have featured as virtuous leaders in this book brought out that, in addition to their mental, emotional and spiritual competencies, they were physically healthy. They believed in regular physical activity such as sports, walks, golf and tennis. Some of them also were regularly doing yoga and meditation.

PART IV: JOURNEY FROM TOXIC TO VIRTUOUS LEADERSHIP

Almost all institutions of governance, whether political, bureaucratic and corporate, are currently experiencing severe crisis of leadership. Things have reached such a level that most people in politics seem to be tarred with the same brush. One of the retired university professors expressed his frustration at the prevalent political quagmire, 'four thieves are fighting the elections from different parties, do you have any choice but to elect one of them? Many of them have criminal backgrounds. They have amassed wealth through illegal and unscrupulous means. How does one differentiate among them, I really don't know!' The scenario in the business sector is not very different. Bureaucrats are busy in perpetuating their own oligarchy, rather than serving the interests of people. They have miserably failed to make constructive contribution to the roles and positions they occupy. They are conformist, careerist and power seekers. In many cases, there is in fact a powerful nexus among the political elite, bureaucrats and businessmen.

The multitude of sordid scams over the last decade amply demonstrate the low level to which the values of corporate leaders, politicians and bureaucrats have fallen. The above-cited nexus among bureaucracy, businessmen and politicians is probably a global phenomenon. However, in India, it has reached unprecedented levels. In summary, the contemporary business world is characterized by crony capitalism, exploitation and defrauding of the public exchequer. This is a depressing scenario about the manner in which most public institutions and corporate sector are managed and governed in India. It is in this perspective that Part IV has been written in the hope that toxic leaders from different walks of life will undertake the pilgrimage from toxic to virtuous leadership.

Great thinkers such as Buddha, Chanakya, Confucius, Aristotle, Plato and such others emphasized that the behaviour of kings and leaders must be aligned with the contextual reality—as per time, place and people. In the light of this perennial wisdom, we now very briefly touch upon the current contextual imperatives, which powerfully influence the needed leadership competencies.

Today, the combination of IT and powerful media has rendered leaders 'naked' in the public eye. In fact, figuratively speaking, leaders live in glass houses and whatever they do is closely scrutinized and observed by stakeholders and above all the media. Stakeholders' expectations from leaders are so high that leaders are expected to be holier than the pope, with teeth whiter than the blood hound.

From the above discussion, it can be briefly concluded that we need leaders who are characterized by integrity, transparency and ethical orientation. They must have competency to tolerate ambiguity, complexities as well as to manage things objectively and pragmatically. They must develop heightened human sensitivity, humility, emotional stability and a participative approach to inspire, galvanize and channelize the energies of their followers towards the larger goal.

This is possible only when leaders move from toxic orientation consisting of dispositional mindsets such as arrogance, close mindedness, being abusive, 'me' centric, sadist, Machiavellian, narcissistic, etc., to virtuous orientation characterized by humility, honesty, heightened human sensitivity, openness, listening, intuitive power, etc.

This part focuses on the following stages of the journey:

1. Identifying blocks to move from toxic to virtuous;
2. Developing gestalt holisticity of mind and
3. Checklist for self-therapy to move from toxic to virtuous

Blocks to Move from Toxic to Virtuous

We strongly believe in the ancient Indian wisdom cited below that all human beings have abundant potential and power to become virtuous leaders:

> *Every Akshara (alphabet) has the power of mantra.*
> *Every plant has medicinal value;*
> *Every human being is a competent human being with a reservoir of vast potential*
> *What he lacks is strong will; determination; the right mentoring; and clarity of life goal.*[5]

In our experience, most leaders do not see life holistically and live in a conditioned manner, mechanically and in an autopilot mode. Position holders with such mindsets are preponderantly governed by the sensory-motor-centric mind, characterized by photogenic lens and video graphic capability—metaphorically speaking. Whatever they see and hear is recorded and imprinted in the mind. Those experiences, events and interactions which cause pain, anxiety, conflict and unpleasantness normally get suppressed into the unconscious level of the psyche and are subsequently expressed in terms of biases, stereotypes and prejudices, significantly affecting our behaviour and interactions. Similarly, certain positive events and experiences may also get relegated to the unconscious for various reasons. Human behaviour, therefore, is significantly affected by contents of the unconscious mind as brought out by the analogy of the iceberg, implying that most of human behaviour is driven by the unconscious self.

Describing the workings of the human being, the Katho-Upanishad—an Ancient Indian scripture[6]—used the analogy of the chariot. It said that the human being is like a chariot, the Self is the

Lord of the Chariot; the intellect is viewed as the charioteer; and the sense organs are considered to be horses. If these horses (senses) are not controlled by the charioteer (intellect), they become wild and pull the chariot (human being) in any direction they wish. In other words, if the sensory centric and conditioned mind is not trained and converted into an intellect and wisdom-centric mind (characterized by volition), there is lack of concentration and lack of a meditative mind, both being essential for tranquillity and mental stillness. Mind without equanimity, peace and tranquillity is restless, hyperactive and devoid of balanced judgement. Describing the workings of the human mind, Swami Chinmayananda in his commentary on the Gita[7] said it is like a tree which emerges from a seed, the source of all evil starts from our own wrong thinking or false imagination. Thought is creative. It can make us or mar us. If rightly harnessed by controlling the sense organs, it can be used for constructive purposes; if misused it can totally destroy us. When one constantly thinks upon a sense object, the consistency of thought creates in him an attachment for the object of his thought, and when more and more thoughts flow towards an object of attachment, they crystallize to form a burning desire for possession and enjoyment of the object of attachment. The same force of motivation, when directed towards obstacles that threaten the non-fulfilment of one's desires, is called *krodha* (anger); from anger comes delusion; from delusion loss of memory, and the destruction of discrimination; from the destruction of discrimination he perishes.[7]

It is in this perspective that Nathaniel Branden's[8] observation is quite meaningful. He says, 'the tragedy of so many people is precisely that to a large extent, they live mechanically; they don't examine their motives, thoughts and actions and react in auto-pilot mode in a robotic fashion. They respond to events through the prism of stereotypes, rather than examining realities and dealing with them'. Therefore, their responses and actions are devoid of reality check.

They wrongly assess themselves and the environment which results in illusions and delusions, misplaced judgements, denial, poor decisions and actions. Such people (and by extension leaders), therefore, lead unproductive and uncreative lives and are unable to successfully meet the challenges which life throws up. In a nutshell, they do not live their lives consciously; they are not in touch with reality and do not live in a fully functioning, productive and creative manner. Needless to say, it is such people who become toxic leaders. To become virtuous leaders, it is essential for them to lead life consciously. This is only possible when there is clarity of life purpose, life goal and life role which, in our experience, many leaders do not possess. The aphorism, 'begin with the end in mind', tells us that we must be clear about where we are headed and steer the ship of our lives in that direction.

Model 4.1 depicts the above aphorism (begin with the end in mind), highlighting the role of philosophy, purpose of existence, values and beliefs affecting leader behaviour and styles. The odyssey to virtuous leadership will, therefore, have to commence from clarity regarding life philosophy, purpose and goal. To be a virtuous leader, therefore, it is absolutely essential to understand and clarify the purpose and meaning of one's own existence.

Unless leaders engage in such reflection and exploration, they would not be in a position to activate their higher level energies, move from *Tamas* to *Rajas* and *Satoguna*, from unconscious to conscious self and from physical and materialistic self to spiritual self as mentioned earlier. Unless they tread this path of exploration and self-discovery, they will not grow as virtuous leaders, notwithstanding the abundance of potential residing in them. They will be consumed with material and physical desires, greed, envy, jealousy, etc., which will keep them in the grip of self-gratification and push them in the toxic direction.

MODEL 4.1

From Philosophy to Behaviour

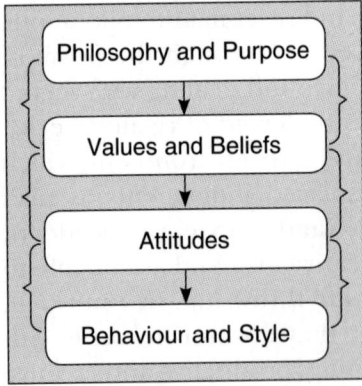

To move from toxicity to virtuousness, understanding the essence of the following prayer is extremely important.

Asato Maa Sat Gama Ya—Lead Me from Untruth to Truth
Tamaso Maa Jyotir Gama Ya—Lead Me from Darkness (Ignorance) to
Light (Enlightenment)
Mrtyorma Amritam Gama ya—Lead Me from Mortality to Immortality

It is important to mention that this prayer is universal in its nature—similar prayers are common across various cultures and religions. The essence of this prayer is generally accepted as the path to becoming a virtuous person and a virtuous leader. This is because it is only truthful persons can be courageous, bold, fearless and overcome all adversities. The enlightened leader can be objective, judicious, unbiased, prudent and can take decisions, giving foremost consideration for equity, justice and fairness. Leaders desiring to be immortal will lead a contributing life and leave a legacy and footprints on the sands of time. Examining the lives of Gandhi, Mandela, Lincoln, Roosevelt, Jamsetji Tata, G.D. Birla, J.R.D. Tata, Akio Morita, Henry Ford, Andrew Carnegie, Fulbright, Einstein, Newton, Edison and many such leaders shows that they amply symbolized the above-mentioned qualities. It is no wonder that in the annals of history, they are considered to be transformational and virtuous leaders, having made immense contributions to make a difference to communities, organizations and nations.

Developing Gestalt Holisticity of Mind

A virtuous leader must be holistically healthy in terms of all the four levels of self—physical, emotional, intellectual and spiritual. Once the leader develops gestalt holisticity—that is integrated self—he attains the highest level of complex capability, as indicated in the following quote by Lao-Tzu—an integral being knows without going; sees without looking and accomplishes without doing.[9] In order to move from toxicity to virtuousness, it is important for role holders and leaders to have a holistic understanding of who they are as human beings. Model 4.2 powerfully depicts all the four levels of self at which development is required to become a virtuous and holistic leader.

MODEL 4.2

Virtuous and Holistic Leader

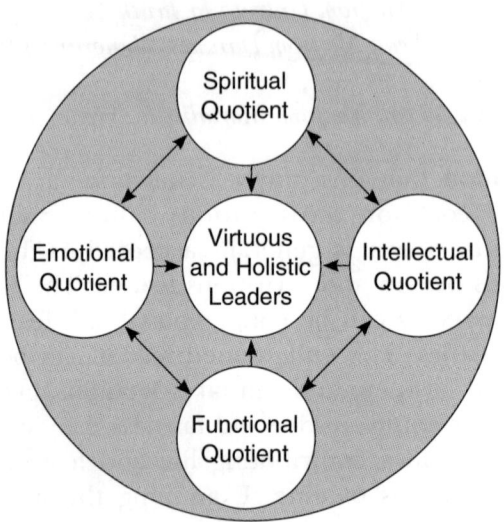

It may be worthwhile mentioning that these four levels of self are closely connected and interrelated and have a significant influence on each other. These four levels need to be aligned and operate synchronously. The state of equilibrium which ensues enables leaders to become virtuous and holistic in their thoughts, feelings and actions. If any of them is not adequate in their functioning, there is a break operational alignment, and it leads to imbalance across all the four self-levels. In other words, we are propounding the paradigm of gestalt holisticity in the functioning of the self. This would operate like a symphony, effortlessly producing melody coordinating across multiple instruments.

The relevance of developing each level of self to become a holistic and virtuous leader is now discussed in greater detail.

Physical Self

In the last 30 years of our work in the corporate world, we have seen that those leaders who have made the difference, those who have been excellence seekers, those who have been contribution centric and those who have left a powerful legacy, used to stretch and work hard, much more than ordinary managers. They believed that hard work alone pays in life and worked long hours stretching into 16 hour work days; frequently travelling nationally and globally (about two weeks in a month) was a way of life for them. They were always connected with their stakeholders through different media—email, SMS, whats-app, twitter—and what is more, they were prompt in responding to messages which they received from them even at odd hours.

Those leaders aspiring to be virtuous leaders have to be in peak physical condition to cope with the ravages of travel, meetings and long hours of work. When the leader's health does not support him, then living such a physically demanding life—which is a reality in today's corporate world—will be well neigh impossible. Many are the cases where leaders have experienced stress-related burnouts at a young age. It is in this perspective that the adage, *Shareer madhyam khalu dharma sadhanam*—the body is the vehicle for the pursuit of dharma—duty, is very apt. Therefore, developing a healthy body is sine qua non for effectively pursuing one's life goal and effectively discharging one's role and in turn laying the foundations to become a virtuous leader. A myriad ways have been suggested for developing physical fitness various techniques of exercise, sports and games, healthy diet and a disciplined life. Findings from the study by Bhandarker and Singh[10] powerfully bring out that those, who led disciplined lives, exercised regularly and maintained a healthy diet, were more capable of managing stress and tension without falling sick. In contrast, those who did not practice the above were less healthy and more prone to illnesses besides being unable to manage their stress.[11]

It may be worthwhile highlighting the role of yoga for building a healthy body characterized by flexibility, stamina and overall fitness. It is possible to develop a healthy body through the practice of yoga *asanas* or yoga postures. We have briefly highlighted below the important role of yoga *asanas* in building health.

Asanas are a form of physical exercise encompassing muscles, nerves and glands in the body. They help to develop a fine physical architecture, which is strong and elastic and not muscle bound. It keeps the body healthy and free from disease and leads to the reduction of fatigue and significantly soothes the nerves. Its greater impact, however, is the manner in which it also trains and disciplines the mind.[12] By performing *asanas* one achieves complete equilibrium of different parts of the physical system. In fact since the physical self, intellectual self, emotive self and spiritual self—as mentioned earlier—are closely connected with each other, achievement of physical health through *yogasanas* also significantly affects the mental, emotional and spiritual self. Deepak Chopra in his book, *the seven spiritual laws of succes*,[13] says that the human body is like a symphony. 'A single cell in the human body is doing about six trillion things per second and it has to know what every other cell is doing at the same time. The human body can play music, kill germs, make a baby, recite poetry and monitor the movement of the stars all at the same time. Because the field of infinite correlation is part of its information field. Human nervous system can command… organizing power through conscious intent. Intent in the human species is not fixed or locked into a rigid network of energy and information. It has infinite flexibility'.

Such healthy and physically fit individuals demonstrate higher capability to handle conflicts, emotional tensions and stress. By practicing *asanas*, dualities such as loss and gain, victory and defeat, fame and shame, body and mind and mind and soul significantly vanish.[14,15,16] It is, therefore, viewed as the fundamental vehicle to pursue dharma, as mentioned earlier.

It is in this framework that we strongly recommend yoga for building a healthy body, which is one of the prerequisites to become a holistic and virtuous leader. It may be noteworthy to mention that the present Prime Minister of India, Narendra Modi, regularly practises yoga and manages to put in long working hours getting to sleep only for 3 hours every day. Today, yoga has gained worldwide acclaim and following and in recognition of the same, 21 June has been declared Yoga Day by the United Nations.

Mental Self

The contemporary business world can be aptly described as a world of competitive wars. In fact, today, we see the Darwinian principle—survival of the fittest—in full-blown form in the corporate world. All the leaders are fiercely battling, combating and competing for their very survival let alone growth. This business war is very complex, uncertain, volatile and turbulent. Leaders are fighting without being aware, either of the enemy or of the territory. Such complexity of the business scenario has contributed to phenomena such as sleep-lessness, tension, mental turbulence, anxiety, fear as well as many psychosomatic diseases.

To become a virtuous leader in such a situation, it is essential to develop a mental state which is steady, tranquil, peaceful and restful. When the leader is able to develop such a mental state, he is able to plan, prioritize and organize effectively to cope with the above mentioned problems, issues and challenges. In fact, human beings are driven by the power of thought and hence it is extremely critical to keep the mind in balance.

There are many modes available to develop mental balance—transcendental meditation, art of living, *Vipassana* meditation techniques as well as relaxation response techniques. However, we will be focusing on *pranayama* as the key technique to develop mental balance. The utility of *pranayama* has also been experienced by the first two authors.

We now briefly write on the role of *pranayama* in developing mental health, moving from sensory motor centric mind to intellect centric and wisdom-centric mind. Pranayama is both science and art of breathing and consists of rhythmic breathing at a slow pace which results in tranquility and peace. The practice of *pranayama* is based on three basic practices of breathing—inhaling, exhaling and holding the breath. By following rhythmic principles of all the three, one develops mastery over the technique. It fundamentally leads to slowing down the pace of breathing, leading to longevity of life. In fact, according to yogic principles, fast breathing leads to shorter life spans. Further, it is worthwhile mentioning that slow breathing strengthens the respiratory system, soothes the nerves and reduces tensions and cravings. Reduction of cravings leads to a steady mind, and puts it in a calm and restful state. In other words, when desires and senses are controlled, the mind is calm and still. In contrast when desires and cravings are not controlled, they lead to disarray, making the mind agitated, restless, unsteady and troubled.

In the practice of *pranayama*, since the eyes are shut, all external sensory stimuli are blocked, thus keeping the mind peaceful, calm and still, a prerequisite for meditation. During *pranayama*, it may be worthwhile highlighting that one experiences lesser and lesser excitation of the thinking process until one transcends thought completely and arrives at the source of thought—pure consciousness. Here the mind is silent. During this process, one finds that breathing gradually slows down, signifying a decrease in metabolic rates. In medical terms, a state of homeostasis or balance is established. As mentioned earlier, it may be reemphasized that the mind, which is peaceful, calm and equanimous, enables a leader to take prudent and objective decisions. A balanced mind is capable of seeing issues at multiple levels, and therefore brings holistic perspective in deciding what is good and appropriate for all stakeholders. It helps individuals to become holistic and virtuous leaders. Contrary to this, an agitated and turbulent mind is incapable of seeing things clearly, holistically and in a detached fashion, leading to unwise decisions. Such a person is likely to be abrasive, reactive and arrogant which impairs decision making. These clearly bring out that the person in such a state can become toxic.

Emotional Self

It is a known axiom that to be an outstanding leader, one needs—among other things—passionate and committed followers. In fact, leadership legitimacy itself hinges upon the leader's ability to create willing followers, who subscribe to the leader's thinking and purpose. In fact, great leaders in history were those who could create such followers who propagated their teachings to different parts of the world. For example, Jesus could build 12 devoted followers; Buddha developed five and likewise Guru Gobind Singh also had five acolytes. George Washington, Gandhi, Mandela, Martin Luther King, Lincoln, Eisenhower and many other such leaders could understand this wisdom and demonstrated tremendous sensitivity towards followers, and made efforts to mentor, coach and develop them.

In today's business world, management thinkers such as Jim Collins, Bennis, Kouzes and Posner, Noel Tichy, Ram Charan, Nitin Nohria and Rosabeth Moss Kanter have unanimously concluded that it is people power which provides sustainable competitive advantage. Other levers of competitive advantage such as cost leadership, quality leadership and customer and innovation centric leadership are able to provide only temporal competitive edge since these pillars can be easily imitated and copied by competitors. It is in this perspective that we would like to highlight the importance of virtuous leaders developing robust capability at the emotional level which is the core requirement to connect with people, as well as to enthuse, motivate and inspire them.

It may be relevant at this stage to ask the question, How can humanistic values, emotional sensitivity and emotional balance be heightened in a leader? This question can be appropriately answered by understanding the dominant locus of emotional power. Emotional power is said to reside specifically in the right brain, which is the seat of capabilities such as interpersonal, holistic, intuitive, innovative, and imaginative.

Besides this intelligence from the heart level has been found to contribute significantly to generating and sustaining positive emotions in a person.[17] It has been found that people who experienced positive emotions had greater mental clarity, significant shifts in perceptions and heightened intuitive awareness. Mystics, thinkers, writers and poets, such as Isabelle Allende, Maya Angelou, Paulo Coelho, Joe Dispenja, Deepak Chopra, Howard Martin, Gary Zukav, Baptist de Pape and Simon Greiner, have evocatively described the power of the human heart in dealing with people as well as in understanding the meaning and purpose of life. The global spiritual guru, Deepak Chopra, in his book, *The Seven Spiritual Laws of Success*, writes, 'most people think, the heart is mushy and sentimental. But it is not. The heart is intuitive, it is holistic, it is contextual, it is rational. It doesn't have a win- lose orientation. It taps into the cosmic computer ... the field of pure potentiality, pure knowledge and infinite organizing power ... and takes everything into account. At times, it may not even seem rational, but the heart has a computing ability, that is far more accurate and far more precise than anything within the limits of rational thought'.[18]

If one listens to the silent voice of the heart, one becomes more attuned to one's holistic self. There is greater clarity about the sense of direction and purpose of life. In other words, it clarifies what one really wants out of life, besides developing awareness about what life wants from him. Deepak Chopra beautifully said, 'If you look at the big problem that humanity faces today—whether it is social injustice or extreme poverty or economic disparities or war or terrorism or climate chaos—this is because we have lost connection with our soul, we have lost connection with our heart'.[19] Shakespeare said, 'my crown is in my heart, not on my head'.[20]

'Unfortunately, in the contemporary world ... we pay more attention to our mind and thoughts in day-to-day life than we do to our hearts. We are often locked inside our heads, having programmed ourselves to rein in our emotions and dismiss intuition.... More often than not, when we face an important decision, we weigh the pros and cons and decide that the rational choice is the best one'.[21] In the whole process, it is forgotten that decision making has two components—rational and emotional—the former affecting quality and the latter affecting acceptance and implementation by the people.

Great leaders such as Gandhi, Mandela, Martin Luther King, George Washington, Aung San Suu Chi heard the inner voice of their heart and soul and despite several trials and tribulations, boldly pursued their difficult and trying agenda. Being in touch with their inner voice gave them the courage, conviction and steadfastness to oppose mighty empires and authority figures for the right cause. The greatest quality of a virtuous leader is that he connects with people, establishes rapport and relates with stakeholders. In fact, it is the power of concern, compassion and love of virtuous leaders towards fellow human beings which manifests itself in this way. We strongly believe that the heart unites while the mind divides. In the contemporary world, there is greater demand for freedom and autonomy, dignified treatment, equity and fairness. Those leaders, who are naturally predisposed positively towards people, are able to respond to these demands. They are able to enthuse, galvanize, inspire and motivate their followers. They are thus great team builders, mentors, philosophers, guides and therefore every follower would like to work with such a virtuous leader. It has been found that the practice of *pranayama* and meditation significantly contribute towards heightening both intellectual and emotive powers.

Spiritual Level

The greatest discovery of humanity in our judgement has been the existence of God, who is believed to regulate the functioning of the universe and that of human lives. According to the ancient Hindu belief, there is a concept of rebirth and that of karma of a previous life, which determine human destiny in a subsequent life. No one knows whether God exists and none can emphatically aver that *punarjanma* (rebirth) is a reality. Perhaps belief in God is like the sheet anchor which protects one and gives hope in times of failure, defeat, loss, shame, etc. In fact, God is also the last resort when the going gets tough and the one who is thanked profusely when things go right.

The following quotes further reinforce the above statement:

1. Every sort of energy and endurance, of courage and capacity for handling life's evils, is set free in those who have religious faith—William James.[22]

2. I could feel no doubt of man's oneness with the universe … it was a feeling that transcended reason; that went to the heart of man's despair—Richard E. Boyd.[23]

3. The beauty of the world and the orderly arrangement of everything celestial, makes us confess that there is an excellent and eternal nature which ought to be worshipped by mankind—Cicero.[24]

4. I cannot conceive how a man would look to heaven and say there is no God—Abraham Lincoln.[25]

5. I triumph still, if thou abide with me—Henry Francis Lyte.[26]

6. If God be with us, who can be against us?—Romans 8:31.[27]

7. Lead Kindly Light … the night is dark and I am far from my home—John Henry Newman.[28]

8. Cast thy burden upon the Lord and he shall sustain thee—Psalm 55:22 (biblehub.com, 2015).[29]

9. Lord is my strength and my shield, my heart trusteth him and I am helped—Psalm 28:7.[30]

10. So by my woes to be nearer, my God, to Thee—Genesis 28:11–19.[31]

11. My faith in God is complete so I am unafraid—William G. Farrow.[32]

12. All who call on God in true faith, earnestly from the heart, will certainly be heard and will receive what they have asked and desired—Martin Luther King.[33]

13. Abandoning all dharmas of the mind, take refuge in me alone; I will liberate thee from all sins—Bhagavad Gita.[34]

This belief system has immensely aided and provided emotional strength and courage to virtuous leaders such as Gandhi, Mandela, Lincoln, Roosevelt and many other great leaders. These leaders took the difficult path, experienced great trials and tribulations and yet came out of it all victorious perhaps because of their faith. Their belief in the saying 'this too shall pass away' kept them mentally and emotionally balanced. They believed that without divine assistance nothing is possible and that with it nothing is impossible. Those virtuous leaders, who believe in spirituality and the existence of an almighty God, are courageous, unafraid to face even death and are able to take great risks for the larger cause of their people. No wonder such leaders could change the course of history, through the power of their faith. We would like to reiterate here that the path of yoga enables people to experience the bliss which lies beyond mental and emotional stillness.

We would like to however caution leaders aspiring to move from their toxic side to their virtuous side to practice yoga and meditation, under the guidance of a Master who can teach them right approach. Finally, it may be worthwhile reemphasizing that one will have to make efforts to develop and evolve all four levels of the self. Such holistic development of the self-helps an individual to become a virtuous leader.

Self-therapy Checklist for Self-assessment and Creation of a Road Map to Move from Toxic to Virtuous

In the foregoing discussion, we have emphasized the role of *asanas*, *pranayama* and meditation to help facilitate the movement from toxic leadership to virtuous leadership under the guidance of a yoga guru. The basic paradigm underlying this recommendation is that all four levels of self-physical, mental, emotional and spiritual—need to be well developed and holistically integrated.

We now recommend self-therapy to move from toxicity to virtuousness. It may be worthwhile mentioning that during our experience as counsellors and therapists, we found self-therapy to be a very important and useful process to bring about the shift from toxic leadership to virtuous leadership. However, self-therapy is not successful in pathologically toxic cases. Experience has shown that in this approach there is greater self-acceptance and lesser defensiveness and denial. This is in line with the wisdom of Nathaniel Branden's statement, 'Know thyself, own thyself and change thyself', which highlights the relevance of living and leading consciously.

We would like to begin with three powerful quotes from Nathaniel Branden:

- Your life is important whether you achieve what you want in life matters; whether you are happy matters; honour and fight for your higher potential. Self-realization—realization of the best within you—is the noblest goal of your existence;
- Your goal is to learn to live at the highest level of awareness, nothing is more important ... than consciousness ... which is the source of liberation, empowerment and increased possibility;
- Living consciously is an act of love for one's own positive possibilities. It is an act of commitment to one's value as a person and to the importance of one's life.[3]

From the above, it can be concluded that to be a fully actualized human being, to be fully productive and functional as well as to become a virtuous leader, the role of self-reflection is paramount. It also emerges that to be a virtuous leader, it is one's own moral responsibility to invest in oneself through deep introspection and meditation to become a fully functional person and a virtuous leader. The checklist for self-therapy will be around the following attributes demonstrated by virtuous leaders (see Chapter 3):

- Life purpose
- Looking within, around and beyond
- Inner directed
- Karma yogi
- Heightened social sensitivity
- Ethical
- Gestalt holisticity (integrating thought, emotion and action)

We now suggest a set of questions which will enable a person to understand self and set the future agenda. During our counselling and psychotherapy sessions, the following questions immensely benefitted role holders. These questions have been developed around the seven virtuous leader constructs which we extracted from the 13 virtuous leader attributes (identified in Chapter 3).

A. Life purpose

1. What is your life purpose? Write down at least three points.

1	
2	
3	

2. If you have to write your epitaph, what will it contain? Mention three key points.

1	
2	
3	

3. How do you want to be remembered by your family members? And by others? Mention below.

1	
2	
3	

4. What, according to you, people must talk when you retire as a leader? Mention below.

1	
2	
3	

5. On a 10-point scale evaluate your *current* efforts:
   a. To reach the statements made in the epitaph

1	2	3	4	5	6	7	8	9	10
Mini-mum				Aver-age					Maxi-mum

   b. To be remembered by family members and by others

1	2	3	4	5	6	7	8	9	10
Mini-mum				Aver-age					Maxi-mum

If your score is less than 5, it means you need to seriously re-examine your life purpose.

B. Looking beyond, around and within

Looking beyond:

1. How much time do you devote to scan and understand the emerging business challenges?

5%–10%	10%–15%	15%–20%	20%–25%

If you are at the top management level, your score should be 20%–25%; in case you are at the middle level, it should be 15%–20%.

2. Kindly mention three emerging business challenges which can impact your leadership efficacy.

1	
2	
3	

3. Kindly mention three emerging business challenges which can impact your organization.

1	
2	
3	

4. How much time do your key people and members of the think tank spend on environmental scanning?

10%–15%	15%–20%	20%–25%

5. If the organization level score is below 20%, kindly pen down steps to be taken by you and your think tank.

1	
2	
3	

Looking around:

1. Identify your key competitors.

1	
2	
3	
4	

2. How much time do you devote to gather (and analyse) market intelligence about your competitors?

5%–10%	10%–15%	15%–20%	20%–25%

If your organization is below 15% on the above, kindly pen down steps to be taken by you and your think tank.

1	
2	
3	

3. What is your competitive positioning vis-à-vis competitor's? Indicate on the 10-point scale below.

1	2	3	4	5	6	7	8	9	10
Very low				Mod-erate					Very High

If you are below 5, kindly enumerate the proposed steps to increase your competitive positioning.

Looking within:

1. How frequently do you reflect, look within?

Monthly	Weekly	Daily

2. How frequently do you conduct a self-level SWOT analysis?

Never	Sometimes	Often	Always

3. If you often do the self-level SWOT analysis, kindly mention your three strengths and three weaknesses as a virtuous leader.

S. No.	Strengths	Weaknesses
1		
2		
3		

4. How often does your organization go on retreats for organizational SWOT analysis?

Bi-annually	Annually	Once in 2 years	Once in 3 years	Never

5. If your organization has done such an exercise, kindly mention five strengths and five weaknesses.

   Identify five attributes stakeholders must talk about your organization hence 3 years in terms of:

a.	Cost leadership	
b.	Quality	
c.	Customer centricity	
d.	People power	
e.	Innovation	
f.	Ethical governance	

C. Inner directed

1. How often do you stick your neck out to change things?

1	2	3	4	5
Never	Rarely	Sometimes	Often	Always

2. Rate your level of courage and boldness.

1	2	3	4	5
Low				High

3. Rate your risk taking capabilities and fighting against the odds.

1	2	3	4	5
Low				High

4. Rate yourself on entrepreneurial innovation (walking the unbeaten track).

1	2	3	4	5
Low				High

5. Rate yourself on your level of being non-conformist.

1	2	3	4	5
Low				High

6. Rate yourself on being unconventional.

1	2	3	4	5
Low				High

7. Identify unconventional role models you have (if any).

1	
2	
3	

8. To what extent do you question established rules, frameworks and practices?

D. Karma yogi

1. Identify a karma yogi whom you have met/admired and worked with. Mention three qualities of this person on a five-point scale given below:

1	1 Low	2	3	4	5 High
2	1 Low	2	3	4	5 High
3	1 Low	2	3	4	5 High

2. How do you rate yourself on the above qualities?

1	1 Low	2	3	4	5 High
2	1 Low	2	3	4	5 High
3	1 Low	2	3	4	5 High

3. Suppose you do not get your due rewards, how will you respond to that situation?

1	
2	
3	

4. Have you ever worked with full commitment despite not getting due rewards?

1 Never	2	3	4	5 Always

5. Write three steps you plan to take to become a karma yogi.
6. To what extent do you possess the following characteristics?

Arrogance	1 Low	2	3	4	5 High
Non-listening	1 Low	2	3	4	5 High
Self-openness and close minded	1 Low	2	3	4	5 High

E. Heightened social sensitivity

1. Think of a person whom you admire the most because of his/her humanistic qualities.

2. Kindly mention key attributes of this person.

1	
2	
3	

3. To what extent do you value people in your team for who they are? Kindly indicate on a five-point scale.

1 Low	2	3	4	5 High

4. To what extent do you feel concern for people and try to help them?

1 Never	2	3	4	5 Always

5. Mention some characteristics to illustrate the above.

1	
2	
3	

6. To what extent do you try to advise, guide, coach and counsel people working with you?

1 Never	2	3	4	5 Always

7. How do you react when someone is being humiliated and abused in public?

- Move away
- Ignore
- Watch
- After the event advise the person to stop humiliation
- Console the humiliated person and help him in recovering

F. Ethical

1. Kindly identify a person whom you admire to be ethical. Mention five characteristics of this person which make you admire this person.

1	
2	
3	
4	
5	

2. Where do you rate yourself on the above five qualities?

1 Low	2	3	4	5 High

3. Kindly evaluate the following statements:

	Strongly Disagree 1	Disagree 2	Neutral 3	Agree 4	Strongly Agree 5
1	Ethics do not pay in life					
2	Successful leaders care about the ends, not about the means					
3	*Satyamev Jayate* (truth prevails)					
4	Ethics pays in the long run					
5	Ethics and business do not go together					
6	Only wealthy people are admired					
7	What matters most in my life is to make money					

If your total score is below 10, you need to reexamine your ethical framework.

G. Gestalt holisticity (integrating complete self)

1. Identify who according to you is a fully integrated and holistic person. Kindly mention three qualities.

1	
2	
3	

2. Rate yourself on the above qualities on a five-point scale.

1	1 Low	2	3	4	5 High
2	1 Low	2	3	4	5 High
3	1 Low	2	3	4	5 High

3. Rate the following:

		Strongly Disagree 1	Disagree 2	Neutral 3	Agree 4	Strongly Agree 5
a	I am capable of bringing together, ideas, people sensitive and execution focus before making a decision					
b	I am too emotional					
c	While handling people I am swayed by my emotions and feelings					
d	I focus all my energies to make the decision of high quality					
e	Many times, I make impulsive decisions on the spur of the moment and regret them later					
f	I do not lose my balance even in my toughest situations					

REFERENCES

1. Frankl, V.E. (2000). *Man's search for ultimate meaning.* Cambridge, MA: Basic Books.
2. Bennis, W. (1997). *Why leaders can't lead: The unconscious conspiracy continues.* San Francisco, CA: Jossey-Bass.
3. thinkexist.com (2005). Bhagavad Gita quotes. Retrieved from http://thinkexist.com/quotation/a_man-s_own_self_is_his_friend-a_man-s_own_self/296926.html (accessed on 15 July 2015).
4. Brainyquotes.com (2015). Socrates quotes. Retrieved from http://www.brainyquote.com/quotes/quotes/s/socrates101168.html (accessed on 15 July 2015).
5. Sanskritpearls.blogspot.in (2015). Samskruta Mouktikaani: Sanskrit Pearls of Wisdom. Retrieved from http://sanskritpearls.blogspot.in/2010/01/january-11th.html (accessed on 15 July 2015).
6. Kuppuswamy, B. (1993). *Source book of ancient Indian psychology.* New Delhi, India: Konark Publishers Ltd.
7. Chinmayananda, S. (2013). *The Holy Gita: Commentary by Swami Chinmayananda.* Mumbai, India: Chinmaya Prakashan.
8. Branden, N. (1999). *The art of living consciously: The power of awareness to transform everyday life* (p, 10). Los Angeles, CA: Touchstone Books.
9. Chopra, D. (1996). *The seven spiritual laws of success* (p. 53). New Delhi: Excel Books.
10. Bhandarker, A. & Singh, P. (1986). Managerial stress: A study in cyclical perspective. *ASCI Journal of Management, 16,* 25–59.
11. Singh, A.P., Srivastava, U.R., & Mandal, M.K. (1999). The role of social support in stress and health outcomes among Indian managerial personnel. In T. Sugiman, M. Karasawa, J.H. Liu, & C. Ward (Eds), *Progress in Asian social psychology: Theoretical and empirical contributions,* Vol. II. Seoul, Korea: Kyoyook-Kwahak-Sa Publishing Company.
12. Iyengar, B.K.S. (2015). *Light on yoga: The definitive guide to yoga practice.* UK: Harper Thorsons.
13. Chopra, D. (1996). *The seven spiritual laws of success* (p. 71). New Delhi: Excel Books.
14. Oshoworld.com (2015). *Introduction to the Path of Yoga.* Retrieved from http://www.oshoworld.com/osho_talk/talks/yoga01.asp (accessed on 15 July 2015).
15. Jaggi V. (2015). *Bharata: Rhythm of a Nation.* Retrieved from http://www.ishafoundation.org/blog/lifestyle/bharat-the-power-of-a-name/ (accessed on 15 July 2015).
16. artofliving.org (2015). Demystifying yoga with Sri Sri. Retrieved from http://www.artofliving.org/in-en/yoga/sri-sri-on-yoga/demystifying-yoga-sri-sri (accessed on 15 July 2015).
17. McCraty, R., & Rees, R.A. (2009). The central role of the heart in generating and sustaining positive emotions. In S. Lopez & C.R. Snyder (Eds), *Oxford handbook of positive psychology* (pp. 527–536). New York, NY: Oxford University Press.
18. Chopra, D. (1996). *The seven spiritual laws of success* (p. 44). New Delhi: Excel Books.
19. de Pape, B. (2014). *The power of the heart* (p. 211). London, UK: Simon & Schuster.
20. goodreads.com (2015). William Shakespeare: Quotable quote. Retrieved from https://www.goodreads.com/quotes/155494-my-crown-is-in-my-heart-not-on-my-head (accessed on 15 July 15 2015).
21. de Pape, B. (2014). *The power of the heart* (p. 35). London, UK: Simon & Schuster.
22. blog.gaiam.com (2015). A Quote by William James on courage, endurance, evil, faith, life, energy, and religion. Retrieved from http://blog.gaiam.com/quotes/authors/william-james/40506 (accessed on 16 July 2015).
23. wikiquote.org (2015). *Richard E. Byrd.* Available at https://en.wikiquote.org/wiki/Richard_E._Byrd (accessed on 16 July 16 2015).

24. lifecoachmary.com (2015). *Inner peace quote: Cicero.* Retrieved from http://www.lifecoachmary.com/inner-peace-quote-circero/ (accessed on 16 July 2015).

25. thinkexist.com (2015). *Abraham Lincoln quotes.* Retrieved from http://thinkexist.com/quotation/i_can_see_how_it_might_be_possible_for_a_man_to/251292.html (accessed on 16 July 2015).

26. Watson, L.E. (1951). *Light from many lamps: A treasury of inspiration* (p. 36). New York, NY: Simon & Schuster.

27. biblehub.com (2015). *Romans 8:31.* Retrieved from http://biblehub.com/romans/8-31.htm (accessed on 16 July 2015).

28. Watson, L.E. (1951). *Light from many lamps: A treasury of inspiration* (p. 39). New York, NY: Simon & Schuster.

29. biblehub.com (2015). *Psalm 55:22.* Retrieved from http://biblehub.com/psalms/55-22.htm (accessed on 16 July 2015).

30. biblehub.com (2015). *Psalm 28:7.* Retrieved from http://biblehub.com/psalms/28-7.htm (accessed on 16 July 2015).

31. enwikipedia.org (2015). *Nearer, my god, to thee.* Retrieved from https://en.wikipedia.org/wiki/Nearer,_My_God,_to_Thee (accessed on 16 July 2015).

32. Watson, L.E. (1951). *Light from many lamps: A treasury of inspiration* (p. 50). New York, NY: Simon & Schuster.

33. brainyquote.com (2015). *Martin Luther Quotes.* Retrieved from http://www.brainyquote.com/quotes/quotes/m/martinluth151424.html (accessed on 16 July 2015).

34. Sethumadhavan, T.N. (2015). *Bhagavad Gita- Chap 18(Part-3) Moksha Sannyaasa Yogah- Yoga Of Liberation By Renunciation.* Retrieved from http://www.esamskriti.com/essay-chapters/Bhagavad-Gita~-Chap-18(Part~3)-Moksha-Sannyaasa-Yogah~-Yoga-of-Liberation-by-Renunciation-1.aspx (accessed on 16 July 2015).

Epilogue

The perennial human quest is for health, wealth, happiness and above all to be immortal and remembered. This is a universal human quest regardless of age and stages in life. We have experienced such a phenomenon while dealing with students, bureaucrats, political executive as well as corporate honchos. However, in reality, few are able to achieve it all. It is perplexing that despite being endowed with great potential, human beings are unable to actualize their cherished life goals. Even in a Maslovian sense, self-actualizing people are in a miniscule minority. Thinkers and scholars globally have been wrestling with this paradox—that despite being endowed with potential, few are successful in realizing the same. This probably happens because human beings live life in a mechanical and myopic way. They are unaware of the blocks and barriers, which arrest them from transcending their limitations.

This raises the following questions:

- Why do human beings lead their lives so mechanically?
- Why are they unable to move beyond their myopic and self-serving routines?
- Why are people unable to recognize their inner blocks and barriers and transcend them?
- Why is it that despite a plethora of writings and advice on the subject, only a few succeed in attaining the holy grail of self-actualization?

The answer—in our judgement—lies in the way human beings lead and live their lives. Unfortunately, they seldom question and reflect on why they do things in a certain way and the likely consequences of their actions. They are, in fact, trapped by their own unconscious conspiracies, the power of habit and their reluctance to confront life's challenges. Many times, they are in the grip of *tamoguna*, id, bad habits, toxic orientation, arrogance, narcissism and focused on self and self-preservation. Most senior-level executives in our experience suffer from the delusion that they are always right and that they are paragons of all wisdom with a monopoly on the truth. They are therefore unable to self-regulate—that is reflect, introspect and re-examine their purpose in life. Thus, they are unable to create escape velocity which is essential for them to move from one orbit of living to the next. They are trapped by the power of gravitational pulls within themselves which restrict them from changing, transforming and becoming fully actualizing human beings.

The biggest block between a person's intention to change and action to achieve this change is the power of one's unconscious conspiracy, which exerts relentless pressure to keep one from changing and transcending to a higher level of self. The biggest challenge is, therefore, to manage one's own unconscious conspiracy. This is possible, as mentioned earlier, only when the person creates escape velocity, like the rocket which moves to the next orbit. In other words, this escape velocity has to exceed the gravitational forces of his toxic side. This is possible by training one's energy to consciously move from the toxic side to the virtuous side—from darkness to light. The most powerful device in this quest is continued self-reflection and mindfulness in thinking ahead regarding the likely consequences of one's actions. Above all, human beings need to clarify their highest life philosophy, meaning and purpose, and to establish clarity on how they would like to be remembered. Such clarity will help them to re-channelize their energy towards becoming a self-actualizing and fully productive and creative human being. This will enable them to discard their toxicity and replace it with the power of enlightenment. They need to continuously confront and challenge themselves in the words of Swami Vivekananda 'to Arise, Awake and Stop not till the Goal is achieved'. They must live life mindfully and consciously at their highest level of Self. This Self must be in charge of the total person so that the energies of the lower self-level can be redirected and channelized meaningfully.

The fundamental reason for writing this book has been to challenge the reader and the leader to move from mere thinking to reflecting, from desire to action and from dreaming to doing.

Unless there is preparation to move with self-awareness, the reader is likely to be the victim of his own desires and self-defeating habits. Such a person is likely to become his own biggest enemy, incapable of invoking and activating the virtuous side.

It would be worthwhile reaffirming that by activating the virtuous side, there is every possibility for a person to become the best that he or she is capable of. It is about making the choice of how one would like to lead life—constantly moving towards the light or moving towards the darkness within one's own nature. This philosophy has been succinctly captured by David Thoreau's lines as follows.

> *Let go of the past and go for the future.*
> *Go confidently in the direction of your dreams.*
> *Live the life you imagined.*
> —David Thoreau[1]

Finally, we would like to end the epilogue by recommending 10 commandments which can immensely help readers and leaders in their odyssey towards virtuous leadership:

1. Clarify the purpose of your existence—think of life beyond self.
2. Be true to yourself and listen to your inner voice.
3. Abandon cynicism and embrace optimism.
4. Be courageous and never give up in the face of adversity.
5. Have faith.
6. Do unto others what you would like others to do to you.
7. Let karma, not reward, be your driving force.
8. Look beyond, look around and look within.
9. Strive to lead a holistic life, integrating your physical, emotional, intellectual and spiritual selves.
10. Lead life mindfully and consciously.

By practising the above commandments we are sure that the perennial human quest for health, wealth, happiness and immortality will be significantly achieved. Further practice of these commandments by everyone will contribute immensely to create a society characterized by greater harmony with nature and with each other; a society where equity, justice and fairness will prevail; where people live with dignity and mutually work for the upliftment of all. It must be emphasized here that the creation of such a society will throw up many virtuous leaders, a sore requirement of this jaded, cynical, corrupt contemporary world.

REFERENCE

1. wisdomquotes.com (2015). *David Thoreau.* Retrieved from www.wisdomquotes.com/quote/henry-david-thoreau-51.html (accessed on 20 July 2015).

About the Authors

Pritam Singh is currently the CEO of LEAD Centre in Gurgaon. Dr Singh is a thought leader with extraordinary insight. Dr Singh is the author of seven critically acclaimed books, three of which are award winning. He has also published over 60 research papers in various national and international journals. He is a globally sought-after speaker and has addressed various Indian and global audiences, including Chambers of Commerce in various countries, notably, Holland, France, Germany, Greece, Russia, UK, USA, Thailand, Mauritius, Egypt, etc.

As an academic administrator, Dr Singh has an unparalleled record. With his entrepreneurial vision and path-breaking innovative methods, Dr Singh turned around the fortunes of both MDI-Gurgaon (where he was the director from 1994 to 1998 and from 2003 to 2006) and IIM Lucknow (1998–2003). He steered International Management Institute (IMI) for a period of three years until October 2014, and during this period IMI improved tremendously in reputation and ranking. Quite fittingly, therefore, he earned the repute of Midas Touch Director.

As the Chairman and member of several policy-making committees and bodies of the Government of India, he has stamped his perspective on policy issues that surround both management education and corporate management in India. He is currently on the Board of 10 reputed private- and public-sector organizations, helping them initiate the change process and charter a winning corporate strategy.

He has been conferred the prestigious 'Padma Shri'—a first in the field of management education. He has also been the recipient of several other prestigious awards, the most notable among them being the 'Global Thought Leader' 2006–2007 by MIRBIS (the Russian School of Business in Moscow), where he was the first

Asian to be thus awarded. Thinkers50 India ranked him 27 out of 50 Indian Thinkers (both in India and globally) in 2014.

Asha Bhandarker is well known in the field of HR and Leadership Studies in India as a scholar, consultant and researcher. Prior to her current assignment as a Distinguished Professor OB at IMI-Delhi, she was the Raman Munjal Chair Professor of Leadership Studies as well as Dean Research and Consulting at MDI-Gurgaon.

She has published 7 books and 40 research papers and cases in peer-reviewed, national and international journals. She was awarded the highly coveted Senior Fulbright Fellowship for research in the United States, where she studied the best business schools and their practices and pedagogies. In addition, she has, over the years, received the Best Paper award, Best Case award and the Best Teacher award.

Over the last 28 years, she has worked closely with the corporate sector in the areas of training, organization development and capability building. She is one of a handful of professors working with board levels and top management teams of many organizations. She is a recognized HR expert and has been invited on many board-level HR committees. Dr Bhandarker is actively associated with professional bodies and has addressed participants of national and international conferences. She has widely travelled across the USA, Europe and Asia and has rich experience of teaching and consulting in India and abroad.

Snigdha Rai is an Assistant Professor in organizational behaviour at the IMI, New Delhi. She has done her PhD from Banaras Hindu University. She has more than six years of teaching experience in Business Schools. Before joining IMI, she has been a Faculty at Symbiosis Institute of Business Management, Bangalore. Dr Rai's current research interests include leadership, workplace ethics, scale development and psychometric testing.